WATCHING WILDLIFE

A Field Guide to the Wildlife Habitats of Britain

GEOFFREY YOUNG
ELAINE FRANKS

Foreword by
SIR DAVID ATTENBOROUGH
CVO CBE FRS

WATCHING WILDLIFE

A Field Guide to the
Wildlife Habitats of Britain

GEOFFREY YOUNG
ELAINE FRANKS

Foreword by
SIR DAVID ATTENBOROUGH
CVO CBE FRS

Published in association with The **RSNC** **W**ildlife **T**rusts **P**artnership

GEORGE
PHILIP

CONTENTS

Published in 1992 by George Philip Limited,
59 Grosvenor Street, London W1X 9DA

British Library Cataloguing in Publication Data

Young, Geoffrey
    Watching Wildlife: Field Guide to the
    Wildlife Habitats of Britain
    I. Title II. Franks, Elaine
    574.941

ISBN 0 540 01262 9

Page design Kathy Gummer
Typeset by Keyspools Limited, Golborne, Lancs
Printed in Hong Kong

ACKNOWLEDGEMENTS

I'm indebted to many books and articles. Books are either a delight to read and will surely pass the test of time, or they are not. Of the former, warmth and enthusiasm speak as much as their factual content, and I'd like to recommend a handful of classic books.

W. G. Hoskins, *The Making of the English Landscape* (Hodder)
Oliver Rackham, *Trees and Woodland in the British Landscape*, and subsequent titles (Dent)
John Gilmore and Max Walters, *Wild Flowers* (New Naturalist Series, Collins)

Authoritative they are. Their content was innovative and eye opening when they were first published. And it says something for the excitement of watching wildlife that new discoveries can still be made and explained. I'd like to recommend the recently published:

Jeremy Thomas, *The Butterflies of Britain and Ireland* (Dorling Kindersley)

which contains new insights into butterfly behaviour on which some descriptions in this book are gratefully based.

Of great value would be books which present clear but detailed analyses of complex surveys and other work carried out by the experts. The publishers T & A.D. Poyser have set high standards, here – R.J. Fuller's *Bird habitats in Britain* is one title, which incorporates and explains the work of the British Trust for Ornithology and others. A parallel for botany and mammal and invertebrate life would be welcome (although the New Naturalist series does of course fill some of the gap).

Of the experts themselves, I would like again to express my gratitude to Oliver Gilbert, Nigel Holmes, George Peterken, Derek Wells and others, who have given me encouragement and ideas in the past, which also find their way into these pages.

Geoffrey Young

FOREWORD SIR DAVID ATTENBOROUGH CVO CBE FRS

For many people, a visit to the countryside is one of the most commonly undertaken leisure pursuits, and with over 80 per cent of Britain's population based near a town or city, the enjoyment to be gained from visiting a favourite wood, river valley, or upland cannot be over-estimated.

For the casual visitor to the countryside it is only natural to want to be able to identify both the types of habitat and landscape features which one can see, plus the often seemingly bewildering variety of plant and animal life which can be seen even on the shortest of countryside walks.

The British countryside has evolved, with man's influence, over thousands of years and now represents a fascinating mosaic of woodland, open fields, coastline, and urban fringe all contributing to the unique nature of the British countryside.

Over the years many books have been published as field guides describing Britain's flora and fauna but here for the first time, Geoffrey Young has provided an easy-to-read and understandable description of the principal habitat types to be found in Britain along with a fascinating insight into the types of wildlife associated with such habitats. He has been able in an easy and informative style to guide the casual observer and visitor to the British countryside to each habitat in turn and enable such visitors to gain a greater understanding of the complexity of plant and animal life associated with them.

Geoffrey Young has been able to do this as an author and journalist well known for his work with countryside and environmental matters over the last twenty years or so, coupled with the superb illustrations produced by one of our most talented and up-and-coming wildlife artists, Elaine Franks.

I thoroughly recommend this book to anyone wishing to have an informative and accessible field guide to Britain's countryside wildlife.

As President of The RSNC Wildlife Trusts Partnership I am delighted that by buying this book you will be contributing to the work of the Wildlife Trusts throughout Britain as a percentage of the royalties is being donated by the author, Geoffrey Young, to help with our work in conserving Britain's countryside and wildlife.

David Attenborough

INTRODUCTION

THE BACKGROUND

The rock

Britain's rock layers lie at a slant, with the lower, older and often harder strata coming to the surface in the west, although by the time the Malvern Hills are reached massive slips complicate this simple picture and bosses of other kinds of rock intrude.

By and large, however, Britain's hard-rock uplands lie in the west and north. Here they were deeply sculptured by the glaciers and ice sheets of the Ice Age. This was, in fact, a series of advances and retreats of the cold, and during the warmer interglacials (we are possibly in one now) meltwaters spread silts and gravels over vast areas of low ground. In places these form the 'bedrock' of the soil today.

The soil

A clod of garden soil typically consists of mineral clay and rock debris mixed with an organic humus of decaying plant matter, but a good half of the clod will be water and air. The minerals give the soil a chemical taste which can encourage or discourage bacteria and other decay organisms. Three main kinds of soil are found: acid, neutral, and basic or alkaline. The first is typical of the uplands, where the bedrock is often slightly acidic and leaching by heavy rain accentuates this; lowland sandy heathland soils are also acidic, however. Typical neutral soils are the silty alluvial soils of river valleys, while chalk and limestone are familiar basic-soil types.

The profile of a soil, such as is seen along a roadside cutting, for example, is modified by this chemistry. Four extreme types are: mull (forest), mor (heathland), peat, and chalk soils.

A mull soil is typically nearly neutral, with active decay releasing new supplies of plant nutrients. It is a rich soil with plenty of earthworms and no sharp boundary between the humus and the subsoil; rainfall is more or less balanced by evaporation, so that the nutrients remain in place. In contrast, acid conditions put a brake on decay bacteria, and peaty undecayed matter remains. This does not have the ability of humus to retain water; the ground tends to become leached of nutrients, and a mor soil develops, poor and with few worms (see pages 152–3). Waterlogging also discourages decay bacteria, and peat is laid down in wetlands (see pages 140–1).

Alkaline limestone and (especially) chalk soils are rather thin and poor in nutrients, which, contrary to what might be expected, can increase the variety of plants growing (see pages 60–1). Bacteria are, in fact, favoured by alkaline or near-neutral conditions, which is why acid farm soils are limed. This liming also flocculates soil colloids, improving the aeration and the 'crumb'.

Second to the soil, altitude and exposure control what plants grow where. The growing period shortens up on a mountain, which affects grazing as well as wild flowers and wildlife (see pages 160–1), but this is really just one face of the influence of climate.

Climate

The climate is the summary of weather, which is itself changeable. Britain is on the edge of the European mainland and exposed to a wide expanse of ocean, and this influence means that generally we have a rather wet but relatively mild climate. Although winters may be bitter on the hills, the sea tempers the cold, and the North Atlantic Drift (the Gulf Stream) with its warm water swings north in winter, and even allows semi-tropical plants to survive on parts of the coast of western Scotland. By contrast, the east is influenced by the Continent, with colder winters but hotter summers: a drier climate altogether.

Nor is the climate fixed. It changes, and relatively warm and dry Boreal and wetter Atlantic periods have alternated since the ice began its last retreat, some 12,000 years ago.

Microclimates

These are local 'climates', where such things as aspect and shelter make one side of a lane differ from its opposite face, one field different from another. At the extreme, a small habitat such as, for instance, a decaying tree will offer its denizens a 'microclimate' rather different from the rest of the wood in which the tree is lying.

The year

Although conventionally divided into four seasons, the habitat and wildlife year is best thought of as five different periods:

winter – water is locked up in freezing conditions, and the threat of this is responsible for minimal plant presence

prevernal – when the first 'spring' flowers are seen, but the trees are leafless

vernal – a general bursting of buds, and woods and lanes have medium shade

summer – the deepest shade, so few wild flowers are seen in woods

autumn – leaf fall, and many fungi to be seen

HABITATS

The definition of the word habitat

From the point of view of a plant or animal, its habitat is the place where it lives. The word can be used to refer either to that kind of place in general or simply to one particular site. In both senses, the word encompasses the whole complex of vegetation and animal life present, as well as the broader factors of soil and the climate.

From the point of view of a living organism, a habitat need not be a major countryside feature. A rotting branch lying on the woodland floor is the habitat of many beetles, for example: referring to the fact that they lay their eggs in its bark, and the grubs which hatch eat their way through the softening timber within, although the adults may fly through the wood at large.

How to recognise habitats

Habitats are, simply, places that we can put a name to: wood, moor, grassland, stream. They have a distinctive plant life and animal life. The plants are usually far more obvious than the animals – they do not move, for one thing – and because of this a habitat is usually recognisable from afar. With more information, we can qualify the name: oak or beech wood, heather or grass moor, limestone pasture, chalk stream. The detailed structure and plant or animal tally of a habitat often reflect the history of its use, as this book makes clear, and 'ancient oak woodland' and similar descriptions therefore have great significance.

The size and shape of habitats

All habitats today are influenced by man, one sign of this being that they have an edge. Neat edges are rare in nature. Thus the physical form of the habitat can reflect its management as much as natural characteristics. A grass field is kept short by grazing, which is obvious enough, and the low profile of a heath is created by undershrubs such as heather and gorse, which, if man did not play a role, would eventually be invaded by trees (see pages 152–3). Natural factors still play a part, of course: a wood has a densely bunched appearance partly because protruding shoots tend to be 'scorched' by exposure, when transpiration speeds up and cells die.

Linked words

The word 'environment' parallels the word 'habitat', but with a bias towards measurable conditions such as temperature and pollution levels, as well as a more scientific assessment of the other living things present. A community is an ecological term for a naturally occurring assembly of different living things in some kind of relationship – a food relationship, for example. Communities can be large or small, and the larger may contain the smaller. The word 'association' originally meant the widest habitat groupings – broadleaved woodland, heathland – but it has often been used of small vegetation groups such as the patch of bluebells and wood anemones which indicate which part of the wood is old (see pages 18–19). However, this kind of minor community, which is the result of particular local conditions, is better called a society.

Climax communities

Growing plants of whatever kind chase the light, and as a result most dry-land habitats evolve until the most successful light-gathering assembly is in place. This is the climax community, and over much of Britain it would be mixed oak woodland, or maybe beech woodland in the south. The climax is often held back, however, by natural conditions such as exposure (scrub is more likely than woodland on a sea cliff, which can be subject to very strong prevailing winds) and by man (grazing,

cutting, trimming and, of course, by ploughing).

Natural and semi-natural habitats

As this book shows, British habitats can be understood only from the standpoint of the history of man's use of them. The process started long ago, for the wildwood was no sooner in place than it was being cleared for fields or changed by livestock, and, apart from perhaps some coastal habitats, there is none which is completely natural. But some habitats in some places now have centuries of unchanging traditional management behind them. They are not natural, but have stable communities and are the next best thing. They are known as semi-natural, and they number among them old woods, meadows and unploughed chalk downland. Their tally of plants and animals can in fact be as varied as that of any natural community, and they may carry rarities.

Together with these 'classic' habitat types are those more obviously man-made and which can also over time become populated by a variety of plants and animals, although you would not expect to find many (or any) rarities. Roadside verges, railway cuttings, hedges and canals are examples. These habitats are also included in this book. Some have in fact been adopted as nature reserves, and receive management aimed at preserving the wildlife they contain.

THE NUMBERS YOU SEE

A deceptive silence

On a walk through the summer wood, you may hear nothing more than a few snatches of birdsong, maybe the echoing 'tee-cher' of the great tits. You may catch sight of a squirrel; or at least the sudden swaying of a branch in the canopy. True, there may be a background humming of insects, but little stirs in the network of paths through the undergrowth. In fact, in a half-hour stroll, you may catch sight of no more than 20 different species of animals, including some of those insects, maybe one or two of which are butterflies.

Of course, the plants are much more easy to spot. They can be sought out in the way that animals cannot, but even so there are probably vastly more than we are aware of. A tally of the more visible and recordable life in one wood in Oxfordshire, for example, showed:

Number of different species			
mosses	12	bees, wasps,	
liverworts	1	ants	5
other plants	206	true flies	8
visible fungi	36		
		spiders	99
insects:		harvestmen	2
crickets etc	3		
lacewings	1	snails, slugs	8
bugs	7		
butterflies	29	frogs, newts	2
moths	167	snakes, lizards	2
beetles	19	birds	44
		mammals	9(+ 1!)

An ecosystem

If the wood were not brimful with life, it could hardly exist. The reasons are not difficult to understand.

Plants come first: they can respond to the energy in the sunlight by creating sugars, which are then elaborated to make starch, woody matter and other materials of plant bodies. In effect, the sun's energy is chemically locked up in these tissues. An animal organism, on the other hand, fuels its body processes with this imprisoned energy: it eats plants or other animals which have eaten plants to gain the necessary food ration. But plants always come first.

In a wood, a large number of animals, including worms and woodlice and many beetles, gain their energy ration by consuming dead and decaying plant and animal matter. This decay eventually releases new supplies of nutrients for new plant growth. The fungi also play an important role as decomposers and really merit being treated as a living kingdom in their own right, equal of plants, animals and bacteria. Bacteria, too, are important decomposers.

Without this network, a wood or any other habitat could not exist as we know it; the gaps would simply silt up with dead material, until plant growth came to an end when the soil nutrients were finished. In other words, there must be a natural cycle, and an ecosystem is simply defined as a self-contained, self-perpetuating and balanced unit of plant-life and animal life, closely interlocked in the way sketched out above. As well as these living 'biotic' factors, physical features such as landform, rock and soil (the edaphic factors) also play a part, as does climate.

Food chains and food webs

A large volume of grass feeds a number of rabbits, which in turn feed a very few foxes. A narrowing food chain of this kind is seen everywhere; the energy package reduces as it is passed on, only about a tenth surviving wastage at each level. The real picture, however, is never a simple chain but much more like a meshed web, because (for example) many animals live in more than one habitat, with different associates, sometimes during different life stages or because they are rather mobile. Nor are predators always restricted to one prey.

Animals in niches

These complex food webs and such things as the time of year and the seasonal climate together create a 'niche' – a role or opportunity – that the species of animal fills. What this means is that voles and shrews in the same grassy field are in effect in different stage sets: the first eats grass and the second insects. They do not compete. Nor do field mice and bank voles when they steal the hawthorn berries in autumn: the former eats the pips and rejects the pulp, which the latter prefers. Nor do greenfly and caterpillars compete: they dine on different parts of the plant, sap and leaf respectively. By and large, in important things, animal species do not generally compete, although many animals are sometimes rivals for the same food, especially if they are scavengers. Each species is fitted to its niche – the famous phrase 'survival of the fittest', which is the key to understanding evolution (see pages 186–7), does not simply mean the survival of the healthiest!

The species

The species is thus a creature of its habitat. It is one which will not normally breed with other species even though they may come from the same parent stock. Islands (see pages 186–7) show how species evolve, although an actual geographical island is not necessary. Within the species, the gene pool is continually being mixed. Local races emerge that could in time perhaps become separate species if environmental circumstances changed to create new niches for which they are the fittest – opportunities in which their 'breed' can live very successfully.

It is much the same for plants. The countless microspecies of brambles provide a nice example (see pages 78–9).

Cropping and pollution

Natural balance is grossly distorted by man. Both farming and woodland management of any kind mean cropping, removing elements of the balanced ecosystem. In farming, if cropping is to continue without a break, the nutrients have to be replaced by fertilising the soil in some way.

Pollution has a rather similar effect, in that the balance of the ecosystem is destroyed. There cannot by definition be a pollution problem on a stone-dead planet; its effect on life is the key. But pollution can result in the vast proliferation of one species of animal (or plant) which can cope with the new conditions, and therefore has less rivalry for food or space (see pages 130–1).

DISTRIBUTION

Keys to habitat

Heather helps to define the habitat of heathland, but it is also found elsewhere, in some pine woods, for example. Animals may occupy different habitats for different periods in their lives, which tends to emphasise the changing seasons. Nonetheless, a number of plants and animals can typify the habitat and act as 'indicators' of it.

Unexpected success

Plants tend to seed outwards, and the seeds germinate and colonise new territory, if favourable. Animals can have an urge to travel as part of their pattern of behaviour, or as a result of overcrowding: with food in short supply, the youngest or weakest may be forced out to find other terrain, grouse being one example (see pages 158–9). Sometimes, however, the new environment fields no real competitors, and the colonisers thrive. There are many 'new world' examples: Japanese knotweed (see pages 98–9) and the collared dove (see pages 102–3) are just two. A fact linked with this is that a habitat is often the richer in plant species when conditions are harsh and vigour dulled, so no species overproliferates to crowd out the others. Fertilising a meadow reduces the number of flowers (see pages 68–9).

Distribution

The close fit with habitat which ensures survival means that species have a geographical range linked to the landform and climate, and to the habitats that these encourage. Most species have a home range, a stronghold, and a boundary zone where they become less common.

Some of Britain's plants are cosmopolitan and found everywhere in the world (chickweed, groundsel); others are Mediterranean (sea holly); or Atlantic and liking a wet mild climate (foxglove, bluebell); or Continental and tolerant of cold winters but liking hot summers (hornbeam, maiden pink). We have northern species such as globeflower and twinflower, arctic species typical of the tundra, and alpine species; most of our cold-tolerant plants are called arctic-alpine, equally at home in tundra or on mountains (mountain avens is one). Much the same is true of animals.

So, terms such as 'rare', 'common' or 'abundant' must be used carefully and locally. Three examples show the point. The barn owl is rare in Britain, with only 5000 nesting pairs across the country, but successful in that it inhabits almost every continent (see pages 102–3). The Adonis blue butterfly is rare and restricted to a few sites, but clouds of these butterflies may fly in some of them (see pages 62–3). Many rather scarce British wild orchids are common enough on the other side of the English Channel.

Another example is the oxlip, a relative of the cowslip, which is restricted to woods in East Anglia, but is seen in woodlands across large areas of central France and elsewhere.

CONSERVATION

The cowslip makes a good example of how distribution is so easily affected by man's activities. This nodding, cheerful flower was once so widespread in Britain that cowslip wine was familiar to all, a common country potion that many households would brew for themselves without a second thought. It's not made today – for the reason that cowslips are now somewhat rare, certainly too rare to be picked for such a frivolous purpose. They've been wiped off the grasslands by modern farming, to the extent that they can now act as a good indicator of undisturbed grassland.

Yet travel south-west from the Channel across France in April and your route will lie between roadside verges still abundantly scattered with cowslips, and the flowers adorn almost every grassy field. Britain too was like this.

Marsh marigold is another example. Its handsome golden flowers were much admired by the Victorians and taken for granted as a token of spring. It too is rather rare in Britain today, and something of a prized sighting.

Conservation is the protection of what remains of this natural heritage. We need to have a fairly expert knowledge of the needs of wildlife. And we need nowadays to understand politics as well as wildlife, and apart from all that, to understand a host of initials as well.

Not too long ago, a group of people wanted to protect a downland colony of Adonis blue butterflies, so they fenced in the slopes where they flew. With the sheep kept out, the grass grew long and smothered the low-growing horseshoe vetch on which these choosy insects laid their eggs (see pages 62–3), and the colony quickly died out.

Real conservation requires a detailed knowledge of both the history of the habitat and the lives of the species within it. As already stated, there is little, if any, natural, virgin terrain in Britain totally unaffected by man. The next best thing, semi-natural habitats, have been created by long centuries of traditional use. Hence conservation often means the imposition or even the re-establishment of traditional land management.

This can lead to local outcry. People lament the fact that the bluebells are not so good as they were, but are outraged when the wood is 'cut down' – when coppicing is restarted. In fact, coppicing helped to create the wood's richness in the first place (see pages 18–19).

Recognising the need to protect fine landscapes, Britain has National Parks in which development is controlled and grant aid available for minimising the effects of the visitors who flock there as a result; the CC (Countryside Commission) is involved here. But this does not protect wildlife. In Britain, the protection of species or habitats is possible only with the agreement of the owner of the land. Even laws which list protected species have declaimers for accidental damage in the course of farming or forestry.

As this book clearly shows, a plant or animal cannot be considered outside its habitat. So the only secure protection (for even benevolent landowners may sell up and move away) is for the ground itself to be a 'nature reserve', owned and managed by a conservation body such as the RSNC (Royal Society for Nature Conservation) and its largely county-based Wildlife Trust Partnership; and for them to have enough money to do a good job. They need money – subscription money, grant money, money from bring-and-buy sales. That is what conservation is founded on today.

Much of the modern destruction of habitats and wildlife has been the direct result of an official campaign of grant aid and propaganda to modernise farming in the years since the Second World War, a campaign organised through MAFF (Ministry of Agriculture, Fisheries and Food) with the support of the NFU (National Farmers Union) and CLA (Country Landowners Association), the pesticide and tractor manufacturers and others. In too many cases, the wild flowers and animals which remain do so by happy accident. They are in the fields and on the farms where the owners have not yet got round to modernisation. And this leads to an anomaly: should any one farmer be penalised and prevented from carrying out modern farming methods simply because other farmers have already wiped those habitats and their associated species of plants and animals off the map?

Part of a solution is to give to farmers and landowners who own prime-grade SSSI (Site of Special Scientific Interest) habitat grants of money *not* to intensify their farming practice but to maintain or revert to traditional management, which is, of course, less profitable. This is now accepted in Britain, although it leads to accusations of 'paying people to do nothing', and in the case of parts of Scotland leads to very large sums of money indeed being paid to prevent the 'coniferisation' of open moorland. This particular approach is now being spread out from SSSIs to areas of more mixed countryside, in what are known as ESAs (Environmentally Sensitive Areas).

Britain is part of the EC – the European Community (the Common Market) – and in fact ESAs are the direct result of the EC, which, in the shape of its CAP (Common Agricultural Policy), promoted intensive farming so successfully that there is now too much meat, grain and other produce. Much of the harvest of the modern prairies of British barley fields now goes straight into store, and even that costs money. To lessen productivity, farmers can apply for grants to 'Set Aside' land – to leave it fallow. Here they are again being paid for doing nothing, but for various reasons this may not benefit wildlife. Britain has now, however, taken the step of recognising ESAs, which are areas where traditional fields still remain and where grant aid can subsidise traditional farming in them. The Yorkshire Dales, with their flowery meadows, and the Suffolk river valleys painted by Constable are two such areas. The methods of assessment and grant award are Byzantine.

Until quite recently, the supervision of nature conservation in Britain was in the hands of the NCC, the Nature Conservancy Council. This has now been split into three separate agencies for England, Wales and Scotland, but EN (English Nature – one new name), for example, is still responsible for assessing SSSIs, notifying the owners and trying to reach agreement on management, and setting the level of grant aid in England.

Another important side to the work of EN and its cousins is the selection, establishment and management of National Nature Reserves.

The EC is now creating new environmental law which in theory supersedes some British law and which Britain has the obligation to respect. The British government argues that the Directives which are beginning to arrive from the EC and which concern protecting habitats are adequately met by the SSSI system. Which they could perhaps be, if EN had enough money to pay farmers large enough 'protective' grants – which is politics as much as ecology!

And as with all politics, there are pressure groups of all kinds. The World-wide Fund for Nature (WWF) as well as grant-aiding purchase of nature reserves by the county Wildlife Trusts and other bodies is also actively involved in propaganda and campaigns, notably on the interface between international concerns and the British situation – on the implementation in Britain of the new EC law for example. Friends of the Earth (FoE) and Greenpeace are also well known and notably active.

READING THE WOODLAND PROFILE

By 'profile' is meant the pattern created by the trees and other plant life along an imaginary section through the wood. This profile can be very revealing.

Definitions

A tree has a single trunk, whereas a shrub is a woody plant with several main stems rising from the rootstock. Undershrub is a term for heather, gorse and similar denizens of heathland (sometimes also of woods) which are woody but never grow to anything like tree size. They are also relatively short-lived. Bush is a day-to-day word for any shortish woody growth. 'Herb' is a shorthand word for a herbaceous plant, one which dies down each winter.

The woodland profile contains height classes. The trees grow tall, and their branching creates a leafy CANOPY below which is an UNDERSTOREY or SHRUB LAYER of shorter or younger trees and shrubs. Herbs and grasses form a FIELD LAYER, below which is a GROUND LAYER of mosses and lichens. Many field-layer plants come into leaf and flower in springtime, enjoying the light before the leaves above them open.

The origin of the wildwood

Twelve thousand years ago, the latest cold phase of the Ice Age was ending and trees and other plants could invade, for Britain was still connected to the rest of Europe across what are now the Channel and the North Sea. Pollen preserved in ancient soils shows that birch and Scots pine were early on the scene (see pages 40–43).

As the climate continued to improve, oak, ash, lime, elm and hazel followed; there was also a lot of alder. They crowded out the pioneers and created a natural wildwood in all except the wettest, highest and bleakest areas. Maple, hornbeam and beech probably became quite widespread in the south, but there was always local variety where soil changes favoured some trees over others. Great areas of eastern England were rich in lime trees, for example. There were also clearings where a tree had tumbled. Maybe one in five trees was dying of old age and there was plenty of rotting timber, which we do not expect to see in today's woods. Then, around 8000 years ago, rising sea levels separated Britain – the beech had been the last across, the last of our 60 or so 'native' trees and shrubs, to which are now added sycamore and other introduced and naturalised species.

Coppice and wood pasture

By 6000 years ago this wildwood was already being attacked by Neolithic tribes. After many centuries of grazing and poor management, the clearances in the lightly

TYPES OF BROADLEAVED WOODLAND

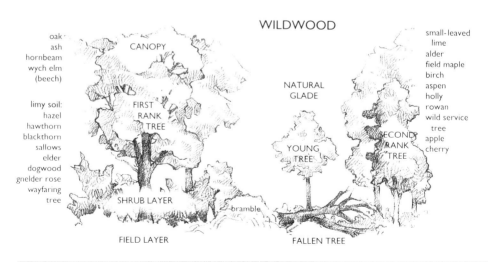

oak
ash
hornbeam
wych elm
(beech)

limy soil:
hazel
hawthorn
blackthorn
sallows
elder
dogwood
gnelder rose
wayfaring
tree

CANOPY

FIRST
RANK
TREE

SHRUB LAYER

FIELD LAYER

WILDWOOD

NATURAL
GLADE

YOUNG
TREE

bramble

FALLEN TREE

SECOND
RANK
TREE

NATURAL
GLADE

small-leaved
lime
alder
field maple
birch
aspen
holly
rowan
wild service
tree
apple
cherry

wooded areas began to evolve into the open heaths and chalk downs of the south and the moorlands of many northern hills. And by Norman times the wildwood had been reduced to isolated patches in the far corners of the parishes. What remained was also by then being hard-used and modified by use, either as coppice or as wood pasture.

Coppicing remained a widespread tradition well into the 20th century. If cut down to a stump or 'stool', most broad-leaved trees and shrubs sprout a head of fresh shoots. These thicken, and after seven to 15 years can be cut to provide a supply of 'smallwood'. Among this 'coppice' a scatter of 'standard' trees was left to grow tall for timber. To prevent livestock and deer destroying the coppice shoots, these woodlands were banked around and fenced.

But grazing was usually allowed in any woodland that was not coppiced and this 'wood pasture' also had a distinctive profile, with well-spaced trees growing on more open ground. These trees were often pollarded (see pages 52–3).

High forest
In recent centuries, 'high forest' management for timber alone has become popular, the trees being close set to grow straight tall trunks. The modern conifer plantation is an extreme example of this. Although open land is often used, many old coppice woods have also been clear-felled to make room for this modern planting.

Semi-natural woodland
Although 300,000 hectares of woodlands remain which are directly descended from the wildwood, they have all been modified in the ways described above, coppicing being most usual. Not only their profile has changed, but also what they contain, for useful species such as oak and hazel have been favoured and planted. An unexpected result is that the most 'natural' feature of a wood may be its spring flowers. Indeed, our sheets of bluebells which are the envy of Europe have been encouraged by the regular coppice cuts opening the woodland floor to the sun. A wood is not, however, made up simply of historical relics; it is a living thing, and diverse, and an old wood is never exactly the same as its neighbours.

Woods at least three or four centuries old which have undergone only traditional changes and which have escaped recent clear-felling and replanting are called semi-natural. They are not natural, but they are as close to it as we have.

Little coppice is cut today, and old coppice woods abandoned or left unmanaged may even regain some wildwood features in their profile.

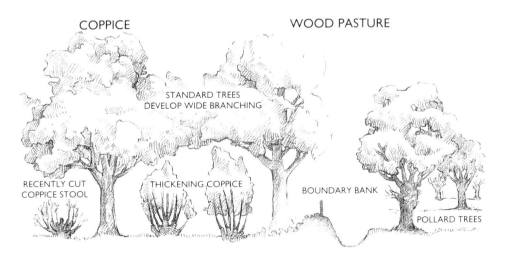

COPPICE

WOOD PASTURE

STANDARD TREES
DEVELOP WIDE BRANCHING

RECENTLY CUT
COPPICE STOOL

THICKENING COPPICE

BOUNDARY BANK

POLLARD TREES

EXPLORING THE MAP OF THE WOOD

Simple mapwork can demonstrate the diverse areas in a wood, and also help to explain why continuity survives in some parts but not others.

Primary and secondary woods

A primary wood is one that has never been anything but woodland since the wildwood formed, although it has certainly been modified by coppicing or by grazing if it was once wood pasture (see pages 16–17). A secondary woodland is one that has seeded itself onto, or was planted out onto, once open ground. Some secondary woods, however, are now centuries old and semi-natural, with a high wildlife tally.

Old woods on the map

Although some are mentioned in earlier documents, woods did not begin to appear on maps until the 16th century. As a general rule, a wood shown on an old map or described as existing three or four centuries ago is called an ancient wood and is probably a primary wood, a direct descendant of the wildwood.

Ancient woods are often moored to the parish boundary far from the village itself, which was sensibly sited in the middle of its best ploughland. In fact, old patches of woodland often acted as a waymark when the boundary was laid out. Names may help; medieval woods are sometimes named

FEATURES OF AN OLD WOOD

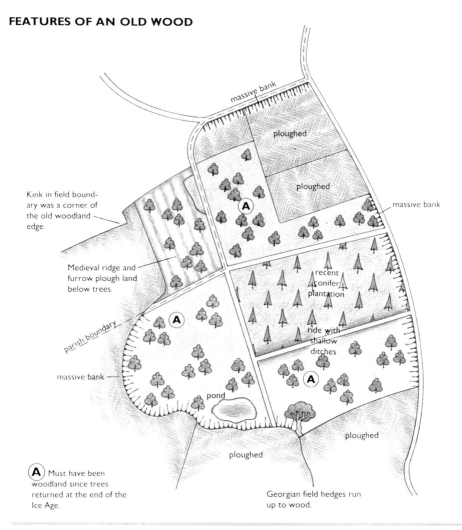

Kink in field boundary was a corner of the old woodland edge.

Medieval ridge and furrow plough land below trees.

parish boundary

massive bank

pond

(**A**) Must have been woodland since trees returned at the end of the Ice Age.

massive bank

ploughed

ploughed

(**A**)

massive bank

recent conifer plantation

ride with shallow ditches

(**A**)

ploughed

ploughed

Georgian field hedges run up to wood.

Some indicators of old woodland		
Very strongly associated with old woodland	*strongly linked*	*Often some link, especially when growing in profusion with others in this chart*
wild service tree small-leaved lime true oxlip (found in East Anglian woods)	herb Paris Midland hawthorn	wood anemone early purple orchid bluebell (on heavy soil) yellow archangel wood sorrel dog's mercury

*Bluebells in a beech wood could indicate a plantation, since beech is usually planted on light, quick draining soil. Ivy and other plants which act as 'storytellers' can be negative indicators (see page 21)

after their parish.. while others may have the name of a former owner, maybe joined with 'copse'. Lynd Wood and Chequer Wood refer to the small-leaved lime and the wild service tree (with spotted berries), both of which indicate old woodland. By contrast, names such as Waterloo Wood betray a recent origin. Although rabbit warrens were medieval, 'Warren Wood' is possibly a secondary, or late wood on the site; 'covert' is also a recent name (see pages 36–7).

The map of the banks

Coppice woodland was usually protected with a fence set along a massive boundary bank, the bank inside the ditch the better to keep deer and cattle out; lengths of this may remain. Following the lines of least resistance, it is often irregular and field hedges which are normally of later date will run up to it. Trees growing on it were usually pollarded, which can be another clue.

Within the wood, there may be slighter banks marking out different compartments of coppice which were cut in rotation to give a regular supply of wood and timber.

A map of the plants

It may also be possible to sketch out a map of different plant communities, each marked by a 'signpost' species. If the trees change – if oak trees and hazel coppice are replaced in one part by sycamore which has seeded itself in – then clearly the management of this area has been different. The wild flowers, which can be more characteristic of the site than the trees (see pages 16–17), mirror their soil preferences, and any area that has evaded the plough or other disturbance is likely to have islands of different soils. Bluebells, although slow to spread on heavy soil, quickly colonise light gravelly soil. Plants sensitive to disturbance and slow to colonise indicate old woodland. The tree lungwort is a lichen confined to old woods in the north and west. But more familiar species can be used.

So, mapwork, names and plants can help identify an old wood. The greater number of positive 'indicators', the firmer the evidence.

As a general rule, the larger and older the wood is and the more varied its profile, the greater its variety of animal life.

Small-leaved lime, its leaves 3-6 cm long, with red hair tufts between veins.

wild service tree

herb Paris

Midland hawthorn – its leaves are not as deeply indented as the hedgerow hawthorn.

MIXED WOODLANDS

The UK has 480,000 hectares (1,200,000 acres) of broadleaved (usually mixed) woodland of which 300,000 hectares are descended from prehistoric wildwood.

The most varied woods

The larger the wood is, the greater the variety of plant and animal life to be expected. A small wood might have 30 different wild flowers and ferns, a large one 200 or more. This is because the latter offers a greater range of conditions: more changes of soil from one place to another, areas with close-set trees, others where the sun reaches the ground, open rides, damp hollows.

The older the wood, the greater the variety likely, since plants and animals have had time to colonise. This is why a modern timber 'forest' is virtually a wood destroyed.

Shade and the seasons

Full daylight rather than direct sunlight is the key to plant growth. Most species of the field layer build up reserves in one year and flower in the next. Their shade tolerance, or intolerance, is linked with the seasons, and many woodland plants appear only briefly in spring before the leaf canopy opens. Beech woods come into full leaf early, which partly explains their bare floor.

Describing a wood

Many things shape the wood as a habitat, and it can be difficult to describe its character precisely. The soil preferences of the trees, shrubs and other plantlife could affect its profile, but soil and structure are often independent of each other, because certain species have been weeded out and others planted in. Wayfaring tree, buckthorn and hawthorn were often grubbed up from coppice, for example. Many southern coppices have been planted with sweet chestnut, brought here in Roman times.

So, although the natural descendant of the wildwood would be mixed woodland with a variety of trees, we find in our countryside today that woods dominated by a single species are common. Nearly pure oak, beech (and ash) woods can be found. The spring flowers may be more typical of the site than the trees and shrubs!

Nor can we try to describe woodland without a sense of history. Many classic ash and beech woods (see pages 28–9, 32–3) grow on what three centuries ago was open

TREES, SHRUBS AND SOIL PATCHES IN A WOOD

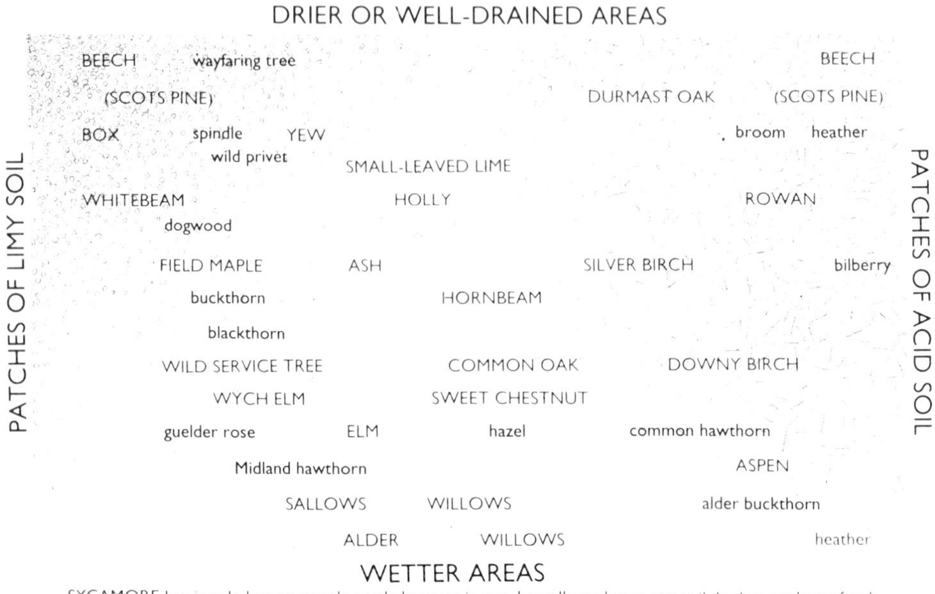
DRIER OR WELL-DRAINED AREAS
PATCHES OF LIMY SOIL
PATCHES OF ACID SOIL
BEECH
wayfaring tree
(SCOTS PINE)
BOX
spindle
YEW
wild privet
WHITEBEAM
dogwood
FIELD MAPLE
buckthorn
blackthorn
WILD SERVICE TREE
WYCH ELM
guelder rose
Midland hawthorn
SMALL-LEAVED LIME
HOLLY
ASH
HORNBEAM
COMMON OAK
SWEET CHESTNUT
ELM
hazel
SALLOWS
WILLOWS
ALDER
WILLOWS
BEECH
DURMAST OAK
(SCOTS PINE)
broom
heather
ROWAN
SILVER BIRCH
bilberry
DOWNY BIRCH
common hawthorn
ASPEN
alder buckthorn
heather
WETTER AREAS

SYCAMORE has invaded many woods partly because it can do well on almost any soil. It also seeds profusely.

pasture. Many ash woods have developed by natural succession (see pages 72–3) quali-fied by grazing, but the Chiltern beech woods were probably planted for timber for the local furniture industry.

Islands of difference

The more 'natural' a wood is, the more diverse it is likely to be, and even a short walk might reveal pockets of different trees, shrubs and flowers, and animal life.

In the jostle for nutrients, light and space, only a slight competitive edge is needed to give one species an advantage over another. It is often the weakness of the competitors rather than exact tailoring to the habitat that allows a species to flourish, this being especially true of the wild flowers of the woodland floor. Many species, however, show a close relationship, either positive or negative, with the chemical flavour of the soil, its dampness and other aspects. The chart shows, for example, that the beech tree favours both chalky and sandy soil – but what it needs is sharp drainage. The link between tree and soil is underscored by fungi, and woods tend to have a typical assortment of these mysterious living things.

Storytellers

Intruders can act as storytellers.

sycamore introduced in medieval times, seeds itself widely to fill once open glades

stinging nettles enriched soil, once open; a site of a hut or cattleshed, or rubbish dump maybe

rosebay willowherb open, disturbed or enriched ground; perhaps the site of a fire in the past

foxglove its seeds can remain dormant for 40 years, to be triggered by fresh light when the wood is opened up in some way

rhododendron planted in Victorian times as pheasant cover; now rampant

bramble can take over disturbed areas and cover the ground (though not flower) in shade

elder rabbits (often numerous but unnoticed in woods) find it distasteful and it may be prominent where their burrows are numerous

ivy can cover the ground in secondary woods and may be restricted to the disturbed ground; it might show up a recent addition to an older wood

snowdrop though wild in Europe, probably a garden escape here (see page 106)

SOIL PREFERENCES OF SOME WOODLAND FLOWERS

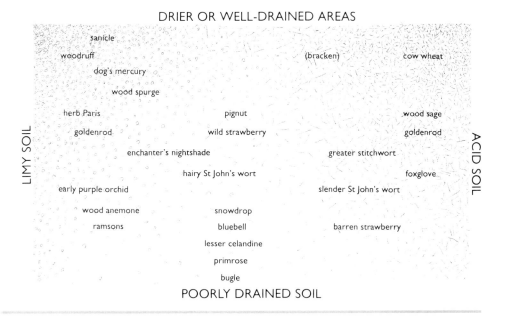

DRIER OR WELL-DRAINED AREAS

sanicle

woodruff   (bracken)   cow wheat

dog's mercury

wood spurge

herb Paris   pignut   wood sage

LIMY SOIL   goldenrod   wild strawberry   goldenrod   ACID SOIL

enchanter's nightshade   greater stitchwort

hairy St John's wort   foxglove

early purple orchid   slender St John's wort

wood anemone   snowdrop

ramsons   bluebell   barren strawberry

lesser celandine

primrose

bugle

POORLY DRAINED SOIL

HOW OAK WOODS SHAPE UP

In the mind's eye, the oak wood is the typical British woodland. As we see here, however, there is more than one kind of oak wood, each with its own character.

Two kinds of oak tree

The oak has been much planted because of its trunk timber and its zigzag branching, which provided ready-curved timbers for shipbuilding. Even without man's influence it would dominate most of our woodland, except in three circumstances: namely, on poor, acid sandy soils; on shallow soils on limestone; and in permanently wet areas. Wind can also stunt it on exposed sites. Beech can compete strongly with oak on well-drained soils, while it gives way to alder in the wet.

There are two distinct native oak species, the common or pedunculate oak and the durmast or sessile oak.

The common oak is linked more with southern, eastern and Midland woods, on heavy, perhaps rather clayish but fertile lowland soils; the durmast with the uplands of the west and north, where the soils are often lighter, better drained and perhaps rather acid. Durmast is also found on sandy soils in the south-east. The common oak,

however, has been more widely planted, even in the uplands, and where the two grow close together they cross-pollinate to produce trees with mixed character.

Types of oak wood

There are four main kinds of oak wood.

1   On heavy but rich soils, the trees grow stately, with plenty of hazel and other shrubs and a varied field layer below with many spring flowers.

2   On drier, rather more acid sandy soils, there are fewer shrubs and foxglove can be a typical flower. Sometimes bluebells carpet the spring wood, to be followed by bracken later in the year (see below); and soft grass (a grass species which lives up to its name) is typical.

3   On very acid soils, the trees are stunted and the canopy lower; there may be many birch trees, and heather and bilberry can form the shrub-cum-field layer.

4   Very wet ground sees the oak patchily giving way to alder and the willow family, with rushes and sedges plentiful.

Other trees

While oak was favoured as the timber standard in coppice woods, this did not

THREE KINDS OF OAKWOOD

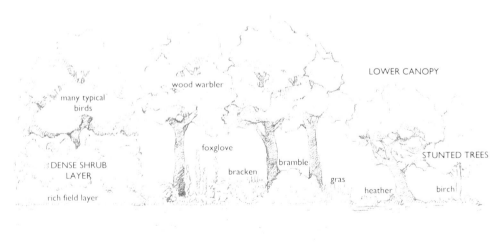

GOOD SOIL   ACID SOIL   VERY ACID SOIL

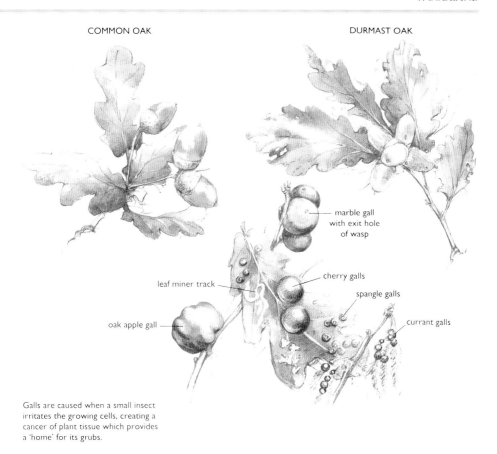

COMMON OAK

DURMAST OAK

marble gall
with exit hole
of wasp

leaf miner track

cherry galls

spangle galls

oak apple gall

currant galls

Galls are caused when a small insect
irritates the growing cells, creating a
cancer of plant tissue which provides
a 'home' for its grubs.

exclude others, and 'oak woods' can also contain ash, hornbeam and wych elm; aspen and maple may also be found. There are some almost pure lime woods in East Anglia. The mixture we see today is usually directly linked with past management, the deliberate choice of centuries.

Hazel and other shrubs

Oak and hazel are frequent companions, the latter creating the coppice below the oak. Hazel is a native shrub, but its frequency results from its usefulness in the coppice. In some southern areas, sweet chestnut has been planted as coppice. Midland hawthorn can be an age indicator (see pages 18–19).

Bluebells and bracken

An oak wood in spring is one of the most powerful of natural images, especially when bluebells carpet the ground. Sheets of bluebells are one of the botanical splendours of Britain; they are an 'Atlantic' species and flourish in our damp, mild ocean-influenced climate. Indeed, in the wetter west of the country they will be seen out on open pastures and along the hedgerows. They do, however, spread faster on quick-draining light soils – on patches of gravelly soil in a wood, for example.

Well-drained wet also suits bracken, and the two make an interesting example of 'companionship', or non-competitiveness. Bluebell leafs and flowers early in the spring, snatching light for a time before the bracken unfurls its fronds overhead. Their competition is also reduced underground, where the bracken rhizomes creep and feed a good deal deeper in the soil than the bluebell bulbs.

A GOOD WOOD FOR WILDLIFE

Ancient woods can contain as many tens of different native species of trees and shrubs. Animal life reflects this, as well as the structure of the wood.

The tree rating

Insect species usually seek certain plant species as food or as host for themselves or their eggs or grubs. The oak tree leads the field, with 284 dedicated species. Moths feature strongly in this tally.

insects:			
oak	284	hazel	73
willow	266	beech	64
birch	229	ash	41
hawthorn	149	small-leaved	
blackthorn	109	lime	31
poplars	97	rowan, maple,	
Scots pine	91	hornbeam	27
alder	90	holly	7
lelms	82	yew	1

Native holly and yew are unexpectedly low. The introduced species sycamore and sweet chestnut, brought here without their dedicated insect life, have counts of 15 and 5. Foreign spruce, larch and fir are similar, with 37, 17 and 16 respectively, compared with native Scots pine's 91.

A well-mixed wood is clearly off to a good start, and to these totals must be added insects which are less targeted: ants and the mining bees and wasps which burrow into banks, butterflies which relate to woodland flowers in the field layer, and spiders, snails and other invertebrates. A large, semi-natural wood can contain over 4000 species of animals. Nevertheless, a simple totting-up of the 'scores' of trees and shrubs might give us an interesting comparison between two neighbouring woods.

The decomposers

If decomposers did not quickly claim fallen timber, in fact any dead matter, the natural wood would silt up with fallen branches and drifts of leaves. A fifth of woodland invertebrates, including numerous beetles, worms and woodlice, rely on decay. Fungi and slimes also play a part here. Their activities release nutrients to feed new generations of green plants, and hence new generations of animal life.

Dead and decaying timber is thus a wildlife bonus in any woodland. This is why it is left in nature reserves, whereas it is cleared from commercial timber-producing woodlands.

Plants and wildlife

The distribution of animals tends to echo that of the plants on which they rely, but

ANCIENT WOODS AS HABITATS

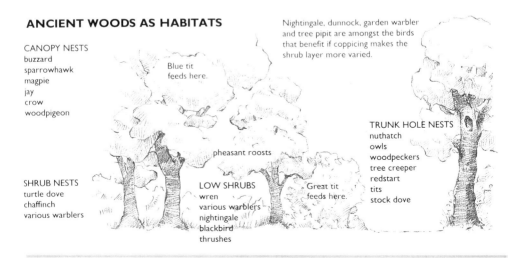

CANOPY NESTS
buzzard
sparrowhawk
magpie
jay
crow
woodpigeon

Blue tit feeds here.

Nightingale, dunnock, garden warbler and tree pipit are amongst the birds that benefit if coppicing makes the shrub layer more varied.

TRUNK HOLE NESTS
nuthatch
owls
woodpeckers
tree creeper
redstart
tits
stock dove

pheasant roosts

SHRUB NESTS
turtle dove
chaffinch
various warblers

LOW SHRUBS
wren
various warblers
nightingale
blackbird
thrushes

Great tit feeds here.

the pattern need not be simple. The birds relate also to the structure of the wood.

Birdsong

Birds need to feed their nestlings with protein-rich, body-building animal food, instinctively opting for woodland areas likely to supply it, and a wood ringing with birdsong is a wood that is full of insect life. Unlike insects, however, birds rely more on the structure of the wood, and whether it provides nesting, preening, singing and roosting sites, and less on the actual species of vegetation. There is vertical stratification, as the sketch below explains. If roe or fallow deer are grazing and weakening the low cover in the shrub layer, the relative abundance of willow and garden warblers, for example, may decrease.

In general, songbirds like woodland that offers both dense cover for safe nesting and a prominent songpost. Birds of one species share out the wood among them, each pair occupying a territory which instinct suggests will provide enough food for their nestlings and from which they will chase intruders. This is clearly seen with the robin, which precedes us along a path until we reach its territory boundary, when it turns back. The delightful songs of many birds are in fact a kind of territorial flag, strongest at the central nest site and weakening towards the edges, and when walking through a wood we pass from one pair's territory and singing area to the next. However, there is no fixed size of territory for woodland birds. A songbird pair may occupy half a hectare in a varied wood, and double that in one poorer in insect life. Predators have large territories: a tawny owl may possess a whole 20-hectare wood.

This 'invisible map' applies only within a species. A songbird will accept others of different species and live wing-to-wing with them without argument. The details of their food-gathering mean there is little direct competition between them. Hence the fact that woods can ring with birdsong.

Mammals

All British land mammals, including bats, are woodland species by origin, although now well adapted to open ground. Deer, badgers and others can leave obvious clues, depicted in most field guides (see How to assess the habitat, pages 194–8).

The wood can be full of burrows of one kind and another, and these, although often well hidden, are worth looking for. Whether the burrow is large or small, signs of recent occupation include freshly dug soil (and perhaps footprints, of course) and a noticeable smell. Cobwebs strung undisturbed across the entrance are a negative sign. Rabbits can be numerous in a wood, though less obvious than in the open countryside.

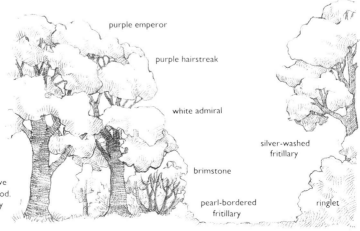

purple emperor

purple hairstreak

white admiral

silver-washed fritillary

brimstone

pearl-bordered fritillary

ringlet

As with birds, butterflies have their own precincts in a wood. Unlike birds, they are closely linked with the actual plant species rather than the structure of the wood.

WILDLIFE TALLIES

Familiar plants and animals can indicate the general age or diversity of a wood. The song of the nightingale mirrors the actual structure of the wood.

Plant indicators

Old, semi-natural mixed woods guard an enormous variety of wildlife, and the larger the wood the better. As explained earlier (see pages 18–19), these woods can often be identified by mapwork and by using flowers and shrubs as indicators. Even the familiar sheet of bluebells may mean that many other wild flowers, some of them rare, can be expected.

Invertebrate indicators

From midsummer on, it is possible to let diversity literally speak for itself – there is no mistaking the hum of an insect wood, especially (but not exclusively) in the sunnier open areas. This busyness may remain on the old woodland edge, even when the centre has been felled and replanted (see pages 44–5).

Digger wasps are one group to look for, making small holes in paths and banks (and sometimes dead wood). The hundred or so species are all predators, matching birds of prey on their own scale, and are thus a key to a thriving insect life in general. Galls are another indicator of similar kind. Cancer-like growths on leaf, stem or flower, they are usually triggered by an insect; over 50 different species create oak galls (some examples are shown on pages 22–3). Because of the interrelationships in nature, a variety of galls indicates a varied insect life in general.

Some easily recognised individual species are also relevant. The once familiar stag beetle, for example, is linked to decaying timber and is now more restricted to older semi-natural woods.

Their exacting needs mean that butterflies can mirror general stability and variety. Regular butterfly walks will be needed, however, to estimate the full picture (see page 203). A renewal of traditional coppicing encourages the field-layer flowers and results in higher butterfly counts.

Insects apart, certain snails make good indicators of old woods, although they are more for the expert, being difficult to find and identify.

Birdlife

Coppicing can also increase the opportunities for birds, and the nightingale provides a classic example. A migrant, it arrives at the end of April in woodlands mostly south of a line from the Severn to the Humber, and sings until mid June. Choosing dense low cover, it is attracted to coppice three years after a cut; numbers climb to a peak when the coppice is seven years old, but then fall away as it is becoming too 'leggy'. The bird is more likely in large woods (with greater structural variety): it is likely in one in five woods of less than 10 hectares, but maybe in half of those of 100 hectares. It may occupy downland scrub, but not young conifer plantations as do some songbirds (see pages 44–7).

The woodland bird tally changes by the season, but the summer's 'top ten' in relative abundance (page 202) in a southerly mixed oak wood might be:

1 woodpigeon	6 song thrush
2 wren	7 blue tit
3 blackbird	8 migrant warblers
4 chaffinch	9 great tit
5 robin	10 greenfinch

If the greenfinch is seen, this of course suggests that the others are present. Nuthatch and treecreeper might have the same abundance as the greenfinch. Although they are present, owls, sparrowhawks and woodpeckers will not be abundant to the same degree.

In the winter wood, birds tend to flock, and mixed flocks of tits and others may roam the canopy. If you fail to spot one flock, you may fail to see a host of species! Only the woodpigeon, robin, wren and pheasant may be conspicuous.

Mammals

Most mammals are fairly tolerant of the structure, but the dormouse is one example of a habitat specialist. To help it when it

THE NIGHTINGALE IN ITS HABITAT

The nightingale also nests in dense scrub, such as that found on downland.

Numbers peak in woodland when the coppice is around 7 years old.

The bird also needs rather open ground on which to feed.

7 year coppice

A range of song posts are nearby, one of which will be regularly used for the night-time singing.

The nest is low in dense cover, often in the sunny south area of a wood or a scrub patch.

The cock bird sings at night when it has established its territory (but it also sings by day).

clambers among the branches, it prefers a well-lit and thus branchy shrub layer rather than straggly, densely shaded growth. It eats catkins, flowers and fruit and so a botanically mixed wood suits it. Its summer nest can be a couple of metres up in a tree fork, while its winter one is on or below ground. Both can be made and lined with strips of honeysuckle bark, and hazel coppice with a lot of honeysuckle suits it well. The squirrels are also habitat specialists in the sense that they like tall trees.

More than many other mammals, the badger actually imprints its presence on the wood. The delights of badger-watching are outlined on pages 196–8.

THE ASH WOOD

The ash tree is common in woodland, often found in coppice and a boon companion to the oak, but the ash tree can also form woodlands in its own right.

Ash in the wildwood

Pollen preserved in ancient soils shows that the ash tree was well established in the early wildwood. Poorly drained, and with fallen branches clogging the streams, this wild-wood was often a soggy place; ash can, in fact, tolerate damp soil so long as it is not permanently waterlogged.

But then the record becomes less certain. What is clear is that there was a decline in elm around 3000 BC, and it is possible that the numbers of ash and of the native small-leaved lime also decreased at this time. Disease may have struck, similar to that which wiped out the hedgerow elms over much of Britain in the early 1970s; but the leaves of these three trees make good fodder for livestock, and perhaps this is early evidence of man's influence. Ash was certainly being coppiced in prehistoric times – ash poles were used for Neolithic cause-ways, preserved deep in the peat of the Somerset Levels – and ash has remained a popular coppice species.

Ash as a colonist

With its wind-blown seeds, ash is early on the scene on abandoned, ungrazed ground and, being fast-growing (to 4.5 metres high in 10 years), it can quickly create a second-ary woodland. Pollen evidence shows that many of the ash woods in the north country are fairly recent (see below).

In the natural order of things, the ash wood would in time be invaded by oak, or by beech on thin limestone soils, and eventually be shaded out by these slower-growing trees. It would remain numerous, however, because it can so quickly colonise gaps when trees are felled by storms; it will take advantage of better-lit patches below the canopy. Although man has changed the composition of many woods, ash trees can remain as a link with the old wildwood.

Ash woods on limestone

Some 'pure' ash woods are found in rocky limestone valleys such as the gorges of the Severn and Wye and in Derbyshire; or on limestone pavement (see pages 66–7), where thin soil and other conditions deter oak and beech. Here ash may be the only canopy tree (and still in the majority even when others are numerous).

THREE PARTNERS OF A LIMESTONE ASHWOOD

ash
wych elm
field maple
(sycamore
  recently
  seeded in)
small-leaved lime
whitebeam
aspen
. . . and others
familiar from
oakwoods

SKIMPY GROUND COVER ON LIMESTONE BLOCKS

BUT A VARIED WOOD ON DEEP SOIL

The winter silhouette reveals that the end twigs turn up.

Large ash stool after a coppice cut.

Ancient ash stool in a wood in
East Anglia; this is one 'tree'

In Derbyshire and up the west coast of Scotland in particular, these woods can occupy what was open pasture abandoned in the farming slumps following the Napoleonic wars. As a result, their trees are likely to be of much the same age. There are, however, pockets of what seems to be older woodland, with ash trees of widely different ages and also containing both common and durmast oak, wych elm and (in England) field maple. Other woody species can include aspen, and (again in England) whitebeam and yew (reflecting the limy soil).

The ash tree grows a fine lace of leaves which lets a lot of light through; and the tree is, anyway, late into leaf and early to lose its leaves, often still green, at the first autumn chills. As a result of this plentiful light, the variety of shrubs and wild flowers in some ash woods is a botanical delight. Wild privet with sweetly scented flowers, spindle and dogwood are three shrubs which might reflect the limy soil.

Ash coppice

The fact that ash was so popular for coppice has had a bizarre result: that some ash coppice stools may be the oldest living things to be found in Britain. Trees do not age in the way of animals, and if they combat disease and other hazards coppice stools can produce heads of new shoots for hundreds of years. The oldest ash stools are found in certain woods in Suffolk, and are probably around 1000 years old. They now look like rings of trees, the central growth having died and rotted away. By comparison, the oldest oak and beech trees are probably about 500 years old (the only sure way of determining age is to count the annual rings in the felled trunk).

Hedgerow ash trees

The ash tree of the hedgerows can display its distinctive profile, hard to discern in a crowded wood. The upper branches form a rounded crown, and the lower curve down, almost vertically in some cases, to turn up again near their tips.

Many field trees, however, have been pollarded, the branches being cut to supply strong but flexible poles and the leaves stripped for fodder. The characteristic bunching of the branches at the top of the trunk is the clue to this.

In this connection it's interesting to recall the vital importance of hedgerow or 'field' trees in the landscape. At the time of the enclosures young tree saplings were planted down the young hedges. They have since grown tall to give us the bosky views we take for granted today.

A HALF-HOUR WALK IN AN ASH WOOD

An ash wood harbours a characteristic suite of shrubs and flowers. Both they and the animal life benefit from the generous light which spreads down below the canopy.

A rich underwood

The purest form of ash woods are those clinging to limestone slopes in the Mendips and Derbyshire: even when fairly young they may contain oak, wych elm and other trees. Some northern woods have bird cherry, a tree only found in East Anglia in the south of Britain – which says something for the complexities of woodland history.

The generous light below the ash encourages a strong bushy underwood, and many of the shrubs will be familiar from the hedges nearby. Wild privet, whitebeam, guelder rose, dogwood and spindle reflect the limy soil and can positively foam with white blossom in spring. Traveller's joy may also lace the edges of the southern woods.

A natural garden

With sunshine dappling the ground, the ash wood offers attractive walks. Wild flowers flourish: where there is some depth of soil, dog's mercury and wood anemone and

ASH WOOD SPECIES

ash

whitebeam

wych elm

stone bramble

baneberry

polypody

garlic-smelling ramsons familiar from oak and other woodlands can be seen. In northern ash woods you may see stone bramble, a slender, weakly prickly bramble with red berries which have only two to six segments; and rare baneberry, with fluffy-looking flower-heads and black berries. One fungus of note is King Alfred's cake, looking for all the world like a burnt bun glued to dead or dying ash.

Gardens of ferns

Where limestone blocks tumble down the hillside below the trees, a host of ferns may luxuriate in the damp shade offered by the angled rock, and the effect can be rather like a carefully planned garden. Some ferns are familiar from other woods. Polypody is one, its simple outline like a child's drawing of a fern; it curls brown when dry, to revive like a Japanese paper flower when wet. Others, such as the Tunbridge filmy-fern, are quite rare. As is the case with other plants, some ferns are strongly linked with soil type, hart's tongue and hard shield fern, for example, with lime; others, such as male and lady ferns, are more general, while hard fern marks the acid conditions of such places as moorland soils.

Birdsong

Surprisingly, the ash tree attracts only a limited variety of dedicated insects (41, as opposed to 284 for oak). True, there will be others linked with the shrubs and field-layer flowers, but what is crucial is the timing of this larder, the time when it is available to birds. Whatever the reasons, the bird balance can be subtly different from that in an oak wood, with chaffinch and willow warbler being relatively more abundant. Northerly ash woods are also at the far end of many migrants' ranges, and out of range of the nightingale, for example.

The keys (seeds) attract bullfinches, and in autumn mixed finch flocks may visit the wood to strip them; unlike beech mast and acorns, the keys tend to remain on the trees. Like the beech, the ash also has abundant and poor seed years, and so varying numbers of birds are expected.

willow warbler

King Alfred's cake fungus

Tumbling butterflies

A sunny ash wood alight with wild flowers could certainly be a good place to spot many familiar woodland butterflies. But, intriguingly, the ash tree has often been linked with the less well-known brown hairstreak. The female travels far along hedges and copses to find suitable blackthorn shrubs for her egg-laying; the butterflies that result are thus well spaced and, to be able to meet and mate, these butterflies tend to congregate at certain tall 'master trees'. The magnificent purple emperor butterfly does the same, but, whereas it selects oak, all known master trees chosen by the brown hairstreak are ash. It is not known why this should be. Sweet honeydew oozing from aphids feeding on the ash leaves could be the magnet, although oak leaves are also usually sticky with honeydew.

You need to take binoculars to see these small butterflies tumbling overhead.

THE BEECH WOOD

The beech is one of our stateliest trees, creating woodlands which resemble natural cathedrals. Apart from woodlands, the tree is often seen planted in narrow shelterbelts.

The puzzle of the beech tree

Fossil pollen shows that the beech tree has been growing in the south of Britain for over 6000 years and was the last of our native trees to colonise (see pages 16–17). Although it can grow to overtop the oak and impose its own woodland, it hardly had time to compete before man was playing a part by clearing, grazing and coppicing the wildwood. It is difficult to be certain if southern beech woods are 'natural'; in the last three centuries beech has been extensively planted in woods and in shelterbelts. It does not set good seed in the north and it is safe to say that, while there is doubt about those in the south, beech woods growing north of Derby have certainly been planted.

A tree of distinct character

Gilbert White considered the beech 'the most lovely of all our forest trees, whether we consider its smooth bark, its glossy foliage or its graceful pendulous boughs'. It is shallow-rooted and greedy, casting a dense shade, and is quite early into leaf. Its leaves are slow to decay, and are still recognisable a year after the fall, to glisten purple in the rains. They may form a hand-deep layer.

Added together, these traits mean that beech often forms pure and empty woods, accompanied only by yew perhaps and a few specialities such as spurge-laurel, for not many plants can survive with the mean ration of sunlight beneath the canopy. The empty floor and smooth grey trunks thrusting up to the latticed canopy might almost have been the inspiration for the fan vaulting of the magnificent late Gothic cathedrals of Britain.

BEECHWOODS

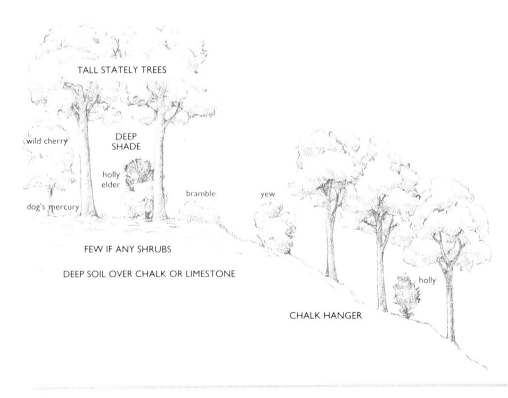

TALL STATELY TREES

wild cherry

DEEP SHADE

holly
elder

bramble

yew

dog's mercury

FEW IF ANY SHRUBS

DEEP SOIL OVER CHALK OR LIMESTONE

holly

CHALK HANGER

The hanger beech wood

Perhaps the most famous beech woods are the 'hanger' woods on chalk slopes in the south of England. To gain a grip, the tree's roots explore every cranny in the face of solid chalk below the thin soil. Just how thin the soil is can be seen when a tree is toppled by a storm. Very distinctive is the way the shallow soils can weather away to leave the roots exposed in tortuous fingers.

Other beech woods

Beech woods are also found on the tops of the chalk downs above the hangers and on Cotswold limestones, and it is these 'plateau' woods on deeper soil that boast the most magnificent trees, rising to the full height of 40 metres. There may be cherry, whitebeam and ash with holly and yew below, but the ground is still largely bare, except perhaps where pillows of bramble sprawl where the canopy is broken.

A third type of beech wood, typified by the famous Burnham Beeches, grows on acid gravel or sandy soils. The key factor for the tree is not soil flavour but sharp drainage. These 'acid' beech trees, however, tend to be misshapen, added to which they have often been pollarded in the past. These acid-soiled beech woods often contain some oak and (hairy) birch, with maybe more of an under-wood and heather and bilberry.

Distinctive ecology

Wild flowers are discouraged both by the shade and by the rather toxic leaf litter and are generally few (and so butterflies are also absent). The sheets of bluebells in some Chiltern woods may be a clue that the beech trees here were planted into oak and horn-beam woods, these last trees having since been felled.

There may be low cushions of green-grey moss on the otherwise bare floor (often taking advantage of nutrients washing with the rain down the nearby trunks). Fungi, present in all woods, can be prominent on the bare floor. Fungal webs whose spore-bearing caps appear as the familiar toad-stools and other shapes are close to the heart of the beech wood's secrets. They are sapro-phytes, feeding from decay. The soil is permeated by their feeding threads, but if the rootlets of the beech tree are exposed (which may mean no more than brushing the leaves aside) they will often be seen to be clothed with a whitish bloom. This, too, consists of fungal threads, closely associated with the root cells, and helping the tree gain nutrients from the decaying mould in the soil. This close association of a fungal web with a plant or tree which has green leaves is called a mycorrhiza, and it is another relationship of this kind which helps to explain the presence of exciting flowers – wild orchids.

In addition, the beech wood also houses higher 'green' plants which have adopted a saprophytic lifestyle, some of them not relying on sunlight for nourishment at all. We also meet them when we step into the shade of the beech wood.

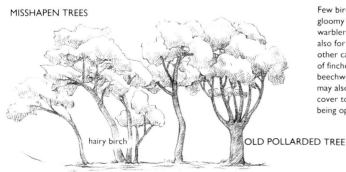

MISSHAPEN TREES

hairy birch

OLD POLLARDED TREE

ACID SANDS AND GRAVELS

Few birds will nest in a tall, empty, gloomy wood, but the wood warbler may be the exception. Look also for crows, woodpigeon, and other canopy nesters. Mobile flocks of finches come to the winter beechwoods, and tits and nuthatches may also come if there is some low cover to ease their anxieties about being open to view.

IN THE SHADE OF THE BEECH WOOD

The beech wood greets you coolly when you step into it, a fact taken for granted, but which explains much of the basic ecology of this lovely wood.

The cool of the wood

The beech wood is cool when you step into it out of the sun. In other words, the canopy is stealing a great deal of the sunshine and its energy. Plants have adopted special strategies to survive in such surroundings.

An obvious one is to be evergreen, to have leaves which can produce food all year round, and especially in winter when the beech leaves have dropped. Yew and holly are familiar examples, but look out for spurge-laurel, a rarish shrub of southerly beech woods. It is recognised by its long leathery green leaves bunched at the tip of the shoots in rhododendron fashion.

Exploring patches of deep shade

A second strategy is more intriguing. Some plants typical of the beech wood have given up photosynthesis and green leaves, and feed on decaying mould in the soil, calling on the aid of fungal webs to do so. One is the yellow bird's nest, a plant of bizarre appearance, which makes use of a fungus of the *Boletus* genus.

Another, similar in appearance but browner, is the bird's nest orchid. This is just one of a number of orchids to be sought in beech woods. Wild orchids may also feed on decaying matter, at least in part, and especially when they are young.

The world of orchids

Our wild orchids have an exotic structure and a fragile and complex lifestyle. They produce a large quantity of dust-like seeds spread by the wind. With nothing in the way of a store of food, germination would mean immediate death were it not for a mycorrhizal association that they strike up with fungus webs in the soil (and this is so for both open-grassland and woodland orchids). The feeding threads of the fungus invade the roots of the germinating orchid, but somehow the orchid manages to control them and in fact milks them of nutrients.

For many orchids, the mycorrhiza is crucial only during germination, before the green leaves appear (which even so can take two or three years). For others, such as the bird's nest orchid and the shallow-rooted helleborines, the orchid remains dependent on the fungus for its entire life.

Orchids also have an intricate pollination which fascinated Charles Darwin. 'In no other plant, indeed in hardly any animal, can adaptations of one part to another be more perfect', he wrote. A bee crawling into the flower triggers an 'explosion', which glues a pollen sac to part of its body. Orchid flowers are structured to receive only those pollen sacs positioned by their own tribe.

Orchids are also attractive to small flies, and Darwin's son was struck by the number of spiders' webs strung near flowering orchids, as if the spiders knew what to expect. This, too, is worth looking for.

Fungi

Although classed as plants, fungi merit being recognised as a living kingdom of their own, equal to the animal and plant kingdoms. Fungi are certainly numerous and far-reaching. Prominent fungi to look for, linked to beech trees, are the oyster, chanterelle and cep.

Birdlife in the beech wood

Although wood pigeons and crows may nest in the canopy, they are using the beech wood only as a hotel, flying out to feed in the surrounding countryside. Songbirds need room service, and require a much more detailed local habitat to supply food. The empty and simple structure of the beech wood deters them, but one notable exception is the wood warbler. This summer visitor nests on the ground, among the scant cover or alongside a grass tussock, and sings its energetic trills from a songpost on a branch high above (it also likes the open oak woods of the hills). Where there is some diversity other species come in, the chaffinch being the most likely. Old trees with rot holes create another opportunity: redstarts nest in New Forest beech woods, for example.

THE ECOLOGY OF THE BEECH WOOD

Wood warbler, a relatively brightly coloured warbler.

Its tail feathers growing again after a moult.

green-purple flowers: broadleaved helleborine

white helleborine

yellow bird's nest

fly orchid

chanterelle

oyster fungus

PATCH WOODS

Small patches of woodland not only add interest to the landscape but are also a haven for wildlife. Many are recent additions; some echo the distant past.

Sporting coverts

A covert is one of many words for a small wood (spinney and copse are others). It was coined only two centuries ago, to indicate that it offered cover for foxes or for pheasants. In the sporting shires, coverts were even planted at the same time as the field enclosures and strategically placed to give good runs for the hounds. The simple fact that it was a patch of woodland was enough for foxes, but shooting coverts often have their own management (see pages 48–9).

Relics of past landscapes

Many woods linger as the relics of the prehistoric wildwood (see pages 16–17), but even in the heart of today's manicured countryside we can still expect to come across some woods which echo more particular periods in landscape history. They mirror the early colonisation of the open land at the end of the Ice Age and can give us a taste of the scenery of those times. Under a steel-grey sky, even a young suburban birch wood has a prehistoric feel.

Birch woods

Birch has ideal pioneering tactics: it has plentiful small wind-borne seeds, is quick-growing and can begin to seed when only 12 years old. On the minus side, it is short-lived as trees go. Today it is often seen colonising derelict sites, and is quickly into heaths when grazing and other management have ended.

The tree is also seen in woodlands, and if clustered may well mark the site of what was once a clearing, although the birch stand will eventually be invaded and shaded out by taller trees.

North of the border, the situation is rather different. In places in the Scottish Highlands, birches form the upper limit of the forests (at about 600 metres), where they may grow among low juniper. Higher up the slopes, a cousin, the dwarf birch,

may hug the ground, but lower down, on more sheltered ground, plentiful birch is probably the relic of mixed oak-birch forest from which the oaks have been removed. There is usually some rowan (mountain ash) growing with these.

Juniper

Juniper is a rather prickly evergreen with scented berries which are waxy blue when ripe. It was once much commoner, in three distinct habitats: on chalk downlands, in northern woods, and high up open hillsides in the north. In the first it is an upright shrub, in the second either a shrub or a small tree, and in the third it often hugs the ground.

The leaves of its seedlings are not prickly and are vulnerable to grazing, and, on the chalk, patches of juniper scrub or low woodland mark grazing land let go. Its success here holds its own demise, however, for both yew and beech can take root within its embrace, and if the soil is deep enough will grow to shade out the juniper. Dead junipers are sometimes found in beech and yew woods here.

Yew and box

Evergreen yew is a fairly common, if scattered, member of a beech wood, but can form pure patchy woods of its own. Here it has managed to colonise abandoned chalk or limestone grazing, and also to grow well enough to shade out any beech or ash which might attempt to invade the same ground. Once in place, a yew wood cannot be replaced by beech until old trees die and open up gaps.

Box, with its hauntingly scented foliage, is easily recognised, and is also a native evergreen shrub or tree. But box woods are even rarer than yew woods. Box Hill (Surrey) is perhaps the most famous, where, together with yew, box clothes a steep, unstable chalk slope; beech cannot get rooted here although it grows nearby. It is a classic example of an important ecological maxim: that the success of a species may not be due to its own individual vigour but owe more to lack of competition.

Alder woods

Although patches of birch can recall forgotten scenery, what is difficult to imagine today is the sheer wetness of much of the landscape in prehistoric days. For much of the year valleys were waterlogged, fallen trees lying tangled and uncleared to create natural dams (and beavers, which were common even into historic times – Beverley, near York, gained its name from them – did their bit by damming up pools). Patches of carr, a wet woodland in which alder predominates, still accompany our remaining fens (see pages 140–1).

Lines of alder trees can also be found alongside rivers and streams in the hills, or marching along seepage lines. Where it grew well, alder was often an important coppice species, its charcoal being used in the manufacture of gunpowder. Neglected alder coppice is probably the most typical type of wet woodland today.

YEW, BOX AND JUNIPER

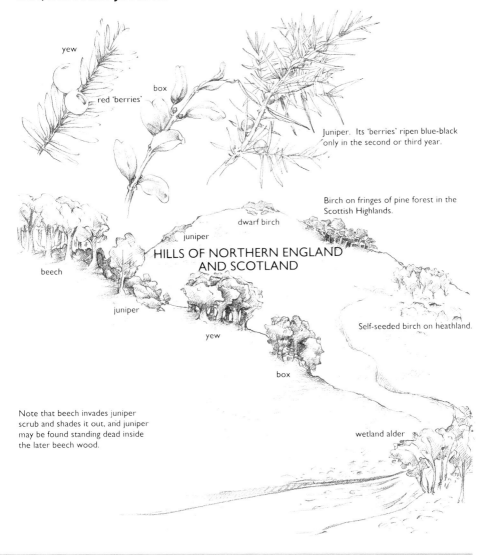

yew

red 'berries'

box

Juniper. Its 'berries' ripen blue-black only in the second or third year.

Birch on fringes of pine forest in the Scottish Highlands.

dwarf birch

juniper

HILLS OF NORTHERN ENGLAND AND SCOTLAND

beech

juniper

Self-seeded birch on heathland.

yew

box

Note that beech invades juniper scrub and shades it out, and juniper may be found standing dead inside the later beech wood.

wetland alder

37

A HALF-HOUR WALK IN A BIRCH WOOD

Favoured for ornamental planting, the birch tree is one of the most familiar of trees. It can create charming woodlands which hold some distinctive species.

Botanical scrutiny of the birch wood

There are two birch trees, and their characters can vary.

The silver birch is perhaps the more familiar, slim and elegant of form, its light leaves dancing on slender stalks in every breeze. It is called the lady of the woods, but is often planted for quick ornament on new developments. It has white papery bark, but note that older silver birch trees may be rough below, becoming knobbly towards the base where the bark may be figured in rectangular bosses.

The silver birch is more typical of the lowlands. Its cousin, the hairy or downy birch, is more tolerant of wet and cold and is maybe commoner in the north and the uplands. This is more variable: it can have silvery-grey bark, but it is often brownish almost down to the ground. In southern and lowland areas it does have hairy twigs which are dull as a result (those of the silver birch seem polished), but the northern form has hairless twigs with sticky brown warts. A further complication is that, when the two grow together, they can hybridise.

Though usually an elegant tree, mean soil and circumstance can produce warped trunks. Do not, however, be misled by this appearance of age, for birch rarely lives longer than 60 years. As a result of its short lifespan, dead boughs and decaying trees are a feature of a birch wood.

A profile of the wood

The birch wood is rather simple in structure. The tree is never very tall and casts only a light shade, so that sunlight dapples the ground. This is sometimes a carpet of fine grass tussocks spun with spiders' webs and scattered with bracken, but, if the trees have colonised heathland, a bushy mat of heather and bilberry remains (and sometimes juniper or rowan, too). Rotting branches are always to be seen scattered through the wood.

Fungus forays

The wealth of decaying timber (and many of the standing trees also are likely to be dying) makes birch woods good for fungus forays. The most obviously typical species is the vivid and poisonous fly agaric, a picture-book toadstool. It is also found in pine woods.

The birch trunks carry brackets. One found on birches in the Scottish Highlands is the tinder fungus. This fungus, dried and soaked in saltpetre, was used as tinder to catch the spark from flint in the days before matches; its shape also gives it the name 'hoof fungus'. Razor strop is more widespread; its dried corky flesh was used, as its name suggests, as a natural whetstone for cut-throat razors.

Witches' broom

This cluster of deformed twigs is a gall. It is caused by a fungus infection, and not by insect irritation as with the majority of galls (see pages 22–3).

Birds in birch woods

The simple structure of the birch wood is not immediately popular with nesting birds, although heathery birch woods rate better than spruce plantations and in Scotland can hold more species than even the old pine woods. The redpoll may nest in a tree fork and its twittering families be seen feeding acrobatically on the gherkin-like seed catkins. The wood also suits the tree pipit, which nests on the ground but likes scattered cover; its parachuting songflight is quite distinctive. Flashes of yellow in the autumn wood will almost certainly be parties of siskins, although for deep winter they very often forsake the birches for alder woods and other larders.

Tits of various kinds may also be expected. How many will be seen is completely unpredictable. Unlike the breeding months, when populations may be guessed, the mobile winter flocks, of siskins (and redpolls) in birchwoods and of finches in beechwoods and of tits in both relies on chance sightings of what are often rapidly moving flocks of birds.

silver birch

redpoll

When seen, the siskin gives an impression of yellow, with bright wing bars.

siskin

razor strop fungus

tinder fungus

fly agaric

earth ball fungus

THE WOODLAND OF THE SCOTS PINE

Once blanketing much of the highland area of Scotland, only 12,500 hectares (31,000 acres) of semi-natural Scots pine forest remain, at 25 main sites.

A scenic tree

With its dusky orange bark and its head of attractive blue-green, the Scots pine is the most handsome of our native trees. It took an early role in the woodland story. Conifers can often grow where the season is too short for broadleaved trees. Being evergreen, they can begin photosynthesis without delay as soon as the days warm up after winter, and they gain added advantage from the fact that their seeds are held back to ripen ànd disperse in the year after pollination, thus allowing time for slow development. Together with birch, Scots pine was soon on the scene when the ground warmed up at the end of the Ice Age. It may have formed extensive forests in some places, but oak, ash and others typical of the lowland wildwood followed to oust it (see pages 16–17). Their advance was halted in the Scottish Highlands, where the pine forests survived to become their crowning glory. The surviving woods are usually on coarse glacial soils which put the oak at a disadvantage.

Scottish pine woods and history

The pine forest disappeared in patchwork fashion, as the clans had always felled small areas for crofts and grazing or fired the trees in cattle raids, but its destruction later came to be closely linked with actual history. Well into medieval times the Scots pine forest still blanketed vast areas of Scotland, giving refuge to wolves and boar, brown bears, lynx and elk. Wolves survived until the 18th century, the time of the Jacobite rebellion against London. When this failed, at the Battle of Culloden in 1746, the English and their puppet clans embarked on a scorched-earth policy against any pockets of rebels. Before long, trees were being felled in thousands and floated down the fast Highland rivers to be sold on as ironmaster's fuel. The destruction did not halt until well into this century. Now only 12,500 hectares (31,000 acres) remain.

An open woodland

Although some areas tend to be close-set, much of this ancient pine woodland is rather open, which may be due partly to fellings in the past, with grazing deer holding back regeneration. Regeneration has been natural, from seeds loosed by trees

PINE WOODLANDS

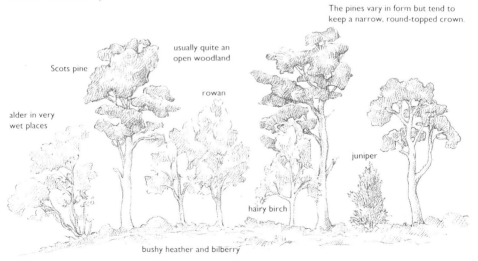

The pines vary in form but tend to keep a narrow, round-topped crown.

Scots pine

usually quite an open woodland

rowan

alder in very wet places

juniper

hairy birch

bushy heather and bilberry

SCOTTISH PINE WOOD

standing nearby. As a result (and quite unlike conifer plantations, even those of Scots pine itself), the trees are very varied, of many different ages and shapes, giving a real feel of wilderness. The typical crown of the native Scots pine is narrow and pyramid-shaped, although it becomes rounded with age – but there is considerable variety to be seen here.

The underwood

Where the trees jostle each other there are few tall shrubs, but where the wood is more open there may be some birch and well-developed juniper with bushy heather, bilberry and cowberry below, and a moss garden on the ground. Some areas, however, are being heavily grazed by both red deer and blackface sheep, and this alters their profile.

Pine woods in the south

The tree gains its name from the Scottish forests, but some natural-looking Scots pine woods are also found in the south on sandy or gravel soils, often verging on heathland. These might be relics of plantations which have been thinned and then let go; but much of this pine woodland has come into existence 'naturally', when plantation trees have seeded themselves out onto heathy commonland nearby.

The seed source used in the southern plantations has often been a European strain, which, unlike Scottish seed, develops a broad, flat-topped crown if the tree is allowed space to grow – something to look out for. And although Scots pines are usually associated with sandy soils, they grow well enough on dry chalk soils, where they are sometimes seen as ornamental borders to farm tracks across the downs.

As a result of structure and content, both northern and southern woods attract a characteristic tally of plants and wildlife.

Other pines were also popular with the Victorians. (The pines are easily distinguished from other conifers by their needles bunched in groups of 2–5 on short spurs). The Corsican pine, native to that Mediterranean island, is one such. It likes warmth and was planted in southern Britain (but it has also been planted on some coastal dunes in Wales and Scotland). Its needles are in pairs like the Scots pine, though they are longer and twisted and the tree's bark becomes fissured and dark grey with age.

The classic birds of pine woods are: capercaillie, crested tit, crossbill, siskin. The first two are Scottish birds, the others are also seen in the south.

The goldcrest and coal tit are more often seen in pine woods than in oak woods. They may be joined by other oakwood birds.

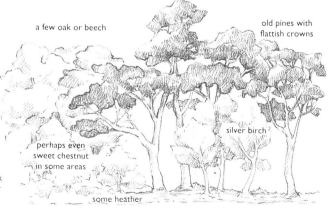

a few oak or beech

old pines with flattish crowns

silver birch

perhaps even sweet chestnut in some areas

some heather

SOUTHERN SELF-SEEDED SCOTS PINE WOOD

A WALK IN AN OLD PINE WOOD

Natural wildlife pathways can take us to the heart of the Scots pine-wood, to discover rare and delicate wild flowers and see some exceptional birds.

Fungi

Although the trees may share the ground with heather and with flowers such as yellow tormentil which indicate acid soil, if

THE WOOD ANT IN ITS HABITAT

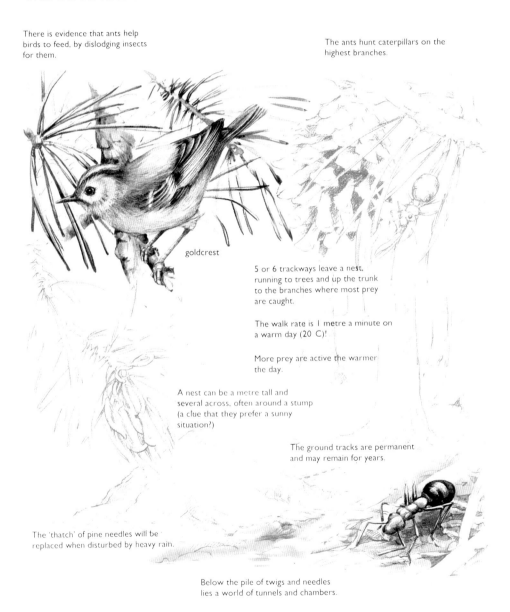

There is evidence that ants help birds to feed, by dislodging insects for them.

The ants hunt caterpillars on the highest branches.

goldcrest

5 or 6 trackways leave a nest, running to trees and up the trunk to the branches where most prey are caught.

The walk rate is 1 metre a minute on a warm day (20 C)!

More prey are active the warmer the day.

A nest can be a metre tall and several across, often around a stump (a clue that they prefer a sunny situation?)

The ground tracks are permanent and may remain for years.

The 'thatch' of pine needles will be replaced when disturbed by heavy rain.

Below the pile of twigs and needles lies a world of tunnels and chambers.

very closely ranked their needles can smother the ground. There could even then be quite a few fungi at various times of year, some of them in relationship with the tree roots as with those under beech trees (see pages 34–5). Fly agaric is common (see pages 38–9), and even decaying pine cones have their own specialist, the tooth fungus. Tufts of caps are typical of decaying stumps. Look out, too, for the false chanterelle, which looks very like its edible namesake of beechwoods (see pages 34–5).

Scottish woods

In any event, southern woods are botanically poor compared with the tally of flowers found below and around the sharply scented juniper and matted heather in the native pine woodlands of Scotland. The latter also illustrate some of the eccentricities of botany which help enliven its rather academic formality. Wintergreens are one example, with pinkish or greenish-white flowers rather resembling lily of the valley and a ground rosette of primrose-like leaves, seen on open ground, maybe near an ant track. Chickweed wintergreen, confusingly named for it is no relation (nor does medicinal wintergreen oil come from these wintergreens!), is also found in these woods. This flower is actually one of the primrose family, but its rosette of leaves is held at the top of the stem; its flowers resemble neither wintergreens nor chickweed, being rather like wood anemone. But these plants certainly live up to their wintergreen name.

There are some interesting orchids: coral root, like the birds' nests of beech woods (see pages 34–5), has given up its green leaves; and creeping lady's tresses has creeping runners. But the prize gem of these woods is the twinflower, a minute shrub growing on the needle litter, named from the pairs of fragile pink bell-shaped flowers it holds over its cushion of leaves.

Main roads through the wood

Deer tracks there certainly will be, which will readily be used by other mammals, including (in Scotland) wild cats and (in the west) pine marten.

Ants

The woodland floor is also crisscrossed by the slight tracks of wood ants. They are worth a few minutes. A colony can number up to 300,000 workers and raid the woodland of 100,000 insects a day, as well as a vast quantity of aphid honeydew. Wood ants reach to every corner of the habitat, and so it may be that, by raiding this larder, they also influence the birdlife. They are clearly in competition with birds struggling to find body-building protein for their nestlings.

Their foraging to the topmost twigs is efficiently programmed. The outward journeys are rambling, until ants begin returning with big catches, when they recruit others (by some means unknown). In this way they focus on abundant prey; and the traffic seems to be heavier in hot weather, maybe because more prey is detectable then. Neighbouring nests do not usually compete (observe their trackways) unless food is scarce.

Birdlife

Summer birds of broadleaved woods can be expected in varying numbers in the Scottish pine wood, although several are not seen for reasons of geography, structure or larder. The nuthatch and nightingale are obvious absentees. There are some species that are rarely seen outside it: crested tit and crossbill (which uses its odd beak for extracting the seeds from the pine cones), and the turkey-like capercaillie, which will spend hours happily perched on the topmost branches before launching itself clumsily through the branches.

An interesting insight into chaffinch ecology is seen where mature pine woods and mixed oak woods are neighbours, as they may be in the south and also in parts of Scotland. The mature birds fill the mixed wood as their first choice, the pine being left to the younger and less dominant. Hence numbers in the oak wood are constant, but in the pine-wood they may vary considerably from year to year. This phenomenon is probably also true of other birds which are found in more than one habitat type.

THE PLANTATION

Although a fairly recent addition to the landscape, plantations now account for 2,100,000 hectares (5,200,000 acres), 7 times the area of older woodland.

The origin of forestry

Unlike other woodland management, forestry had a definite date of birth. It is not an evolution from traditional coppice-with-standards, but a complete break, trees being planted close together to grow a tall 'high forest' of straight trunks.

The first plantation was in 1580, in Windsor Great Park. The trigger at that time was concern over supplies of timber for naval ships. Plantations followed in other forests: many fine oak groves of the New Forest were originally plantations, although they have had trees removed to open them up somewhat. By Victorian times, 'plantationing' was booming, and by then Scots pine was also favoured, as well as larch and Norway spruce (the Christmas tree), precursors of today's conifers.

The Forestry Commission

During the First World War, reliance on home-dug coal (then vital to the whole economy) required a huge supply of pit props needed for the frontline trenches. Over 200,000 hectares (half a million acres) of mature trees were felled, and in 1919 the Forestry Commission was founded to guarantee future supplies. Land was bought (often moorland and heathland) and subsidies awarded to private estate-owners to blanket their land with conifers. Few were mature enough in time for the Second World War, and a third of the remaining old oak woodlands were then felled. New goals were set, and since 1945, as well as planting on open ground, more ancient woodland has been felled and 'coniferised'. The fringe of old wood left around the plantation often disguises this.

Clear-felling and block-planting

A plantation is quickly recognisable by the trees being of only one kind, in rows, and all of one age. When a forestry compartment is felled, it is usually clear-felled, and the ground often sprayed before new saplings planted. The link with the past which maintains the diversity of a semi-natural wood is broken.

Management of the conifer plantation

The young plantation is often fenced against rabbits or deer. The first thinning is usually when the trees are 6 metres tall.

THE CONIFER PLANTATION

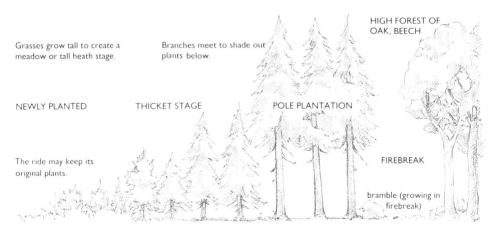

Grasses grow tall to create a meadow or tall heath stage.

Branches meet to shade out plants below.

HIGH FOREST OF OAK, BEECH

NEWLY PLANTED   THICKET STAGE   POLE PLANTATION

The ride may keep its original plants.

FIREBREAK

bramble (growing in firebreak)

STAGES IN THE GROWTH OF A CONIFER PLANTATION

They are brashed, that is cleared of side branches to gain knot-free timber, when about 15 years old. They are usually felled after 50–70 years.

How ranked conifers rank as a habitat

The young plantation can encourage wild-life: the flowers of the old woodland can flourish in the light, but usually grasses grow tall to create a 'meadow' for butterflies and other insects and which is also quite attractive to voles and some birds.

Then the saplings rise to create a scrub or thicket stage. As birds respond more to structure than to the actual species of tree (see pages 24–5), this can attract songsters. The general trend (for broadleaf and conifer plantations alike) is for numbers of both species and individual birds to increase, but at some stage – at brashing in the case of conifers – to drop away, to leave only those birds which will nest in the canopy but feed outside the plantation altogether.

Many woodland birds linger in the broad-leaved fringe which is often left around the conifers. The rides can be important, offer-ing relic vegetation of what was there before and hence a feeding ground. All in all, partial coniferisation of a wood may not have a marked effect on the variety of bird species. All bird species show a preference for some particular stage of growth, and so a jigsaw of compartments of different ages can encourage diversity in the plantation as a whole. But a conifer plantation even at its richest is far poorer than an oak wood, although its early stages may be richer than, say, a beech wood.

Although the rides between the tall trees may carry relic plants from either the glades of the previous wood or the previous heath or moor (and many plantations are on sand-dune systems), firebreaks are usually much poorer and swamped with brambles, which the wheeled and foot traffic of the ride keeps down. Firebreaks are sometimes ploughed, when arable weeds come in; and in Thetford Forest, Norfolk, the stone-curlew, a once common rare bird of rough open ground, is found lingering on the ploughed firebreaks.

This really is a last ditch stand, if it can be put that way. The stone curlew with its surprised-looking visage is a bird of open spaces such as chalk grass and the grassy heaths of Breckland. It was once found also on ploughland and even the shingle of Dungeness and elsewhere. It remains amongst the conifers as a kind of unforseen living fossil!

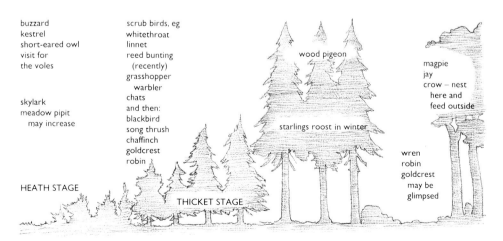

THE BIRD LIFE OF THE CONIFER PLANTATION

A BRIEF LOOK AMONG THE FIR TREES

A conifer ('fir') plantation has a pace of change unmatched by native broadleaved woods, and the different stages each have a distinctive wildlife tally.

The rides

If planted onto heathland, heathers, tormentil and other typical flowers (even orchids) may survive along the plantation rides. Where an oak wood has been felled and replanted with conifers, the existing woodland rides are often kept in the new plantation. The plants often create a grassy meadow community, and there could be brown and skipper butterflies in large numbers, and yellow underwing moths with their flashy bursts of flight when the grass tussocks are disturbed. The short-eared owl (which hunts by day) will visit to raid the growing numbers of field voles. In fact, these rides may have been enriched themselves, flowers and butterflies being concentrated by the acres of ranked conifers around them.

On a broad ride, thicket growth can add interest, imitating the edge of the old wood.

The scrub stage

In the plantation compartments themselves, there will at first also be a meadow stage, when the grass grows tall around the newly planted saplings. Skylark and meadow pipit are attracted, and again the short-eared owl after the voles. Songbirds begin to be more noticeable when the young trees reach waist height. The cover now suits scrub birds such as grasshopper warbler, tree pipit, redpoll, reed bunting and yellowhammer. The nightingale, however, is more noticeable by its absence. The nightjar is also heard now, on warm summer nights. In moorland settings even the hen harrier may nest here, although it will remain dependent on the open landscape around for hunting.

Brashing

Bird diversity tumbles after brashing, when the scrub birds leave. Even the ubiquitous wren has by now been shaded out. From a nesting bird's viewpoint, the tangle of branches left littering the ground after brashing is of little interest.

THE WILDLIFE OF A YOUNG PLANTATION

yellow underwing moth

The field vole is not the distinctive reddish brown colour of the bank vole; it also has a shorter tail.

grass tussocks and vole runways

Short-eared owl nests on the ground.

Some moorland species may nest here but they rely on the surrounding open ground for food.

The forbidding forest

Quite unlike an oak wood, where scrub birds remain in the underwood, a mature conifer plantation keeps only those birds that are linked with the canopy. Surprisingly, alien conifers can sometimes match the bird rating of the Scots pine in this, perhaps because spruce, for example, with its dense foliage of needles, offers a high density of insects. Twittering parties of goldcrests move through the canopy, where the insect life is found, and firecrest and crossbill have both extended their range in England as the earlier plantations have matured. There is much more mobility in winter, and family parties for tits, for example, may make daily tours of 40 kilometres, searching all woods, plantations included.

For some birds, the plantation in its older stages becomes more of a hotel or night stop. Pigeons now coo unseen from the canopy, and flocks of starlings typify the change, coming from afar to roost noisily each evening.

The derelict plantation

There are already some derelict Victorian conifer plantations of great wildlife value; these have been thinned in the past but not completely cleared. Rot holes offer sites for tree-nesting birds. Fallen trees are a bonus here, not only for bark and other beetles but also because they open up space into which birch and ash and other broadleaves could seed themselves. The great storms of October 1987 and January 1990 may have brought an unexpected bonus; it is worth looking to see what is now growing in the wrecked plantations where they remain uncleared. In view of the terrible toll taken of old woodland this century, it would be better to allow these devastated woods to renew themselves naturally, but they are usually being cleared, replanted and 'managed'.

A young oak growing in one of these open areas will be worth considering, for how did it arrive? Oaks are normally spread by squirrels (and maybe crows) burying the acorns for a future larder some distance from the parent tree. It is also interesting to see just what the seed source in the soil is producing in the way of wild flowers in these fortuitous newly opened clearings in the conifer 'desert'.

GLADES AND RIDES

Open rides and clearings in a wood are always worth investigation. Apart from their wildlife interest, they may also throw light on the history of the wood.

Deciphering the geography of a wood

A simple map of the wood can sometimes be read to reveal some of its history (see pages 18–19). The sites of huts, or even whole farmsteads, of rubbish dumps, open pasture land and even fish ponds may be identified. But, unless kept open, a clearing is usually quick to fill; a stand of silver birch or ash in a wood may mark the site of one (see pages 28–9, 36–7). Thus an opening, even in semi-natural woodland, is usually a sign of some kind of occupation or management activity. The exception could be clearings or thinnings created by heavy grazing by livestock: examples are the grassy lawns or 'launds' found in wooded parts of the New Forest. Fallow and other deer in a wood can thin the shrub layer (and as a result affect the populations of nesting songbirds).

It is interesting that, in the course of time, a handful of plant species have become typical of rides: ragged robin, devil's bit scabious and greater burnet saxifrage are three to look for.

Woodland rides

Because of the decline of traditional woodland management, the original rides of old woods may now be difficult to discern. Lack of any mention in medieval documents, however, suggests that they are a fairly late feature of woodland. Before then, simple tracks wound between the coppice stools, as can still be seen in some woods today. The word 'ride' was first coined only in 1805.

Rides imply some formality, not only of line but also of structure, with perhaps drainage ditches alongside. That they seem to meander can be more an impression than a fact, and due to the growth of vegetation from each side. These snaking paths are better for butterflies, because a straight ride tends to be something of a wind tunnel.

Rides are planned into the layout of conifer plantations where the forestry regime anticipates frequent periods of thinning and felling. Firebreaks, also a feature of these modern plantations, tend to be narrower, and bramble, while kept at bay in the ride by traffic (even foot traffic can be enough), often grows in dense tangles in the firebreaks. Here it is regularly cut, of course, and the firebreak may also be ploughed.

Worked woodland

The woodland compartments served by the ride often show distinct differences. Coppicing is still carried out in some woods (and is now often being reintroduced into woods which are managed as nature reserves). Coppice compartments are usually rather regular in shape, and when newly cut (it is a

GLADES AND CLEARINGS

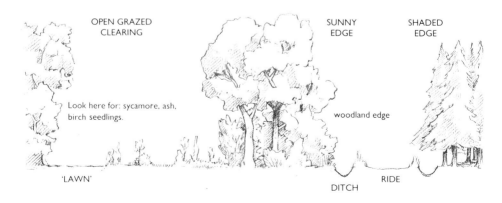

OPEN GRAZED CLEARING

Look here for: sycamore, ash, birch seedlings.

'LAWN'

SUNNY EDGE

SHADED EDGE

woodland edge

RIDE

DITCH

winter job) their knobbly stumps make them immediately recognisable. Compartments were traditionally cut in rotation so that the wood as a whole yielded a continuous supply of smallwood, and as a result the compartments of coppice woodland were of varied heights and bushiness.

Coppice may also contain tall-timber standard trees, traditionally felled in their prime at 70–120 years. If the wood is being managed as high forest, however, the compartments will often be clear-felled and be empty of all except clean-cut tree stumps. These stumps may be bulldozed and piled in one corner to open the ground for the next planting.

Shooting woods

Sporting interest can coincide with other management, or involve its own planting. Today's form of pheasant-shooting started in Victorian days when rapid-firing breech-loaded guns came into general use. The 'guns' now stationed themselves outside the wood instead of walking through it, the birds being flushed to fly out of the wood and above them. This is best achieved with a wood of special form. The beaters typically walk through the trees to move the birds to open 'flushing' areas or very broad rides or avenues. Taking wing here away from the disturbance, the birds rise over a belt of tall shrubs, which may be coppice growth, and then have to accelerate over the trees beyond, finding themselves high over the guns outside.

Rhododendron was often planted to thicken the wood to give better cover for the birds themselves: on acid soils this has often become rampant and now chokes the wood. Honeysuckle, snowberry and even cotoneaster were also planted. These shooting woods can also be recognised by the round metal food hoppers and by the gamekeepers' gibbets hung with the corpses of squirrels, crows and magpies.

Fallen trees

Smaller glades might be the creation of storm-tumbled trees. Many of these remain uncleared after the great storms of October

1987 and January 1990, their shattered limbs claimed by velvet green moss and a myriad of fungi and insects. They may be embraced by head-height growths of ash or sycamore saplings urgently racing up to the light. The dead tree is a habitat feature in its own right (see pages 54–5).

GRASSES, RUSHES AND SEDGES

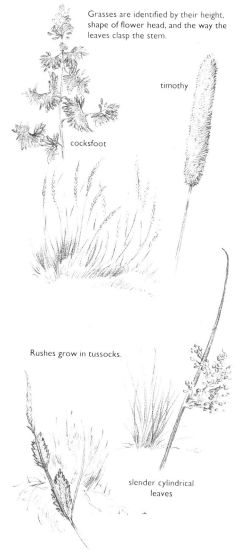

Grasses are identified by their height, shape of flower head, and the way the leaves clasp the stem.

timothy

cocksfoot

Rushes grow in tussocks.

slender cylindrical leaves

Sedges are grass-like, with solid stems which are triangular in cross-section.

BUTTERFLIES IN THE SUNNY GLADE

A fritillary basking to gain heat.

The handsome white admiral.

Keeping cool: the butterfly will rise on its legs facing the sun and close its wings.

Insect life is often (literally) buzzing in the warmth and shelter of the sunny glade. The glade provides a wonderful chance for butterfly-watching.

Established colonies

Old and semi-natural woods usually have well-established colonies of butterflies along the rides and in clearings. Butterflies have intricate relationships with their habitat and its plants, and the wood makes an ideal observatory for this. Each species has its own periods of adult existence during the year, giving unbroken possibilities for observation from early spring to late autumn.

Butterfly morning

Butterflies will roost in various places overnight, and in early morning crawl to a nearby sunlit spot. It is here that they are first seen, basking with wings opened and often held flat to catch the sun to warm themselves up. They need to raise their body temperature to above 32 C (90–95 F). Together with the late afternoon, when the air temperature is again marginal, this may be the only time to see the wings fully opened, the glorious patterns revealed.

Although this wing patterning may be partially a defensive mechanism, either with warning colours or with camouflage,

dark colours can help the absorption of sun warmth at these crucial times.

Territories

Once warm, the aim of the males is to mate with as many females as they can. Some merely perch in a prominent place, surveying a 'territory', and launch out at any butterfly that enters it: if it is a male of the same species, there may be a skirmish, with the intruder retreating. Others patrol their territory, while yet others fly widely and actively in search of mates. The territories are, of course, a way of spreading the species through the wood; they also give us a good chance of seeing the butterflies themselves!

The instinct which guides the choice of territory is often intricate, and the brown species seen on well-drained rides may be different from those on wet, where the ringlet is typical. But usually a sunny spot is chosen as focus: the large skipper and comma will occupy the open junction of two rides. The speckled wood likes dappled shade, and overgrown coppice suits it.

Courtship

If the passing butterfly is female, and willing, courtship may occur. This can be a rather secret affair, with a staged 'dance', something often hidden by the lush grass.

FRITILLARY COURTSHIP

courtship dance

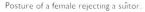

mating

Posture of a female rejecting a suitor.

courtship concluding

The female quest

When mated, the male returns to his vigil, awaiting further females. But the female will spend the remainder of her short life seeking suitable plants for egg-laying. She lands frequently and briefly, tapping and 'tasting' them with her legs, searching out a vigorous plant rich in body-building protein food for the caterpillars that will hatch from her eggs.

Those jewels of insects, the fritillaries, illustrate just how subtle her choice may be. All fritillaries lay on dog violets, but the pearl-bordered likes sunny patches with only low growth nearby (newly cut coppice, for example), while the small pearl-bordered likes slightly older, rather more shaded clearings. The silver-washed fritillary likes her violets in the sun, but, as she lays her eggs in the bark of a tree nearby, deeper woodland suits her instincts better.

Perhaps the most magnificent of all likely sightings is the white admiral gliding through the trees. The female seeks spindly, shaded honeysuckle, and one unforeseen benefit of the ending of coppicing (in which the honeysuckle is cut away) is the increase and spread of these butterflies in recent years.

Visitors from the canopy

Butterflies normally resident in the canopy may sometimes visit the ground. Hairstreaks and the purple emperor are sometimes seen 'drinking' the minerals of muddy puddles and droppings.

A CHOICE OF VIOLETS

pearl-bordered fritillary

small-pearl-bordered

silver-washed fritillary

WOOD PASTURE, FOREST AND PARKLAND

An ancient pollard tree may be all that remains of centuries of wood pasture, once a widespread land use but today lingering only in a few forests and parks.

Wood pasture

Together with ploughland, meadow and coppice woods, wood pasture was part of the commons holdings of the old village. It was often known as 'waste', and it did have a ragged abandoned look. It was basically rough grazing for everything from horses to geese, but in the old make-and-mend fashion it was also used in other ways. Armed with their commons rights, the peasants could loot it of fallen timber for firewood or building, and cut its heather and bracken for bedding. Indeed, many, if not most, of today's commons (see pages 76–7) were originally wood pasture.

The pollard tree

Pollard trees are lopped of their branches at head height, the stumpy bolling (rhyming with 'rolling') growing a renewing head of branches. This head makes them immediately recognisable, even when last cut tens (or maybe hundreds) of years ago and where the head of shoots is now grown into ponderous branches. Willows along river banks are still pollarded, but pollarded trees were once of much wider significance. They were typical of wood pasture, providing as they did a means of gaining smallwood of coppice type where animals grazed the ground.

And in areas of old countryside with hedges enclosing old pasture fields, hedgerow trees have also been pollarded. Local custom varied, however: there are few hedgerow pollards in the ancient and ornamental countryside of Herefordshire, for example.

The forest

'Forest', one of the most emotive words in the language, was in reality very different from its greenwood image and signified simply land made over to deer rather than trees. It was originally a tract of land, often vast, set aside by the Norman and Plantagenet kings for the royal hunt, a royal playground in other words. There were 80 royal forests in all, maybe wooded in part, but a forest would also include much heathland (or moorland), marsh and swamp, a very varied landscape. The New Forest is a good example. Chases were similar, but for the benefit of the greater magnates rather than the king.

Although forest law was harsh, and even disturbing the deer could lead to blinding or

WOOD GRAZING IN ITS HEYDAY

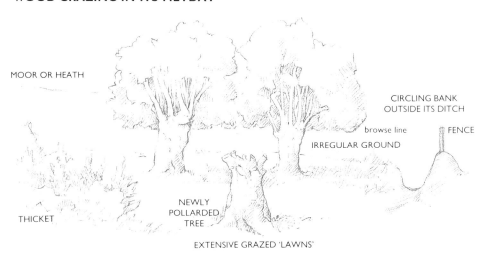

MOOR OR HEATH

CIRCLING BANK
OUTSIDE ITS DITCH

browse line   FENCE

IRREGULAR GROUND

THICKET

NEWLY
POLLARDED
TREE

EXTENSIVE GRAZED 'LAWNS'

THE RELIC WOOD TODAY

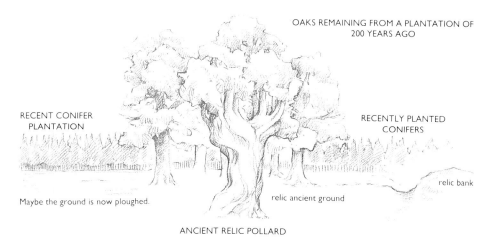

OAKS REMAINING FROM A PLANTATION OF 200 YEARS AGO

RECENT CONIFER PLANTATION

RECENTLY PLANTED CONIFERS

relic bank

Maybe the ground is now ploughed.

relic ancient ground

ANCIENT RELIC POLLARD

execution, a forest was integrated with local commons rights, and pollarding of the trees was quite usual. Ancient forest pollards are still alive today, though only scraps of original forest land still remain. Over the centuries, much has been sold off by hard-up monarchs and much has become farm-land, although, by the end of the 17th century, plantations were already being set in place (see pages 44–5). Most 'forests' now carry blocks of conifers in one part or another.

The park

The word 'park' also had a precise meaning in landscape history. By the 14th century, there were 2000 baronial deer parks in existence, to 80 hectares (200 acres) in area and stocked with fallow deer. They were meat farms of a kind, the deer often being hunted down (and sometimes released into the countryside around for the hunt). Parks were surrounded by a fence or 'pale' which ran along a massive bank, which, unlike that of coppice woodlands, lay *outside* its ditch to make it harder for the animals to leap to freedom from within. Traces of such banks might be found enclosing a vestige of woodland today, or be seen running across unploughed pasture nearby. Park trees were usually pollarded as a matter of course

and, like all trees in grazed landscapes, might develop a distinct browse line about man-height above the ground.

In Regency times, many deer parks were 'improved' – trees were planted, not for timber but in carefully planned clumps to improve the view. It was at this time that many hilltop trees were planted, as eye-catchers for the mansion below. But some of the old park pollards may remain.

Ancient trees

Pollards yield poor trunk timber and, when they started to become prized for their stately appearance, they were often allowed to continue life even when boughs weak-ened and died. They were not worth the labour of felling. As a result, many of our oldest standing trees are old pollards, a fact often clear from their leafless winter profile. Even Major Oak in Sherwood Forest is probably an old pollard; Knightwood Oak in the New Forest, maybe Britain's oldest tree, certainly is. These old trees, associated today with commons, 'forests' and park-lands, offer a mini-habitat of decaying wood.

It's interesting that these parkland plant-ings put in hand by the English landscape gardeners were largely informal, for people had by then begun to admire what seemed to them to be 'natural'.

A HALF-HOUR STOP AT AN ANCIENT TREE

An old tree can be not only a signpost to an old habitat, but also itself an intricate habitat. From the bark in, innumerable forms of life take advantage of it.

A world from the bark in

Crumpled and deeply cut, the old bark can carry a garden of lichens (the origin of the expression 'hoary with age'). There may be 30 or more different lichen species, mostly on the main trunk 3–5 metres above ground; one, the tree lungwort, is found only on large old trees, and may be a direct relic of the wildwood. They are found more on living trees, as dead and softening bark weakens their grip. They are not a sign of disease, but in reverse their absence can point the finger towards air pollution (see pages 90–91).

Neither are moss nor festoons of ferns a sign of disease. Bark that becomes deeply fissured with age can also offer pockets of soil for these sturdier epiphytes, those plants that are specialised to sharply draining soil. Polypody is a common fern more often seen on trees and rock faces than on the ground.

These epiphytes do not lessen the bark's important function as a protective layer against fungal attack, but this can occur as a result of insect activity. A good many of the 284 insect species dedicated to the oak tree bore through the bark. A metallic green hoverfly and a cardinal beetle (with black head and a blood-red body) are two gaudy examples. Pieces of fallen bark often show beetle burrows, each species with its own intricate pattern. Distinctive in another way is the finger-thick hole of the goat moth caterpillar, in old ash and poplar more than in oak, named from its foul smell. Other insects claim already decaying timber. A third of all invertebrate species in woodland rely on dead wood, whether or not it remains standing.

Stag-headed and hollow oaks

Dead boughs are often raised like antlers above the oak's green crown, the result of a combination of circumstances. A warm early spring can encourage vast numbers of leaf-eating caterpillars, such as the green oak roller which is often seen suspended on a thread when dislodged. It can defoliate the tree unchecked, because the broods of blue tits and other birds are not yet hatched and their parents are not yet so active. The tree will put out a second flush of leaves, but is weakened, and a dry summer can heighten its vulnerability to fungal attack. Squirrels may open the tree to infection by stripping bark. Boughs die, but a new canopy thickens below – a kind of natural pollarding.

That trees do not age like animals is also demonstrated by hollow oaks. Death of areas of the living bark has allowed entrance to fungi, though these do not damage the remaining sapwood, which continues to nourish the crown above. A lightning strike sometimes starts the process, leaving a sharp, sword-like cut.

Fungi

The largest bracket fungus to be found on British trunks is dryad's saddle, growing to 60 cm across, while the beefsteak is characteristic of old butts of oak. Like all the fungal growths we see, these are the spore-producing bodies of a hidden mesh of feeding threads permeating the bark, sap tubes or timber. Some are found only on dead timber; and many fungi have a relationship with only one particular species of tree, but the exact dovetailing can be intricate, with the fungi specialising not only on different sizes of dead wood but also on wood at different stages of decay. Some fungi are even confined to open parkland, growing in grass but only when associated with old trees, and are rarely to be found inside woodland. *Boletus leonis* is one of these.

Some grudgingly allow the tree to live, but clusters of honey fungus caps, piled like cornflakes at the foot of the trunk, are a sign of a death warrant. The main reason why burrowing beetles are such a hazard to growing trees (and why dead timber is cleared from commercial plantations) is that, in flying from one tree to another to burrow below the bark, they may carry fungal spores with them. Dutch elm disease, which in the early 1970s wiped out most of the hedgerow elms, was spread in this way.

Birdlife

The tears and ravages of an old tree also offer nest sites for a considerable number of birds. Woodpeckers will actually dig out a hole or even just a shallow refuge behind the bark, but many birds (and bats) simply exploit gaps which are opened up when branches have been torn away by storms. Look for the nuthatch, one of the most handsome of all our birds.

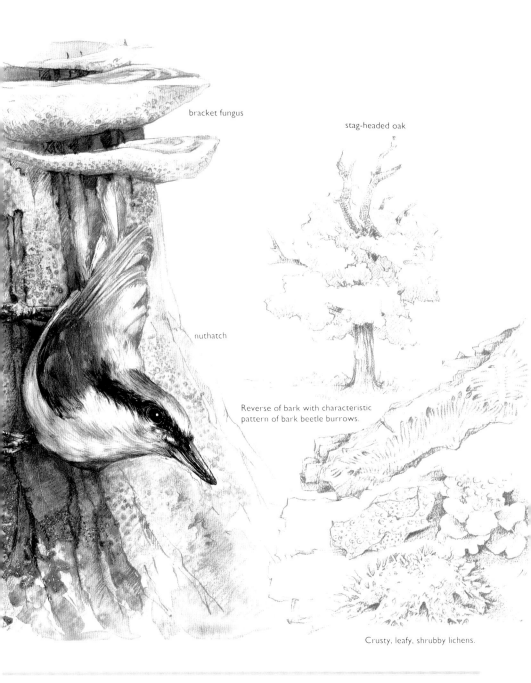

bracket fungus

stag-headed oak

nuthatch

Reverse of bark with characteristic pattern of bark beetle burrows.

Crusty, leafy, shrubby lichens.

GRASSLAND

RECOGNISING OLD GRASSLAND

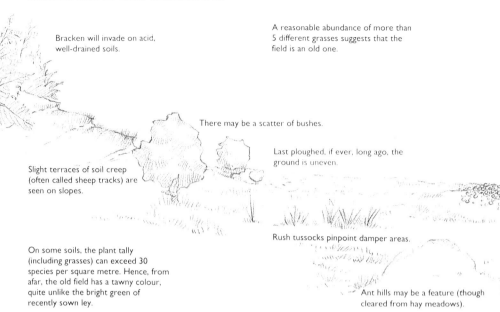

Bracken will invade on acid, well-drained soils.

A reasonable abundance of more than 5 different grasses suggests that the field is an old one.

There may be a scatter of bushes.

Last ploughed, if ever, long ago, the ground is uneven.

Slight terraces of soil creep (often called sheep tracks) are seen on slopes.

On some soils, the plant tally (including grasses) can exceed 30 species per square metre. Hence, from afar, the old field has a tawny colour, quite unlike the bright green of recently sown ley.

Rush tussocks pinpoint damper areas.

Ant hills may be a feature (though cleared from hay meadows).

About three-quarters of farmland is grassland, but only a small proportion of this is old. Its wildlife value is lost if it is agriculturally improved.

The origin of grassland

Although our wet and rather mild climate encourages grass, only in some exposed places will it be the natural ground cover. In time, however, regular grazing eliminates even shrubs and saplings while allowing grass (which has a low growing point) to survive. Deer grazing can create open 'lawns' in woods, and from early prehistoric days livestock grazing helped to open up the woodlands and destroy the young saplings which would replenish them. The open chalk downs as well as many areas of heathland and moorland had this origin.

A semi-natural community

Although held artificially in check by grazing or mowing, old unploughed grassland counts as a semi-natural community (see pages 16–17). Apart from the wild grasses, its plants cope with the grazing. The flowers seen will reflect the soil type as well as other conditions: old grassland is so fascinating a habitat partly because its plant geography can change by the metre (see pages 58–9).

Traditional and ley grassland

Up to and beyond Tudor days, grassland was proudly valued, whether as part of the rough 'wastes' (see pages 52–3) or as meadow (see pages 68–9). Both remained unploughed. But in recent times 'taking the plough around the farm' has become normal, the soil being turned, fertilised and reseeded at regular intervals. Seven years is a usual interval for these grass 'ley' fields; if they are left unploughed for longer farmers call them 'permanent pasture', although (see overleaf) their semi-natural quality will have been lost. These modern grass leys are often 'paddock grazed' in strips controlled by electric fencing.

Another recent change is that little hay is cut, only enough to feed horses and perhaps a few sheep in winter. The grass is instead cut young and green (and often more than once a year) for silage. Stored under black sheeting held down with old tyres, it pickles itself, to provide tangy rations for cattle.

SOIL PREFERENCES OF SOME GRASSLAND SPECIES

DRY, WELL DRAINED

LIMY SOIL

ACID SOIL

horseshoe vetch
bulbous buttercup
common mallow
kidney vetch
gorse
cowslip
burnet saxifrage
hairy plantain
tormentil
rockrose
carline thistle
ORCHIDS

harebell
wild thyme
meadow cranesbill

yellow rattle
meadow buttercup

ribwort plantain
lady's mantle
birdsfoot trefoil
great burnet
red campion

ragged robin
creeping buttercup

rosebay willowherb

oxeye daisy
devil's bitscabious
lousewort

cuckoo flower

WET, POORLY DRAINED

Wiping out the wildlife

Ploughing unbuttons the plant communities of old grassland, but as much damage can be done chemically. Herbicides, of course, kill the wild flowers for the sake of the grass, but, contrary to what might be expected, treating grassland with bulk artificial fertilisers can also wipe out the flowers by encouraging the more rampant grasses to grow at their expense. The sedges go first, closely followed by the rosette plants, and then the rest. Artificial fertilisers are embargoed on grassland nature reserves, where the tone is kept by grazing or mowing.

Some indicators of old grassland:

Recognising old grassland

The field holds a great variety of plants, more than 30 species to the square metre sometimes, including several wild grasses. This mixture of plants tends to give the field a tawny colour, quite unlike the bright green of the sown ley. Never ploughed (or last ploughed decades, if not hundreds of years, ago), the surface of the ground tends to be uneven, and ant hills may be common. The plant communities jigsaw, reflecting pockets of different soils; and with grazing erratic there are likely to be scatters of hawthorn and other shrubs.

Age indicators		
Restricted to old grassland	*More likely on old grassland*	*Sign of disturbance*
yellow rattle	cowslip	nettle
horseshoe vetch	mushrooms	thistles
rough hawkbit	knapweeds	plantains
	many orchids	ragwort etc
Bracken comes in on acid soil, if the drainage is sharp		

A HALF-HOUR STUDY OF THE GRASS

Ancient grassland usually has several interlocking plant geographies. These reflect not only the plants' own soil preferences but also the grazing regime.

The plant count of old grassland

What seems from a distance nothing more than a grassy field can contain a surprising number of grasses and flowers, sometimes over 30 species per square metre. Not all are in flower at any one time, and their leaves may be inconspicuous, but it is this mix which gives old grassland its tawny colour. Fungi are also to be found; mushrooms and fairy-ring toadstools are the best known. Lichens, too: dog lichen with thick fleshy 'leaves' is typical of old grassland.

Yellow rattle is one of those flowers which can be used as a handy signpost to old grassland (see pages 56–7).

Surviving grazing

Some plants survive because their sour or poisonous taste deters grazing animals – buttercups in fact gained their name because they covered the cow pastures for that reason. Others survive because of their low growth. Plants with runners such as clovers, or prostrate plants such as thyme and bedstraw, or with flat rosettes of leaves such as plantain and daisy, survive grazing. Have a look at a path. Regular treading has much the same effect as grazing, creating a fine sward dotted with rosette plants.

Soil geography

The three buttercups are one example: they pick out areas where they compete best. Extra soil nutrient is often marked by lusher, greener grass growth, and by nettles.

Ant hills create other conditions (and the larger and more numerous they are, the older grassland is likely to be). They tend to be flat on acid soil, more rounded on chalk. Only small annuals and thyme might survive their sharp drainage to grow on the tops. Cowpats create their own world of bacteria and soil-dwellers within the crust. Thistles and other coarse and unpalatable plants seed into them, as they may into fresh mole hills.

The longer, rougher grassy areas will be sculpted by the surface tunnels or runways of field voles. Recent use of these can be signposted by green droppings and piles of cut grass stems.

Grazing geography

In the farmer's eyes, a grazing regime which balances manuring with cropping gives the best sward, otherwise less demanding grasses may take over the site (the easily recognisable Yorkshire fog is one example). Poorly managed grazing produces nibbled bare areas which are invaded by thistles, ragwort and other non-grassland flowers (often familiar as garden 'weeds'). These also invade areas where the turf has been ripped or 'poached' by heavy-footed cattle.

Sheep and rabbits create a very fine close sward, while cattle and horses tear patches. Cattle can break down the coarse dead winter litter but may damage the turf; while horses will not eat dung-tainted grass and it may grow long in their latrine corners, where perhaps there may also be some 'meadow' plants. This all affects the wildlife and the conservation management of the field: horses are too selective, and they also tear out the roots of tussocks, a site favoured by craneflies and other insects.

Animal life

As butterfly walks (see page 203) show, it is a general rule that blue butterflies are linked with short turf and browns (which lay eggs on grass) with longer areas, where grasshoppers also abound. Spiders' webs show up in long grass, but short turf also has a good many.

Grasslands have their own list of nesting birds, described on following pages. The relative abundance of species is delicately linked with the state of the grass. The familiar skylark and the wheatear (which is the earliest of the summer migrants to arrive) like short turf, but the latter leaves if it grows longer, to be replaced by the meadow pipit. Skylark and meadow pipit remain if sparse bracken (or very light scrub) invades, but as this thickens the meadow pipit leaves, well ahead of the skylark.

SOME GRASSLAND PLANTS

Plants and soil are often hand in
glove, as these examples show.

Meadow buttercup. Smooth stalk,
second to flower.

Bulbous buttercup. The green sepals
turn down; grooved stalk, dry
ground, first buttercup to flower.

Cowslip. Usually found in old
grassland (though now sometimes
sown on motorway banks).

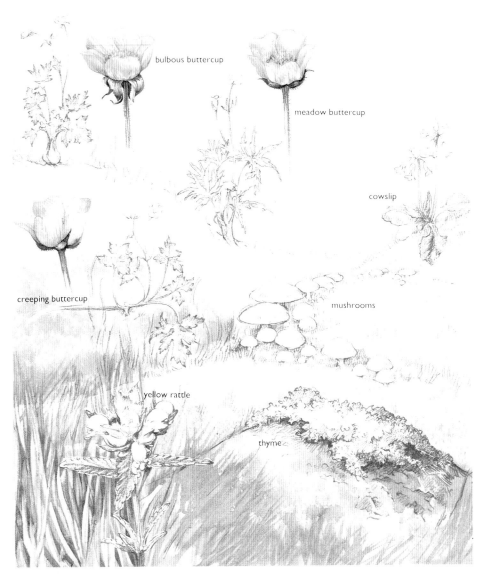

bulbous buttercup

meadow buttercup

cowslip

creeping buttercup

mushrooms

yellow rattle

thyme

Creeping buttercup. Runners,
furrowed stalk, wetter ground,
maybe with rushes nearby; last
to flower.

Yellow rattle. An indicator of old
grassland.

Thyme will often mark out dry areas,
such as the top of an ant hill.

Mushrooms: more likely to be found
in pastures manured by horses.

CHALK GRASSLAND

Old chalk grassland is one of Britain's most threatened habitat types: at most only 9500 hectares (24,000 acres) remain and further losses are to be expected.

The ancient downlands

Chalk, which is a fine form of limestone, grasps England's heartland like an ungainly spider, its body creating Salisbury Plain and legs stretching as the Dorset Downs, the South and North Downs and the Chilterns, which extend on into Norfolk and then further as the Lincolnshire and Yorkshire Wolds. 'Down' is an old word for hill, but 'wold' comes from wood, a name lingering long after the trees have gone.

Some of this open ground dates back to the early Neolithic farmer-pastoralists, who chose to settle first where the wildwood was thinnest, on the river gravels and on these sharply drained downs. It is on the downlands that many of their burial mounds are found; and, if the area is now ploughed, the downland wild flowers and insects may survive only on these tumps and mounds and similar banks.

Sheep and rabbits

Except for a time during the Napoleonic wars (and even then not much was affected), downland traditionally escaped the plough. It was grazed by sheep, which, under the watchful eyes of their shepherd, followed their appetites across the unfenced ground to create a mosaic of turf which was lightly dotted with scrub.

But things have drastically changed during this century. Little remains unploughed today, and even where it does much downland grass has been treated with herbicides and fertilisers, which has eliminated the wild flowers. The ploughlands may be green with grass, but it is sown ley, and empty of flowers and butterflies.

FEATURES OF CHALK DOWNLAND

Abandoned grazings become scrubbed up.

Fields are ploughed up to the limit, leaving grassland only on the steeper slopes.

Dense, yellow patches of tor grass appear when grazing stops.

steps of soil creep

fine grazed sward

Overgrazing may lay bare the chalk below; mosses grow and then coarse grasses which shelter scrub seedlings.

ant hills

Old, 'unimproved' downland turf often remains only on slopes too steep to plough or reach. Even when farms gave up sheep altogether, these slopes were kept open by rabbits, but when the rabbits were hit by disease, in the 1950s, the open grass started to become scrubbed up. The first sign of this may be the spread of clumps of tough tor grass across the turf, which die down to straw-coloured domes in winter. The shorter wild flowers are soon swamped by this rank growth. Even where downland remains unploughed on army ranges, it is becoming scrubbed up.

Fine-turfed downland is truly secure only in nature reserves where management follows traditional lines, although distant breeds of sheep such as Welsh beulah may be kept today.

Downland soil

By the way they grow, many plants can survive grazing (see pages 58–9). Old downland turf carries a marvellous variety of wild flowers, but this is not because the soil is rich. It is in fact rather poor and thin (newly ploughed fields nearby are a startling white), but this impoverishment does retard the competitiveness of ranker species, and so allows a myriad of slighter forms to survive. Over 30 different species (including wild grasses) can sometimes be found in a square metre. Variety is also added by the alkaline soil chemistry, which prevents the release of metals which would poison many plants. Many of them combat the dearth of nutrients with root nodules in which bacteria 'fix' atmospheric nitrogen.

With its sharp drainage, chalk soil is also rather dry, and as a result even small plants can have long roots – those of rock rose can reach for almost a metre. Others avoid the problem by being annuals, seeding before the summer drought.

Intriguing botany

Taking into account such things as slope and exposure, botanists recognise seven different types of chalk grassland, but there are always pockets of difference. Ant hills can often carry annuals and thyme, for

The distinctive profile of quaking grass (totter grass).

A wide variety of wild flowers and wild grasses grow on old, short turf of chalk downland. There are often many orchids, some widespread such as the bee and common spotted orchids, others very local or rare, such as the man and monkey orchids. Other classic short flowers are:

gentians	clustered bellflower
birdsfoot trefoil	small scabious
yellow wort	carline thistle
cowslip	lady's bedstraw
rockrose,	squinancywort

Lack of grazing means that taller flowers like knapweed and wild carrot may be seen. Of the birds, skylark and meadow pipit; lapwing, wheatear and (if a song post) woodlark may be seen, the 'classic' bird of the habitat, now rare, is the stone curlew.

example, while longer grass can harbour yellow rattle (see pages 58–9). Clay may have been washed into hollows in the chalk, and the leaching of this may also create a confusing and intriguing botany. The chalk may in fact be masked by thin patches of acid sandy soil, so that 'chalk' flowers grow alongside 'heath' flowers, as they do in Norfolk's Breckland. Elsewhere, long roots may reach down through the surface acid soil to reach the chalk below.

Insect life and birdlife

There is generally a low density of birdlife, both in summer and in winter. This is more than made up for by the vibrant and busy populations of butterflies and other insects.

COUNTING THE LIFE OF CHALK TURF

Old unimproved chalk turf can tax the eye with its wealth of wild flowers. Its butterfly life can match them, being intricately linked in unexpected ways.

A half-hour count

Many of the clues of old grassland are to be found. The minutely varied small leaves tax the eye, as there can be more than 30 different species to the square metre; in all, 60 plant species are exclusive to chalk swards. It is interesting to spend half an hour counting and comparing various areas (best done on hands and knees), for the species each exploit fine differences which are to their advantage.

This high count is largely because poor soil and close grazing reduce the competitiveness of rampant growths which would otherwise smother the others. Clearly, these tight communities were a long time forming: it is known that horseshoe vetch cleared from one site took over a century to re-establish itself, and that was with a seed source nearby. On the slopes, the lime may be leached out, leaving conditions in which fewer plants compete more strongly. But it can normally be very dry here, and the plants need strategies against drought – rock rose and horseshoe vetch have surprisingly long roots and do well. Look at the grasses to see if any respond to water loss by rolling or folding their leaves.

It is worth comparing short turf with longer-grass areas. Competitive suppression does imply that, where the grass is longer, fewer flowers will be seen. Some new ones come in, however: yellow rattle and eyebright may be found as they parasitise vigorous grass roots, though they can grow alone if the soil is moist enough.

Ant hills

The rounded ant hills also create their own conditions: they are usually evenly scattered, marking the territories held by the meadow ant, yellowish in colour (but rarely seen as it forages underground). Like other ants, this species is sensitive to temperature and the mounds are built up year after year on the side facing the morning sun, which may give them a noticeable alignment. The hot, dry top of the mound is perhaps decked with thyme, squinancywort and annuals, and with rabbit droppings (see pages 58–9).

The most elegant grass

Several wild grasses are seen, the most elegant being quaking grass (not restricted to chalk soils, however). Upright brome and tor grass quickly take over large areas if grazing stops.

Seasonal colour

There is an as yet unexplained seasonal colour change in the chalkland tapestry,

THE ADONIS BLUE – FINE TUNING IN THE HABITAT

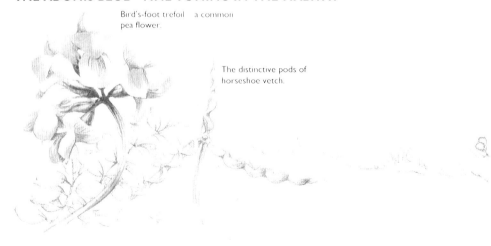

Bird's-foot trefoil a common pea flower.

The distinctive pods of horseshoe vetch.

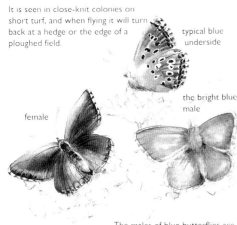

It is seen in close-knit colonies on short turf, and when flying it will turn back at a hedge or the edge of a ploughed field.

typical blue underside

the bright blue male

female

The males of blue butterflies are often the easier to identify.

the spring flowers being mainly yellow, while summer brings in blue, pink or white, and purple and mauve appear in late summer. There is also some yearly change in vigour, reflecting the previous weather. Orchids have their own rules here; and this is the place to look for these intricate flowers, for over half of Britain's orchid species are found on the chalk downs.

The story of the Adonis blue
Blue butterflies are almost certainly to be seen dancing over the turf. They are linked with the small flowers of short turf, but their relationship can be very complicated.

The Adonis blue, for example, is on the wing early in March, and again in late summer when other butterflies have often gone. As is normal among butterflies, the female makes a particular choice when laying eggs, in this case selecting only short sprigs of horseshoe vetch growing in secluded pits and depressions in short turf on south-facing slopes, real sunny spots to provide warmth.

Blue butterflies often have a close relationship with ants, which, in return for sweet honeydew, protect the caterpillars against other ants and prevent small parasitic wasps from implanting eggs in them. This armed guard follows the caterpillar down to the soil when the day's feeding is done, and with some species even buries it for safety.

If the ant guard is to be present and active when caterpillars need guarding in March and other early months, and again in the autumn, it must be warm enough for them. This will be the case only in real sun spots. Hence the choice of the female Adonis blue: her caterpillars are seen only on closely grazed plants where the ground is warmest. If the grass and the horseshoe vetch grow tall, the ants forsake the site. So old grassland, grazing and special hollows are all needed for the survival of this butterfly. Where it does fly, however, it can be seen in good numbers.

The males spend their time hovering, flying over the turf looking for females.

Once mated, she searches out short sprigs of horseshoe vetch in nooky spots.

22 C (72 F)

17 C (62 F)

In full sunshine, the temperature is high beneath the short plants.

The caterpillars live where the ground is warmest and the ants are busy early (and late) in the year.

It is cooler beneath 8 cm high vetch plants.

LIMESTONE GRASSLAND

Limestone rock is not only a memorial to past life, but also creates magnificent scenery. It furnishes a specialised set of wildlife habitats. Grassland is one.

Limestone geology

The constituent mineral of limestone was extracted from ancient oceans by life forms ranging from plankton to large corals and shellfish. Chalk (see pages 60–1) is a soft limestone formed by the smallest of organisms, but some hard limestones are made up of little but fossil shell fragments.

Hard limestone surfaces in many places in Britain, notably the Mendips, the Avon Gorge and across into South Wales, in parts of North Wales, and in the Cotswolds, Derbyshire and parts of the Pennines and the Lake District. Scotland also has some limestone areas.

Limestone scenery

Although chemically similar to chalk, the hardness of limestone provides very different habitat features. It creates a rugged and often a high landscape – much of the Pennine limestone rises past 300 metres – with gorges and rock outcrops scattered over the slopes, and in some places exposures of limestone 'pavement'. Some areas have been quarried and mined.

This countryside was, as others, cloaked with wildwood, but together with chalk downland it was lightly covered and probably cleared quite early in prehistoric times. Certainly the Mendips and the Derbyshire limestones have magnificent prehistoric stone circles and tombs. Some woodland remains, which may sometimes be relic patches of the mixed wildwood, but ash woodland is typical (see pages 28–9).

The fields on the limestone are usually divided by drystone walls. These, like the lowland hedges, may date from several periods. Some which are barely visible as a line across pasture could be of late prehistoric date (Bronze Age and Iron Age). Most of the older walls are of medieval date, however, and create a huddled network around the farms and hamlets in the valleys, while the most recent are those which stride in straight lines across higher open ground. These last often date from the Georgian enclosures, when much of the open, unfenced common rough grazing was turned over to fields, here as elsewhere.

FEATURES OF A LIMESTONE COUNTRYSIDE

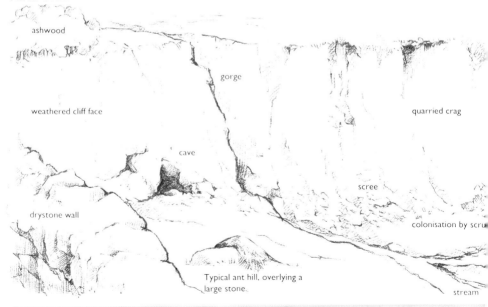

ashwood

gorge

weathered cliff face

quarried crag

cave

scree

drystone wall

colonisation by scru

Typical ant hill, overlying a large stone.

stream

Many of these fields are grass: usually pasture, although there is some meadowland. If unploughed, they can have as much botanical interest as old downland turf.

Indicators of limestone

Many of the flowers of chalk downland which are useful indicators of a limy soil also grow on limestone. As with downland, the reason is not simple, and not merely because their metabolism needs lime, but rather because this soil inhibits plants which normally compete strongly for light and space. If there is no competition (in a garden bed, for example), many 'lime-loving' (calcicole) plants will grow and flower without it, while some lime-haters (calcifuges) normally found only on acid soil can also be grown where it is chalky.

In fact, many calcicoles are not so particular on the Continent, but only in Britain, which is at the edge of their natural range and where slight differences can affect their ability to compete. Much of our limestone lies in northern Britain, and so this could be an important factor. But this northern limestone also carries some flowers not seen further south. The scrubbing-up of abandoned pasture is usually slower than on the chalk, probably because of the height and exposure of many limestone areas.

Screes

A scree, the tumbled blocks at the foot of a cliff or slope, is always worth exploring. Lichens quickly pattern exposed rock faces, but in time soil gathers and sheltered corners can quickly become gardens of mosses and ferns, with flowering plants soon making an appearance.

Limestone pavement

This extraordinary feature is seen exposed mainly in South Wales and the Craven area of the Pennines. Beds of limestone rock initially smoothed by the ice sheets of the Ice Age have then had their cracks opened out by water (rainwater is slightly acid, and it slowly dissolves limestone). The rock surface is today cut into blocks or 'clints' by deep gullies or 'grikes', which offer a sheltered haven for plants.

Rather unexpectedly, heather may sometimes be found growing in soil pockets. Here the heavy hill rains have leached out the lime to leave a rather acid soil.

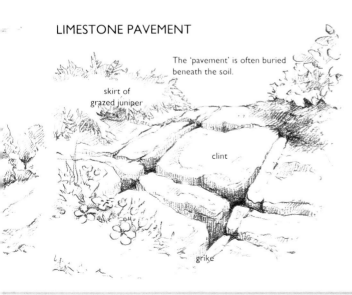

LIMESTONE PAVEMENT

The 'pavement' is often buried beneath the soil.

skirt of grazed juniper

clint

grike

Sheep-grazed limestone grass has many chalk species such as sheep's fescue grass, thyme and carnation grass. Species found only on the moorland limestone include bird's èye primrose, lady's mantle, the yellow- or blue-violet-flowered mountain pansy and blue moor grass. This lovely grass flowers early, so many visitors see only the dead heads. And in the sheltered grikes even dog's mercury and cuckoo pint have been found.

LIMESTONE SPECIALITIES

LIMESTONE FLOWERS

greenish-flowered
lady's mantle

pink-flowered
bird's eye primrose

mountain pansy

Bird's eye primrose and this wild pansy
aren't seen on the southern chalk.

Limestone grassland carries many of the same flowers as chalkland, qualified by height and northern situation. Limestone pavement creates its own world.

Limestone turf

Three special flowers to look for are globe-flower, bird's-eye primrose, and lady's mantle with its 'crying' leaves which exude drops of water which linger like dew. Here, as with the chalk, details of local geography can produce different mixes of flowers: bird's-eye primrose, for example, prefers rather peaty soils fed by limy springs. Plant counts can reach over 20 to the square metre. Like all habitats, there are good and poor growing years, although some species such as rock rose, which is shared with the chalk, have very even growth year in year out, replacing the leaves it sheds.

What cannot be realised except by peering closely on hands and knees is the sheer vitality of it all – it is frantically busy with insects and other animals. Even when walking, you will miss as much as you see.

Story-markers

These are as familiar here as on other grasslands. Even thistles and nettles can be interpreted (see pages 56–7 and 58–9), the creeping thistle usually being the one to take advantage of areas of disturbed soil here.

Glacial drift

Even shallow limestone pavement can hold pockets of acid soil (see pages 64–5); and, on the larger scale, many limestone areas are covered by glacial 'drift', a flour scraped from the rocks by the movements of ice sheets and pushed along by them or carried by the water flooding from beneath them. It can have a quite sour acid character and is often quite deep, even deep enough to bring in different flowers and wild grasses. Instead of blue moor grass with its blue-tinted head indicating limestone and alkaline conditions, for example, there may be hay-scented sweet vernal grass with yellow tormentil flowering with it as indicator of acid soil conditions.

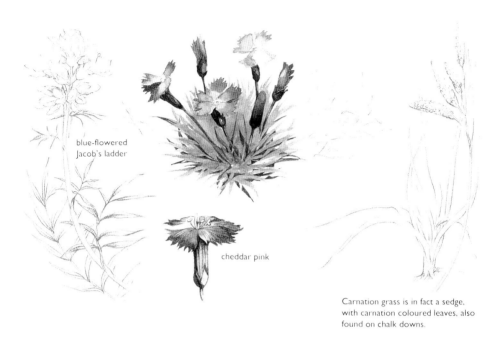

blue-flowered
Jacob's ladder

cheddar pink

Carnation grass is in fact a sedge,
with carnation coloured leaves, also
found on chalk downs.

Limestone pavement

This is literally like a giant's rough stone floor, uneven in surface and cut by deep cracks. Though seemingly inhospitable, the relatively sheltered cracks or grikes can contain a natural rock garden.

Because of the moist shelter, many of the plants in these grikes are in fact woodland species in origin, and perhaps they remain from a time when trees did root themselves here. When they were felled, the shallow surface soil was easily washed from the smooth rock and later from within the grikes. One survey found wild arum and herb-Paris, a notable indicator of old woodland (see pages 18–19). Being a poor seeder, this plant may have been isolated in its grike for hundreds of years.

Other pavement flowers are grassland plants, here protected from grazing, of course. Trees and shrubs will be grazed as soon as they appear at the surface, and this can have an odd effect, creating 'skirts' of species such as juniper growing prostrate over the surface.

None of these plants is confined to pavements, but several are what are known as 'specialists'. That is a subjective way of putting it, but what is meant is that they are more often found here, on limestone pavement, than elsewhere. Some ferns belong to this group, rigid buckler fern being one rarity that is.

One rather separate feature to be found in such limestone scenery is a marl pond or lake, with clear pale blue water (see pages 116–17) and containing dense beds of submerged aquatic plants. One of the best known is Malham Tarn in Yorkshire.

Cliff plants

Limestone cliffs have their own short list of specialists, many found in only one location. The Cheddar pink which colours ledges in the Cheddar Gorge in summer is one; the blue Jacob's ladder of The White Peak is another. On these ledges they are safe from grazing, and largely escape the competition which would overwhelm them in open grassland.

THE MEADOW

HAY MEADOWS AND FLOOD MEADOWS

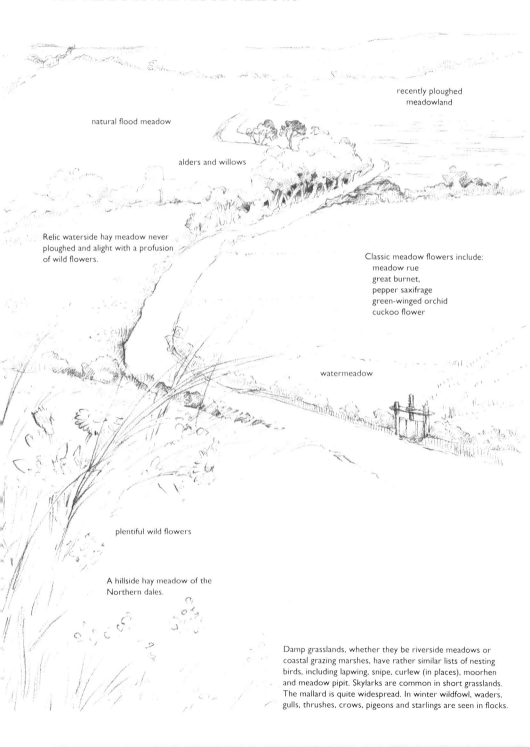

recently ploughed
meadowland

natural flood meadow

alders and willows

Relic waterside hay meadow never
ploughed and alight with a profusion
of wild flowers.

Classic meadow flowers include:
   meadow rue
   great burnet,
   pepper saxifrage
   green-winged orchid
   cuckoo flower

watermeadow

plentiful wild flowers

A hillside hay meadow of the
Northern dales.

Damp grasslands, whether they be riverside meadows or
coastal grazing marshes, have rather similar lists of nesting
birds, including lapwing, snipe, curlew (in places), moorhen
and meadow pipit. Skylarks are common in short grasslands.
The mallard is quite widespread. In winter wildfowl, waders,
gulls, thrushes, crows, pigeons and starlings are seen in flocks.

The traditional meadow is one of the most flowery of habitats, but in today's countryside fewer than one in 20 has escaped damaging 'improvement' in recent years.

The meadow

Meadow is an old name for a field which provides a cut of hay as well as grazing. Grasses usually like damp feet, and so the village hay meadows were traditionally alongside rivers, or where springs or flushes watered the soil; and in time the word became attached to other waterside grass fields that are grazed only. In the eyes of the modern ecologist, meadow grassland is 'neutral' grassland, in contrast to the acid and basic grasslands of heaths and chalk downs. As well as hay meadows, the category of neutral grassland includes East Anglian washlands, flood meadows and some water meadows.

In the Domesday Book, hay meadows were valued above ploughland. In those days, before the advent of turnips and silage, hay was vital for keeping the livestock alive when the grass stops growing, which happens when the winter temperature dips below 6 C (43 F).

The meadow may have been grazed early in spring, but whether it was or not it was then locked up to allow the grass to grow waist-high in June or July, when it was mown just before energy was diverted into seed production. After the cut, the livestock would normally be allowed back to graze the 'aftermath' until the touch of winter again slowed growth.

The smell of hay

Haymaking means hay-drying, letting the sun reduce the water content until it is too low for fermentation. The heady scent of cut and drying hay is given by an aromatic substance called coumarin which is found in grasses. Sweet vernal grass, found on many soils and especially on rather acid hill pastures, contains much coumarin.

A flowery meadow

In early summer, a traditional hay meadow can be recognised from afar by its tawny colour, and at close quarters by the profusion of wild flowers among the tall grass. The timing of the cut allows the flowers to set seed, and the soil, fertilised only by the manure of the livestock and the silt brought by the winter's floodwater, provides a good bed, but not so rich that the more rampant growths can flourish (see below). As to be expected, there are insects aplenty, and the cover of the tall grass is also welcomed by ground-nesting birds.

An endangered habitat

The hay meadow's colourful variety is immediately lost if the field is drained and ploughed and reseeded. Even artificial fertilisers reduce the variety of flowers, by encouraging the greedier grasses which grow and smother the other plants. During the last half century, over 95% of old hay meadows have been destroyed by ploughing and draining for corn or for ley grassland, or by digging for gravel.

Flood and water meadows

Much has been changed by modern river engineering, but washlands and flood meadows are names given to riverside pasture fields which tend to flood each winter. The water keeps the frost off the grass, allowing growth, and this was used to advantage in special water meadows. These were in their heyday a century or more ago in southern chalk counties, where the rivers rarely run out of control.

Here the riverside grazings were cut with channels, and by using sluice gates the grass was kept thinly flooded (or 'floated') in early spring. The silt fertilised the field, but the main benefit was that the grass grew to give an early bite for the lambing sheep. The process could be repeated at the back end of the year to extend the autumn grazing. Even if now derelict, the ridging and maybe the old sluice gates can often still be seen.

This regime was not, of course, by itself especially beneficial to the tall hay-meadow flowers, which would be nibbled down when grazing commenced. Nonetheless, if the turf has escaped the plough, it may carry some interesting species.

STRATEGIES OF THE MEADOW BROWNS

Tattered wings are sometimes seen.

At rest, and well camouflaged.

The small dots on the hindwings trick birds to peck here, rather than at head or body.

If disturbed, it raises its forewings and the gleaming eye spot suddenly appears, to alarm the bird and give the butterfly precious seconds to fly away.

As many as 15 different wild grasses and 60 wild flower species can bedeck an old hay meadow. The wildlife, especially the butterflies, can match this profusion.

A changing pageant

Many of the wild flowers reach as high as the swaying grass. This profusion has been reached after long centuries of traditional management, but it can be (and has been) wiped out in an hour or two by ploughing or by the use of herbicides. Up to the cutting of the hay, sequences of flowers are seen. Marsh marigold flowers early, but wild orchids maybe not until June. The three buttercups can reflect soil differences, and also the month.

A mosaic of plant communities

Buttercups, oxeye daisy, meadowsweet, ragged robin and grasses such as purple moor grass will be found in many different grassy places. There will be a mosaic of very slightly different plant communities because colonisation has been slow and inter-species competitiveness varies with changes in the unploughed soil below. Even slight hummocks raised above the general level will be leached to become slightly acid, and yellow tormentil or even heather may be seen in what is generally thought of as chalk countryside, for example. Each meadow has its own character, so that

while one is locally famous for green-winged orchid another is notable for meadow saffron; and another has cowslip and pepper saxifrage as abundant species, but no great rarities.

Of all of them, however, it is the fritillary which symbolises the sadness of the lost beauty of our meadows, although it can still grow thousands-strong where it does remain. Half a century ago, 27 counties had fritillary meadows, but today only a handful keep them.

Indicator species

The variety of wild flowers speaks for itself, but a handful of plants can be used as 'indicators' of hay meadow – and they may be enough to identify a relic corner which has escaped modern 'improvement'. They include adders tongue fern, pepper saxifrage and great burnet.

A typical orchid is the southern marsh orchid, but these intricate and exotic-looking wild flowers can reflect the particular regime of that meadow.

Insect life

Traditional management created a semi-natural meadow community which included in its relationships a host of small animals as well as plants. A meadow is a prime habitat for butterflies and for butterfly-watching. Browns are typical, generally laying their eggs on grasses of various kinds; their colour identifies them as members of this family, as do the eye-spots on the forewings (and sometimes the hindwings, too). But the marbled white, a brown, too, although its speckled black and white colours belie the fact and it also lacks the eye-spots, is also frequently seen here; it is not at all clear what evolutionary advantages there are in these very individual markings. Other butterflies such as the common blue, small heath and small skipper are common on most kinds of grassland.

Grasshoppers will also be common (see pages 98–9), and dragonflies (see pages 122–3) frequently seen.

Birds

Surveys have shown that the most likely breeding birds are moorhen, reed bunting, mallard, lapwing, snipe and skylark – all to be expected in three out of four unploughed meadow fields. The first on the list is due to the fact that meadows usually lie alongside water. The frequency list continues with redshank, sedge warbler, yellow wagtail, swan, partridge, coot and meadow pipit – all to be expected at more than half of sites surveyed. Swallows swoop low for the insects, and the heron is also a frequent visitor. It fishes from the bank or in the shallows, but young herons are also seen on open grassy 'nurseries' near their woodland nesting colonies, some way from water.

The winter birdlife may be rather different. Some areas such as the Ouse Washes are famous for their pintail, teal, wigeon and other duck, but at more usual village meadows you could expect to see mallard, woodpigeon, fieldfare, redwing, starling, heron, moorhen, snipe, pied wagtail, crow, kestrel, lapwing, black-headed gull, skylark, teal and meadow pipit. A list to make a diversion well worthwhile.

THREE INDICATORS OF OLD MEADOWLAND

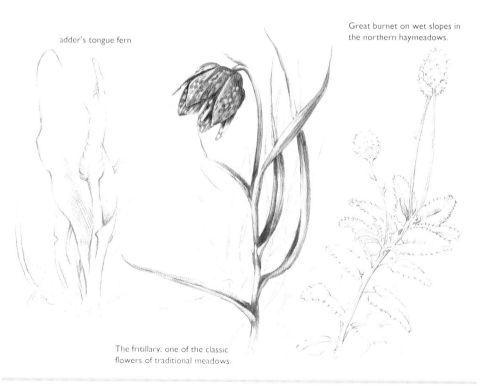

adder's tongue fern

Great burnet on wet slopes in the northern haymeadows.

The fritillary, one of the classic flowers of traditional meadows.

SCRUB

Scrub is a familiar feature, even in well-manicured countryside. Ecologically, however, it is usually a transient, halfway stage to something else.

The word 'scrub'

In some ways, scrub is a portmanteau word. The patches of scrub found on windswept heaths, those verging wetland, those invading open chalk grassland and those in corners of derelict land are each rather different. Thicket is also rather an imprecise word, although it does imply thicker and more tangled growth. For some reason of landscape history, the word thicket (unlike scrub) is often found on the map.

As a word, scrub is derived from shrub, which botanically is a tall woody growth with (unlike a tree) several main stems rising from one rootstock. Undershrubs are plants such as heather and gorse, woody but low and straggly and short-lived. Scrub is usually taken to mean an area of land occupied by shrubs and young trees, with nothing taller than, say, 8 metres, when it becomes a wood. In fact, in the natural course of things, scrub does evolve into woodland unless the area is too cold or windswept for trees.

Scrub can have something of the layered structure of the shrub or underwood layer of a wood. The branching in scrub is often tighter and denser, however.

Scrub as a succession stage

It is clear from a number of habitats, including limestone scree (see pages 64–5) and some derelict land (see pages 112–3), that plants can colonise even bare rock or rubble. As soon as lichens and mosses have created a small depth of soil, grasses and other low plants can invade, usually annuals at first but later more long-lived species, and in time woody shrubs and trees reach the site to form scrub, which then evolves into woodland as the trees grow tall.

The experts call this primary succession. The scrub we usually meet, however, is a stage in what is known as secondary succession, where shrubs and trees reoccupy ground that was originally wooded but was cleared for pasture or ploughland or for smallholdings or other uses. Secondary succession is seen on heathland, for example (see pages 152–3).

A more interesting insight is that each stage invites its successors, encouraging the growth of seedlings of species which will in

SUCCESSION

SUCCESSION ON VALLEY AND CHALK SOILS

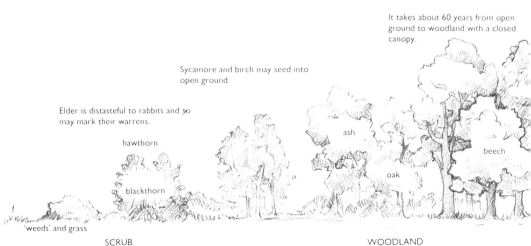

It takes about 60 years from open ground to woodland with a closed canopy.

Sycamore and birch may seed into open ground.

Elder is distasteful to rabbits and so may mark their warrens.

hawthorn

ash

beech

blackthorn

oak

'weeds' and grass

SCRUB

WOODLAND

time outgrow it. Typical scrub species such as hawthorn and blackthorn (or sloe) are armed with spines which protect them against deer, sheep and cattle, but they then also protect any young oak, ash or beech trees growing among them.

These spines, however, are no real defence against rabbits. Rabbits can keep grassland free of scrub, as they did on the chalk downs (see pages 60–1). On the other hand, elder will scrub up rabbit grazings because the rabbits find it unpalatable.

The climax community

Except where the ground is too wet, plant succession in the lowlands normally ends with woodland, which is the climatic climax. The harsher conditions of the hills or coast can restrict the climax to scrub, but normally even wilderness areas such as heaths and moors will, unless 'held' by grazing or cutting, become scrubbed up and eventually become woodland.

The trees, too, strive for primacy, and, given enough time, the beech would eventually shade out the oak.

From open grass to quite tall woodland can take about 60 years, in the region of our own animal lifespan, and so this succession often escapes notice. Most of us live for some years at an address before moving, and the neighbouring patches of scrub can seem unchanging permanent features.

Spreading seeds

One puzzling thing is that, if at the end of the Ice Age the oak extended its range from what is now Brighton to Edinburgh in, say, a generous 5000 years, that represents an advance of at least 100 metres a year. Birch and Scots pine are pioneer trees by strategy, producing light seeds which can be blown quite a distance by gales; ash may be rather similar. Scrub species such as hawthorn and blackthorn (sloe) could be spread by mice and birds eating the fruit and voiding the pips. But would the oak have to rely on squirrels and jays burying the acorns in larders far from the parent tree, as they can sometimes be seen doing today?

A consequence of their strategy is that scrubland species are commonly seen also in hedges. The exact tally reflects the soil, and the age of the hedge (see pages 84–5); you would expect to find a greater variety on chalky soil than on clay. Some species are found really only on chalk and limestone.

oak and beech

pine

birch

gorse

heather

SCRUB

WOODLAND

Although on many soils scrub is a rag-bag of species, the scrub invading ungrazed limestone or chalk can have hawthorn plus characteristic species, i.e. dogwood, maple, buckthorn, privet, guelder rose, spindle, juniper and wild roses, and traveller's joy festooning all, this climber is a classic indicator of chalk soil.

THE WILDLIFE OF THE THICKET

*Thicket and scrub are really a pair of
interchangeable names. They have much in
common with hedges, but some basic ecology
of their own.*

The shrub count
It is worth counting the different species of
woody growth in the scrub, and along its
margins. Here wild roses can be an attractive feature.

More species are to be expected on chalk,
where dogwood, spindle and privet come in
to join the widespread hawthorn and blackthorn (see soil chart, pages 20–1). They are
in fact good indicators of chalk soil, but they
are rather restricted to the south; on chalk
in the Yorkshire Wolds, for example, the
scrub is poorer, often with only hawthorn
and blackthorn. The reasons for this are not
clear. These lime-liking shrubs are also less
frequent in limestone scrub in the north,
possibly because here the ground is too high
and bleak for them.

Unlike trees, which are generally wind-
pollinated, most of these scrub species are
insect-pollinated and their flowers are an
attractive feature. Their berries also add
dashes of bright colour in autumn.

Climbers
A few woody or partly woody climbers are
also typical of scrub. Honeysuckle is one,
and clematis or old man's beard another,
distinctive of chalk and limestone soils. The
two bryonies and other climbers bear gaudy
berries in autumn.

Butterflies and other insects
The thicket can be an insect metropolis.
Leaves and flowers (and fruit, too) attract
many nibblers, and the flying adults enjoy
the open sunshine bathing the scrub, where
in woodland they are restricted to open
glades and rides and other sunny patches.
There are usually plenty of butterflies to be
seen, many linked with grasses and other
plants, but some laying eggs on the leaves or
shoots of the woody species. Colonies of the
brown hairstreak are linked in this way
with blackthorn in a few locations in the
south, although usually this is blackthorn

growing in bushy hedges or woodland
edges. The more familiar brimstone
searches for buckthorn, which is often
found in scrub. The green hairstreak is
strongly linked with gorse and with heathlands, but it will also seek out bramble and
even dogwood, a typical chalkland shrub. It
has one of the widest ranges of choice of all
butterflies.

Birdsong and the thicket
Thicket birdsong is a welcome feature of
spring, but the species count is not as high
as in woodland in general. At the start,
when grassland becomes invaded and open-
canopy scrub develops, linnet and yellowhammer replace meadow pipit and skylark;
but they then phase out gradually as the
scrub thickens. Willow warblers and dun-
nocks remain common right through scrub
succession to closed canopy. Other birds,
such as chaffinch, will not nest until the
scrub is tall and dense. But tall scrub (the
best for birds) might have only around ten
different species, compared with the 30
expected of mature oak woodland. The
density of birds nesting is also lower than to
be expected in woodland. Large birds are

This is a scrub bird, a bird of
commons and farmland, but also
of the scrub of dunes and cliffs
by the sea.

Yellowhammers may become 'woodland birds' if the tree
canopy is broken.

PROFILE OF A SCRUB BIRD

Linnet and yellowhammer colonise when open scrub has been established, replacing the skylark and meadow pipit of the earlier stage.

The linnet nests in low cover; unlike many scrub birds, it has not become a garden bird.

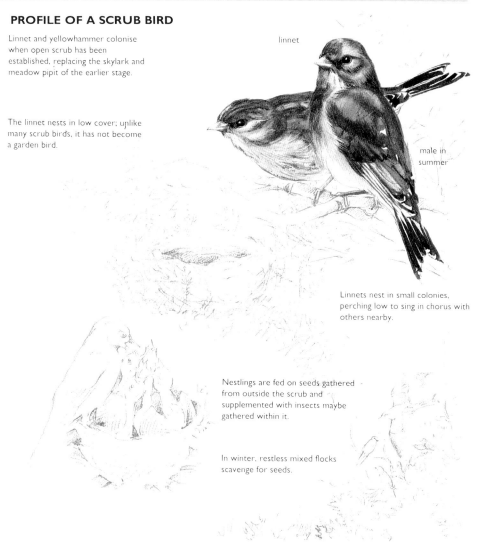

linnet

male in summer

Linnets nest in small colonies, perching low to sing in chorus with others nearby.

Nestlings are fed on seeds gathered from outside the scrub and supplemented with insects maybe gathered within it.

In winter, restless mixed flocks scavenge for seeds.

fewer. Those that may nest in scrub, such as magpie, crow and birds of prey, feed outside it on open ground and along the hedges.

The thicket in winter

Flocks of birds searching for berries are a familiar sight in winter, but this 'winter' behaviour can start well before the first frosts. Flocks of thrushes congregate in this way as early as July, and later on, in October, they are joined by migrant redwings and others coming from northern Europe. What is interesting is that the so-called 'resident' thrushes, faced with this competition, may hold territory to protect their thicket larders as they do when nesting in spring, and they can be observed approaching intruding birds with threat postures. The berries exhausted, the thrushes tend to give way to tits and others searching the branches for hibernating insects and spiders.

Apart from its importance as a larder, scrub also offers some shelter for winter roosting. There is some evidence that certain roosts preferred by tits, for example, may act as hotels, with a clientele of different individual birds each night.

THE COMMON

Our 0.6 million hectares (1.5 million acres) of common land not only have major wildlife importance, but are also historically interesting in their own right.

Early memories

Images of blackberry-picking on a common of a Sunday afternoon are with us from childhood. (And why are the best, the juiciest, always just out of reach?)

But commons also have a prominent place in folk memory. They occupy a unique corner in the history of the countryside.

A motley array of commons

Common land in England and Wales occupies an area about 15 times the size of the Isle of Wight (commons as such do not exist in Scotland). They are seen in the mind's eye as open grassy public places, often on the doorstep of a town or only a short drive away for a Sunday afternoon, but they are really quite varied and diverse. Epping Forest, Bodmin Moor, Clapham Common in London, many of the open Lake District fells – they are all commons. In Norfolk, many commons are ribbons of

COMMONS IN THE COUNTRYSIDE

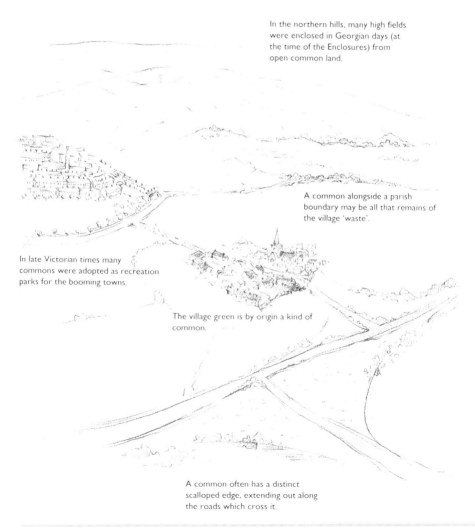

In the northern hills, many high fields were enclosed in Georgian days (at the time of the Enclosures) from open common land.

A common alongside a parish boundary may be all that remains of the village 'waste'.

In late Victorian times many commons were adopted as recreation parks for the booming towns.

The village green is by origin a kind of common.

A common often has a distinct scalloped edge, extending out along the roads which cross it.

green bordering the roads and there are also some of this kind in parts of Dorset. The village green was also in origin a common.

Commons rights

Contrary to belief, commons are not generally in public ownership, although most common land is open to the public. Many commons are now owned by a council, or by the National Trust or other quasi-public bodies, but they are basically privately held land, and today's landlord is the legal descendant of the feudal lord of the manor.

It was in medieval times that the customs of common land reached their peak. Under the manorial system, the parish land was jointly worked in common. The best soil was ploughed in the great shared open fields or set aside for hay. Some woodland was managed as coppice-with-standards, supplying the village with timber and wood for other needs. In addition, every manor had 'waste' land, which provided rough grazing (see pages 52–3) and which could include areas of heathland or moorland. The villagers' commons rights also unlocked this resource, to help them supplement their meagre livelihoods. The rights varied from place to place, with the pasturage of horses, cattle and geese the most widespread, and estover (cutting heather or bracken for fuel or bedding) and husbote (collecting fallen timber) also important. Pannage (feeding pigs and other livestock on acorns and beech mast), turbary (the digging of peat) and piscary (fishing) were other options.

The loss of the commons

By 300 years ago, the ancient commons rights were beginning to be eroded. New Enclosure Acts authorised the more go-ahead villagers to seize the common village lands and fence them up into fields in which they alone could farm. The best soils were taken first, but 1·8 million hectares (4·5 million acres) of open commons were lost before alarm was felt. The Commons Act of 1876 called a halt, protecting the surviving commons. At the same time many scraps of common near or in the growing towns and cities were adopted for public recreation.

The last chapter of the story was the registration of commons in 1970, establishing the identity of both the owners and those claiming commons rights – these had over time usually become linked with the ownership of cottages or farms in the neighbourhood. The reverse of the coin was that, if these rights were not claimed, the owner of the common could find other uses for the land, and many wild commons were 'improved' for farming, dug for gravel or even built over as a result.

Recognising a common

One clue could be the name on the map, and perhaps the local bye-laws governing its use are posted up. Its shape can be another. Unlike a traditional woodland or parkland, a common often has a scalloped boundary, curving out along the roads as they leave it. A common in one parish may well join up with that of a neighbouring parish in this way.

But (and from a wildlife aspect this is important) it can have an old-fashioned look. Never ploughed, it may carry the scars of centuries, including old diggings for peat or marl maybe. Very often, grazing is slackening or has ceased and the land is scrubbing up: this is the place for the blackberry thicket. Rabbits could keep the scrub at bay, but they were decimated by disease in the 1950s when much of today's scrub started to establish itself. Incidentally, many commons do have the name 'warren' (or sometimes 'coney') linked with them or with one part. Rabbits were brought to Britain in Plantagenet times to be bred for meat and fur, and were reared in fenced-off warrens; the first choice for these was the 'waste' rather than the more valuable arable and hay land. It is interesting that very often soft-soiled prehistoric burial mounds or the ramparts of Iron Age forts were called into use as warrens; they were more likely to remain in the wastes. Although rabbits had been here for centuries and presumably often escaped to breed wild, it was not until Victorian times that there were reports of their becoming so common that they became a nuisance.

COMMON SIGHTS

Because of its history, the common can offer many different wildlife sightings. But even the most familiar can be rather more complicated than at first appears.

The scampering of rabbits

A stroll with the dog sends the rabbits scampering off across the common, scuts flashing as a warning to others of their kind. They seem to be scattered at random when they feed, with a hop here and a hop there, but no further than a short dash back to their burrow. In fact, they have a rather particular geography of their own.

They are sociable animals, living together in 'warrens'. In medieval days, special fenced warrens were laid out for them in areas of soft soil. They mark their territory in more than one way: with a scented secretion from a chin gland, with urine, and with droppings. The last are the most obvious, being scattered on mole hills, ant hills or other raised bumps. And it seems that the rush back for the safety of the burrow may not be simply one of blind panic. Some observers claim evidence that the path is exactly marked out on some kind of mental map: not only can the rabbit race along it without wasting a moment's thought, but paws strike ground at the same spots on each occasion so that there is no loss of momentum. Perhaps your own observations will confirm or refute this, but mental mapping is certainly not unknown in the animal world.

Bramble

There are perhaps 60,000 hectares (150,000 acres) of brambles – blackberries – in Britain, found in virtually every habitat. They even grow in woodland shade, although they are rather spindly here and flowering and fruiting only in the dappled patches of light.

Because brambles are generally self-fertilising, clones are the rule – separate populations with their own character. The differences are usually detailed ones: not simply in the numbers of leaflets (three to five) in the leaves, but in the exact shade of the petals and the shape, colour and flavour of the berries, and the shape and direction of the prickles. There are differences in the way stems arch or lie along the ground.

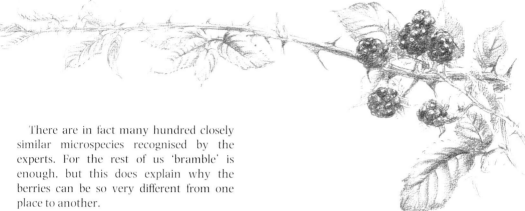

There are in fact many hundred closely similar microspecies recognised by the experts. For the rest of us 'bramble' is enough, but this does explain why the berries can be so very different from one place to another.

Look also for summer leaves coloured and dying from rust fungus, this before the autumn when leaves in general become gaudy with the red and yellow waste products. Look also for the scars of leaf miners within the leaf, some sinuous, others simply blotches. The small grubs of these beetles or moths eat out the juicy middle flesh of the leaf and kill it.

Bramble-watching

Large numbers of insects visit the brambles, and sometimes queues, or at least sequences, can be noticed. One often quoted is that wasps arrive first, with jaws strong enough to tear the skin of the ripe blackberry. Once this has been torn, then hoverflies and others can arrive to suck up the juice. Butterflies prefer it a little later, when it has begun to ferment.

Gorse

On some commons, gorse is first into the scene, upstaging even bramble. Despised by many, it is a handsome plant if allowed to mass itself. And it is worth inspecting for some botany.

Gorse is, like the bluebell, one of our 'Atlantic' plants, thriving in our damp and rather mild climate (it cannot stand much frost, which is why it is a plant of heathland rather than moor). It is a 'switch' plant with its leaves reduced or absent, and photosynthesis takes place in the green stems. Water loss through evaporation is cut down in this way, because it is the leaves which carry the small pores through which the plant 'transpires'. This is an adaptation which is also seen in desert plants.

The question as yet unanswered is why a plant which thrives in a wet Atlantic climate should have evolved as if it needed to save water. Although admittedly its favourite heathlands can be rather dry places, hawthorn and other unspecialised shrubs can grow perfectly happily on them. Gorse is in fact a member of the pea family, and its seedlings have the familiar clover-like leaves.

Bracken

Bracken is by origin a plant of open woods on rather acid soils, often seen under birch and in some oak woods. It spreads rapidly with far-creeping underground stems and is a successful invader of grassland, heathland and also some moorlands, but it likes sharp drainage because its roots cannot stand waterlogging. So it may be seen covering a hillside but ending with a sharp line at the wetter foot of the slope. It is common on commons today.

Its success on such open ground often reflects the fact that the use of the land has changed. In the hills it can mark grazings that are less dutifully cared for, or perhaps now managed rather differently; cattle will eat the young shoots and control it, sheep will not (nor will rabbits). Once in place, it is difficult to eradicate.

THE PLOUGHED FIELD

Although it has a relatively narrow spectrum of wildlife, arable land is the most abundant habitat in Britain, with 4·5 million hectares (11 million acres).

The first farming revolution

In the 'ancient and ornamental' countryside to be found mainly in Devon, West Dorset, Sussex, Essex and the Welsh Marches, the fields are small and irregular, and often seem to have been cleared directly from woodland. But a second type of countryside is more universal, with fields larger and more regular in grid-like pattern. Their origin lies in the largely open (i.e. hedgeless) farmlands of the medieval manor.

These open fields are familiar from school history. Three ploughlands embraced the village, one being left fallow each year to recover its strength and be manured by livestock. The soil was ploughed in long hauls by the ox teams to create a ridge-and-furrow corduroy pattern, still seen in some places running across today's pasture fields.

These open farmlands in time became enclosed, divided up into smaller units by fencing and hedges (or drystone walls where stone was available). Much of this took place in Georgian times, under the licence of Acts of Enclosure, which allowed the more entrepreneurial villagers to take over the common village lands for their use alone. It was in effect a farming revolution making scientific farming possible, with new rotations of crops, new crops such as turnips for wintering the cattle, and new breeds of livestock. Birds and other wildlife, however, could skip the hedge to find refuge not far away. And the fields were still dotted with cornflower, corn marigold and other wild flowers.

The second revolution

Hedges have been grubbed up in recent decades to create larger fields for modern harvesters and other machinery, but this is only one sign of what has been a new farming revolution. Mechanisation now allows most land to be ploughed, so that most grassland is now an arable crop. To favour cereals, the fields are now dried with new buried drains running to deeply dredged streams and rivers (see pages 124–5). There is emphasis on the use of chemicals, in pest control, as fertilisers, and to control the ripening and seeding of some crops.

PLOUGHLAND

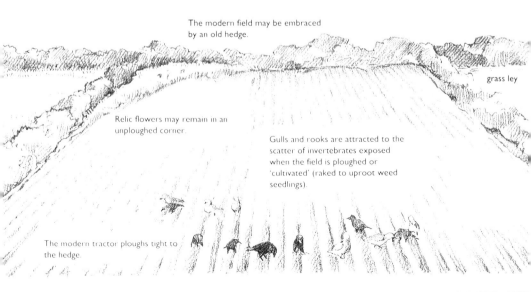

The modern field may be embraced by an old hedge.

grass ley

Relic flowers may remain in an unploughed corner.

Gulls and rooks are attracted to the scatter of invertebrates exposed when the field is ploughed or 'cultivated' (raked to uproot weed seedlings).

The modern tractor ploughs tight to the hedge.

The figures speak for themselves: where the medieval peasant might expect a fifth of a ton of skimpy wheat an acre, the harvest was just over 1 ton in the 1950s and can nudge 2 tons today.

The harvest

Gathering the harvest is now a rapid mechanised task, and the once familiar stooks or stacked sheaves of corn are now seen only where long-stemmed wheat is grown for thatching straw. Grain-driers in the sheds mean less reliance on good weather. And as well as high yield cultivars of wheat, barley and other crops, cash subsidies also promote new harvests, of oil seed rape, for example, which colours the fields vivid yellow when in flower.

Autumn sowing

There is little time nowadays for the traditional harvest-home festivities. The race is on to plough and sow winter wheat or barley before autumn rains make the land unworkable. Dealing with unwanted straw and stubble is a time-consuming business and it has often been burnt where it lay. The flash fires have scorched hedges.

The survivors

The few wild plants which do remain to be characteristic of modern ploughland have a particularly tenacious strategy. Common couch and field bindweed can grow again from even a small fragment of buried root or stem. There are some benefits to being an annual in threatening surroundings: annuals can quickly take advantage of the slightest opportunity. The poppy, for example, may produce 20,000 small seeds a head, which, if buried by ploughing, seem to become 'drugged' by the relatively abundant carbon dioxide in the soil atmosphere and able to remain dormant but viable for decades. When deep ploughing, perhaps for a new field drain, brings them to the surface, they germinate and flower. Only a few species, such as fat hen and charlock seem resistant to modern weedkillers.

It is a parallel tale for animal life. The soil is no longer a rich powerhouse of worms, soil beetles and others, and although some may remain the numbers of 'open-field' birds which rely on them have plummeted. As a general and rather obvious rule, mass plantings of a single species over a large area will attract relatively little wildlife.

Classic 'weeds' of ploughland included wild flowers which could create a splendidly showy mass of colour. Charlock and red poppies are still seen but corn marigold and cornflower are much rarer. Corncockle is only now seen in gardens, grown as a curiosity.

Rooks and starlings follow the plough to feast on the insects exposed (most scrub and hedge birds are shy of venturing too far from cover), as does the black-headed gull – it least deserves the term 'seagull'.

The crop may be sprayed 10 or more times with herbicides, fungicides or insecticides – and usually all three. A farm might use 30 different chemicals on its fields.

The fact that modern sprays are aimed at particular plants can mean that others become typical of that farming regime. Hemp nettle, with coarser hairs than dead nettles, is no stranger to potato fields.

hemp nettle

THE NATURE OF PLOUGHLAND

Dedicated wildlife is the exception rather than the rule in this habitat. Modern farming deters all but the most opportunistic and ingenious plants and animals.

Cornfield weeds

Weeds are simply wild flowers growing in the wrong place. Traditionally they were pulled out of the crop by hand, but most have now been wiped out by herbicides. Corncockle and other classic cornfield flowers were often Mediterranean in origin, brought with the seed corn of prehistoric farmers. Cornflower was an important exception, for it was certainly growing here on open ground when the Ice Age ended.

Some of these flowers grew tall with the corn, and so were visible from afar: red poppy and both yellow and white charlock are still sometimes seen. Others such as scarlet pimpernel hug the ground. Many that survive are annuals, producing masses of seed and poised to take advantage of any opportunity, but ephemerals carry this strategy further. They can germinate, grow and set seed more than once a year: groundsel and shepherd's purse are examples. An alternative approach is that of bindweed and couch grass, both able to grow from very small fragments of underground stems broken off after ploughing (and it is interesting that their stems are weak rather than tough).

Soil 'improvement' has also had its effect. Corn marigold positively liked unimproved acid sandy soils. The deep drainage of today's arable also removes the competitive edge of some plants.

Invertebrate explosions

Sprays eliminate not only pests but also their predators, and population explosions of aphids are quite common, needing more spraying to control them. Arable fields are normally wildlife deserts devoid of much interest, but an exception which proves (i.e. tests) the rule is the clouded yellow butterfly, a migrant from Europe to the south of England, and which lays eggs on clovers. Clovers are often seeded into grass leys (see pages 56–7), and as a result this particular butterfly is unique in being the only one that can have a direct interest in modern ploughland.

Rabbits and other croppers

Within living memory, the harvest finished with a ring of men armed with shotguns circling the last quarter acre. Few rabbits managed to escape this cordon. There is little for them in a ripening field today, but in spring they will nibble the grass-like winter wheat sown the previous autumn.

Deer, too, may graze the young grain fields, and in coastal areas grazing wild geese make many a farmer angry.

Birdlife

The rook is a species of 'parkland' bird which has adopted ploughland. The black-headed gull follows the plough today: note that its dark breeding hood becomes pale in winter, when it is most often seen in these fields. It is a modern opportunist, recorded only in the Thames estuary in Victorian times but now seen exploring rubbish dumps and man-made lakes as well as ploughed fields across Britain.

Many birds are in dire straits as a result of modern farming. The linnet banked on spilled grain lying on the soil, but little of this is left behind today. Gone are the thousand-strong winter flocks of finches, buntings and tree sparrows of the past; today the flocks searching for spent seeds are fewer and much smaller.

The lapwing illustrates another face of loss. It likes to lay its eggs on rather bare ground, but by March the autumn-sown winter wheat is often too dense – and too green. It has been found that, given the choice, its instincts point it to dullish green fields rather than to the vivid green of lush growth, presumably because the former signifies skimpy grass, more likely to remain short. The chicks of the lapwing, like those of most waders, must feed themselves when they hatch. But sown ley grasslands have little in the way of insects, and unploughed grasslands (which are far richer) are now rather unusual. As a result numbers have dropped.

CORNFIELD WEEDS

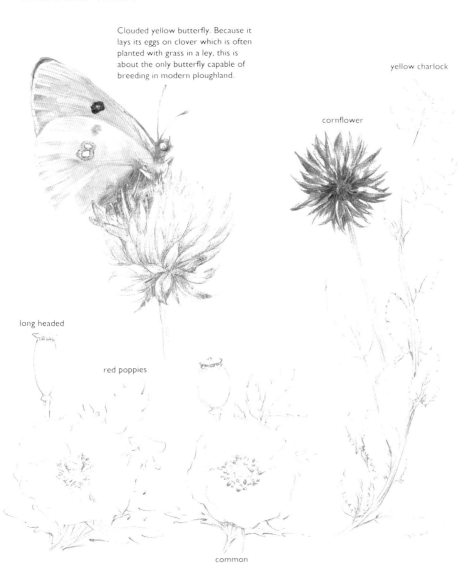

Clouded yellow butterfly. Because it lays its eggs on clover which is often planted with grass in a ley, this is about the only butterfly capable of breeding in modern ploughland.

yellow charlock

cornflower

long headed

red poppies

common

Many birds will still explore the field from their territories along the hedge. The grey partridge is a ground nester, choosing an edge where it may be undisturbed by the tractor. Its decline is linked more to the elimination of sawfly and other grubs from the sprayed soil; these supplied the chicks with their body-building protein. They have better luck if the corn is undersown with clover and grass, as it sometimes is.

The skylark, however, is a true 'steppe' bird, singing high over its territory. It will quickly nest again if the first nest is lost to the tractor, though it is doubtful whether the chicks are able to withstand regular doses of chemical sprays. The corn bunting may escape as it tends to nest slightly later, from May through to the end of July (most spraying is done on the young crop when it is more effective).

THE HEDGE

Estimates vary, but there are probably 560,000 kilometres (350,000 miles) of hedgerow. This is about half the total of 1945, but the loss has slowed in recent years.

Hedges

Hedges line the fields from the Cliffs of Dover to Cape Wrath and are found even in stone-wall countryside. They are commonly about 2 metres wide and up to 1·5 metres high, a kind of linear scrub, a row of shrubs and young trees with some climbers and with other growth at the foot (although in Cornwall field banks are also called hedges).

A hedge can have three possible origins. First, it may have colonised itself as a line of scrub onto a strip of unused ground, such as a parish boundary bank. These hedges can be of great age. Second (and commonest) is the hedge that has been planted around a field or other form of enclosure. Third is the 'assart' hedge, originating with a strip of woodland left when fields were cleared away at each side.

Planted hedges

Julius Caesar described defensive hedges thickened up in the way that they are 'laid' today. But our word hedge is Saxon in origin, from the same root as haw (thorn); spiny hawthorn and blackthorn make ideal hedging, and hawthorn can also be quickset – its cut green shoots will root if pressed into the soil.

The oldest planted hedges are perhaps medieval, enclosing night paddocks near farm or village. There were a good many hedged (or walled) sheep pasture fields even by Tudor times, but the bulk of the hedges we see today date from the 'enclosures' of Georgian and early Victorian times, when Acts of Parliament authorised go-ahead villagers to take over the open common land and fence and hedge it for their own use. The fencing was backed by rows of hawthorn saplings, which have grown into the hedges we see today. There were local fashions: there are almost pure blackthorn (sloe) hedges in places in the south-east and holly hedges in Staffordshire (its leaves provide iron rations for winter livestock).

Tree saplings were also planted along the hedge, for supplies of timber. Oak and ash were favoured, but also elm, which suckered to create a tall row along the hedge. There were some 30 million elms growing along the hedges, but most died of disease in the 1970s. Their cut stumps remain, and in places young trees grow again from the old rootstocks. Hedgerows are also the place for ornamental trees such as horse chestnut, rarely planted in woodland.

HEDGEROW LORE

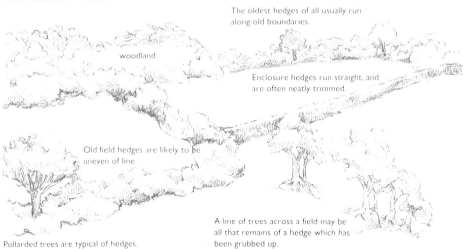

The oldest hedges of all usually run along old boundaries.

woodland

Enclosure hedges run straight, and are often neatly trimmed.

Old field hedges are likely to be uneven of line.

A line of trees across a field may be all that remains of a hedge which has been grubbed up.

Pollarded trees are typical of hedges.

Assart hedges

These originated with strips left when woodland or scrubby waste was grubbed up to create open fields on each side. Many are found along roads, when the field behind was cleared, sometime in the 19th century. As a result, the hedge we see today may contain plant indicators of old woodland, even small-leaved lime (see pages 18–19). The individual plants are often the successors of the original stock. Old hedges which abut old woodland may also have bluebells, wood anemone, and dog's mercury which have slowly migrated down it.

Recognising an old hedge

An old hedge can look old, with ancient trunks and hollow ivy tods, but its variety will also be greater, chance having brought in seeds from elsewhere. A way of estimating the age is to pace out 30-metre lengths and count the number of different species of woody shrubs in each length (down one side), ignoring climbers and treating all rose family as one; the average multiplied by 100 is the age in years. Thus a Saxon boundary hedge may have an average of ten species, a Tudor hedge five or six, and a recent enclosure hedge one or two. Some old hedges have fewer species than expected, possibly because soil or other conditions give some of them a competitive edge over rivals for space. The trees are almost certainly younger than the hedge, which is another way of estimating a minimum age.

Hedge management

A blowsy hedge is not necessarily an old one; its overall appearance will reflect when it was last trimmed or last 'laid'. Trimming is fairy common – and, if done with a flail, torn and split ends result. Laying is a traditional craft. The hedge is cleaned of waste growth to leave an upright row of stems. These 'pleachers' are partly severed with an angled cut at their base and bent over on the hinge of uncut bark. This strip allows them to put out new dense growth, and hedges laid many decades ago can be recognised by the slant of their main wood. Sometimes hedges are coppiced, cut down to stumps to grow again.

Hedges which are let go tend to become blowsy and then gappy. In time the hedge becomes a row of short trees, perhaps now rendered stockproof with barbed wire between them.

Hedgerow trees were pollarded (see pages 52–3). Local custom was strong in this: hedgerow pollards are unusual in Herefordshire, for example, but common in Oxfordshire and East Anglia.

A hedge is a ribbon of scrub habitat and is a haven for woodland and shade-loving plants. On chalk, special shrubs may grow. Hazel and dogwood are two more commonly found in old hedges. Dog's mercury, bluebell, yellow archangel, maple, male fern, spindle and Midland hawthorn are species which do not spread rapidly and so may indicate an old or an assart hedgerow.

profile of a recently laid hedge

A hedge laid many decades ago. The original slanted pleachers can still be recognised, though now grown thick.

THE LIVING WORLD OF A HEDGE

Ecologically, a hedge is a double-sided woodland edge, and plants and animals have in their own ways seized the opportunities it offers to them.

The plant tally

It is worth comparing a hedge's central lengths with its ends where it joins a copse or wood to see if woodland species appear to have migrated down it. Otherwise, nothing very rare can be expected: of our 300 rarest plants, only ten could benefit from hedges. About 200 species occur frequently enough to be labelled 'hedgerow plants', although they are also found elsewhere. Wild arum is one familiar example, as are cleavers and ground ivy, while Jack-by-the-hedge is one of those that have adopted the name tag. In some regions, distinct suites of flowers are seen: for example, the bluebells, red campion and white stitchwort of springtime hedgebanks in the West Country.

Hedgerows are grand places for roses – the dog rose is often seen. The name dog, rather a derogatory word, was given to the flower by 16th-century herbalists to distinguish these wild roses from the grden blooms which were becoming very popular at that time. The dog rose is the commonest, with pink flushed petals, and is often sweet smelling. The field rose, with white petals and scentless, is also quite commonly found in hedges, usually on the shaded side, in the south of England.

Effects of trimming

Dense growths of brambles are often a sign of regular clearing-out, as they grow vigorously from cut stumps; bryonies are more abundant in unmanaged hedges. Clipping seems to encourage the growth of honeysuckle and wild roses.

By removing next year's buds, autumn trimming eliminates next year's flowers, and hence a great deal of insect life. Normally, hedge shrubs can have a high individual insect count (see pages 24–5) and are busy in both spring and summer.

Ivy is often left to grow undisturbed. It does no harm to the tree, being firmly rooted below and using the tree only as support.

Hedgerow birds

Hedgerow berries attract family parties of mistle thrushes and others in winter, but nesting requirements are more precise. Ecologically, hedges are new on the scene, and birds nest in them because of features which echo a woodland edge, or the edge of a glade. Hawthorn is early into dense leaf, and can be inviting (especially on a warmer south side to a hedge). The most frequent nesters are:

Also common in woodland	Also typical of scrub
robin	whitethroat
song thrush	dunnock
blackbird	yellowhammer
chaffinch	

When the hedge develops bushy outgrowths and more resembles woodland, goldfinch, blackcap, garden warbler, wren and lesser whitethroat join the list. Around 30 species might now be found, compared with six or seven in a hedge kept tightly trimmed. It is easy to estimate numbers and territories, a walk down a hedge to count the birds singing being all that is needed. One survey, for example, revealed 34 pairs of 19 species in 1000 yards (900 metres) of thick hedge, compared with five pairs in 1000 yards of knock-kneed gappy hedge.

Crows nest in hedgerow trees, and trees become important for others when they are old and offer holes or the cover of dense growths of ivy. Birds of open country, such as partridge, corn bunting and reed bunting, nest in the tangle at the hedge bottom.

A prize sighting will be a sparrowhawk coursing the hedge. The origin of this (medieval) name is puzzling, for sparrows are not a particular prey; perhaps the reason is that sparrow was a general name for any small bird, in the way that we use duck for waterfowl today. The sparrowhawk is an interesting example of a species adapting its behaviour to new opportunities.

MAKING USE OF THE HEDGE – THE SPARROWHAWK

By origin a woodland bird, the
sparrowhawk has learned to course the
linear hedgerow.

A high prospecting flight may be followed
by a steep dive to the hunting area.

female
sparrowhawk

A quick dash along the hedge, up and over
to catch by surprise.

Sparrowhawks are perhaps smaller than
expected; the male little larger than a
blackbird (and bluish-grey above), the
female about the size of a woodpigeon.

They twist in pursuit of prey.

The kill

Prey are taken to a stump or plucking post
around which the feathers scatter.

THE STONE WALL

Miles of stone field walls take the place of hedges in many areas of Britain. Though not so ecologically varied, they are a distinct habitat in their own right.

Ruins in the countryside

Landscape-drawing became a hobby with Georgian and Victorian gentry, and their pictures show us what the countryside

PROSPECTS IN A STONE WALL

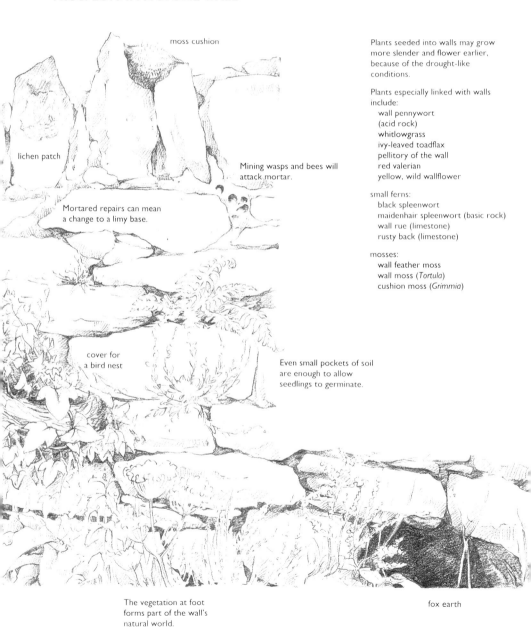

moss cushion

lichen patch

Mining wasps and bees will attack mortar.

Mortared repairs can mean a change to a limy base.

cover for a bird nest

Even small pockets of soil are enough to allow seedlings to germinate.

The vegetation at foot forms part of the wall's natural world.

fox earth

Plants seeded into walls may grow more slender and flower earlier, because of the drought-like conditions.

Plants especially linked with walls include:
  wall pennywort
  (acid rock)
  whitlowgrass
  ivy-leaved toadflax
  pellitory of the wall
  red valerian
  yellow, wild wallflower

small ferns:
  black spleenwort
  maidenhair spleenwort (basic rock)
  wall rue (limestone)
  rusty back (limestone)

mosses:
  wall feather moss
  wall moss (*Tortula*)
  cushion moss (*Grimmia*)

looked like in those days. Sporting prints also provide good evidence of the new appearance of the enclosure fields we take for granted today, marked out with hurdles, the hedges barely started into growth.

Much of what is shown is tumbledown, and ruins of one kind or another are common. There were innumerable ruins. Although many castles had been kept up and altered as family homes, most abbeys and other monastic houses had lain derelict since they were closed down by Henry VIII. Added to these were countless empty farmsteads. Ivy-covered tumbled walls were a familiar fact of life, and highly praised by poets. A liking for ruins was part of the Romanticism which underpins many of our feelings for countryside today.

Today we are hard put to find an ivy-clad ruin. Those not demolished have been tidied up, and entry is by ticket. Thus important habitat type has all but disappeared. Its place is taken by the stone wall.

Field walls

In areas where stone is easy to win from the ground, stone walls take the place of hedges around the fields (although there are often many hedges in stone-wall countryside). The oldest stone walls are older than the oldest hedges, embracing prehistoric villages on Dartmoor and elsewhere. Like hedges, many older walls mark a network of medieval paddocks near farms and villages, but the commonest are the most recent, the Georgian and Victorian enclosure walls, which are, like the enclosure hedges (see pages 84–5), laid out in grid-like lines. They even career over the felltops in the Lake District and other upland areas.

The make of field walls

Field walls are generally drystone walling, built without the use of mortar. Constructed of local stone, which may also form crags nearby, they seem as 'natural' a part of the countryside as hedges. The pale grey of weathered limestone walls matches the hues of cottages and crags both.

There are many different types of stone wall. Some of these are made simply of well-balanced rounded surface stones. Others, such as many seen in the Lake District, are intricately made with sharp-edged pieces of quarried stone layered in two sloping faces packed with rubble between, and with longer 'through stones' to bind them all together. Some have slanted coping stones along the top to deter sheep and to lessen the effects of rain.

The wall as a habitat

The stone faces themselves offer firm anchorage for rootless lichens. These slow-growing plants may take decades to reach appreciable size, and they can sometimes be used to 'date' stone structures. Walls also give lodging for mosses, and provide 'niches' for ferns and some wild flowers.

Here the word 'niche' is used to mean toehold – a pocket where wind-blown dust lodges to provide a spoonful of soil for a few roots. This meaning must not be confused with another, important, one in ecology. In ecology, a niche is the 'address' of the animal or plant in the ecosystem: describing how it and its way of life fit into the total picture of physical, chemical and living influences, including climate and weather, soil type, and the surrounding vegetation and animal life together with competitors and predators.

The plants actually seen growing will often, of course, reflect the fact that field walls are usually more an upland feature than a lowland one. But with skimpy soil, whether the stone is basic (alkaline) or acid could be an important factor.

Walls are never an inviting habitat. Nonetheless, several species have become closely identified with them, being found more frequently on walls than elsewhere. Ancient walls can harbour ancient colonies of plants: the clove pinks which flower on Rochester Castle in Kent are one example.

Cracks, crevices and holes offer physical niches as night or day shelter for a wide range of animals, from the very small to birds and even mammals. Although they are unlikely to tunnel into the stone itself, soil in the cracks may be compact enough to attract mining bees and wasps.

ASPECTS OF WALL LIFE

The wall makes a good natural stage, of convenient height and size and with perimeters which are rather better defined than with many other habitats.

Natural pollution indicators

Lichens are an odd association of two partners, a fungus and an alga. They do not have roots, but rely on rain to wash down slight traces of nutrients. The fungal cells speedily absorb these, whereupon the green algal cells, in the way of any normal plant, produce food which the fungus partner then shares.

This enterprising partnership, however, exposes them to danger if the rain is carrying a poison. The rain may, for example, be 'acid rain', carrying sulphur dioxide emitted from home fires (even oil burners), power stations and factories.

There are three main kinds of lichen to be found on walls and tree bark and on other hard surfaces. Crusty lichens look like miniature crazy paving on bark or stone; the lichen usually creates a coloured patch. Leafy lichens have lobed plates flat on the stone. Shrubby lichens stick out or up from their anchorage, usually rather like miniature tassels.

The simple rule is that the higher it sticks up, the cleaner the air. All three are seen where the air is pure, but shrubby lichens are very sensitive to air pollution and will quickly die off with slight regular contamination. Leafy are less so, while crusty can tolerate quite a bit and may even be found on walls and trees in built-up areas where the other two types cannot survive. 'Onion-ring' lichen maps have been drawn, to show the extent of the problem, around Newcastle and similar cities.

As to be expected, lichens are commoner where the rainfall is heavy, and (as with mosses and ferns) there can be differences in the colonies on sunny and shaded sides of the wall. Many also have a link with the type of stone: one common orange crusty lichen, for example, is familiar on limestone rock faces. In a town, asbestos roofing can provide an attractive, if somewhat surprising, bed for them.

Mosses

With their vivid green growth on stone, bark and shaded banks, mosses are really rather handsome plants, although identifying the actual species is a job for the expert. The colour and shape of the fruiting capsule is often the clue. There are two main types: cushion mosses have short, tightly packed upright stems, and feather mosses have long trailing stems. Some, such as wall feather moss, are typical of walls, and are more likely to be found on the shaded north side. Wall moss forms low cushions on the wall top, and is more often found here than in any other habitat throughout the countryside.

Ferns and a beautiful grass

Some ferns, too, are typical of walls, and reflect the rock type, basic or acid. Identification relies on the way the leaf is divided and subdivided. Polypody, which likes sharp drainage and is typical of walls and tree trunks, has a simple pattern rather like a child's drawing. Observe how it shrivels up when it becomes dry but expands again when damp, just like a Japanese paper flower.

At the same time look for silvery hair grass found on dry sandy soils and also growing from soil pockets on wall tops; it is one of Britain's most finely beautiful grasses.

Strategies of wall plants

Pellitory of the wall is native to sea cliffs and finds matching conditions on walls, but many of the flowers seen on walls are annuals whose small seeds were blown in or carried on bird feet, and have no special qualifications. Note that red valerian and yellow wild wallflower are garden plants from dry climes, now naturalised on walls and dry places in the south of Britain. A truly exceptional specialist is ivy-leaved toadflax. After flowering, its seed stalks curl to escape the sunshine and fumble their way across the rock surface into cracks, where the seed becomes deposited. It, too, was originally brought to the British Isles as a garden plant.

THE LIVELY WALL

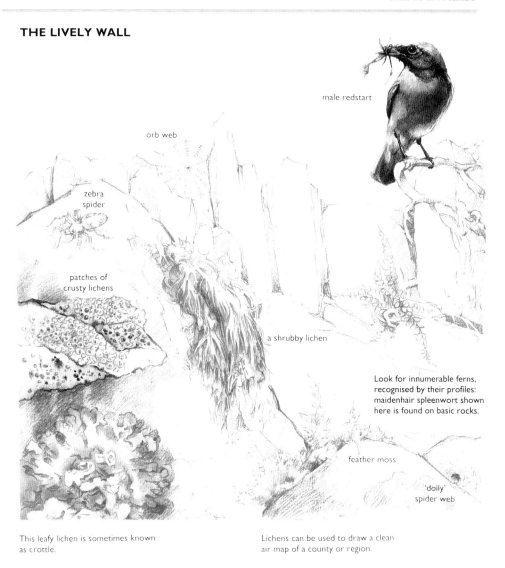

male redstart

orb web

zebra
spider

patches of
crusty lichens

a shrubby lichen

Look for innumerable ferns,
recognised by their profiles:
maidenhair spleenwort shown
here is found on basic rocks.

feather moss

'doily'
spider web

This leafy lichen is sometimes known
as crottle.

Lichens can be used to draw a clean
air map of a county or region.

Animals

We can observe some interesting examples of animals making do, adapting to what the wall offers. The hedgerow bank vole can adopt walls, especially in the north of the country (where walls outnumber hedges), and weasels and stoats will course a wall as a matter of common sense, for the voles and mice and rabbits which take advantage of its shelter. One bird to look for is the redstart, which will nest away from its normal woodland and out in open countryside if wall holes are available. The wheatear of the uplands also makes use of walls for nesting, and on the moors walls act as handy plucking posts for merlins.

Walls are ideal for spider-watching: Look for *Amaurobis* with its tangled lace-like web around its tunnel, and *Segestria*, which runs trip wires; they are both common and familiar. Zebra and other hunting spiders make forays across the open stone.

LANE AND FOOTPATH

A PATH RIGHT TO THE HEART OF THE COUNTRYSIDE

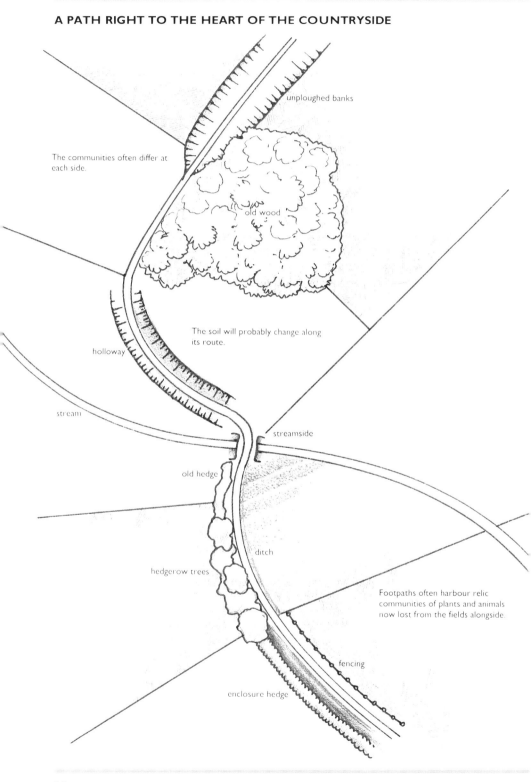

unploughed banks

The communities often differ at each side.

old wood

The soil will probably change along its route.

holloway

stream

streamside

old hedge

ditch

hedgerow trees

Footpaths often harbour relic communities of plants and animals now lost from the fields alongside.

fencing

enclosure hedge

In England and Wales, there are 224,000 kilometres (140,000 miles) of lanes and footpaths which are public rights of way a route to the heart of the countryside.

Footpath law

The public have rights to a footpath which originated when the use of the countryside was essential for the livelihood of most of the population. Many paths and lanes seem almost a natural part of the countryside. Some think they could be, arguing that they could have originated as badger and deer tracks. But our countryside has been fashioned more by man than by nature, and they are part of the pattern of farming.

Legally a footpath can be used unhindered for 'quiet purposes' and has its use restricted to walkers (plus horses if it is a bridlepath). The landowner has obligations: to keep the path open and keep stiles and gates in good repair. His or her rights can, however, include the use of traffic at his discretion, covering occasional cars but also (and regularly) tractors.

Roads and lanes

Road is a word with rather a confused meaning. Legally it can carry wheeled traffic but it need not be tarmacked. Many favourite footpaths are in fact roads in this sense, and as a result they can also be used by cars and motorbikes. A lane is a day-to-day name for a quieter country route, which can be tarmacked or remain as a green track and a footpath.

Wiping out the path

Unploughed and unsprayed, a green track, however it be named, can be a sanctuary for wild flowers and wildlife now lost from the intensively farmed fields alongside. Regular tractor use will of course destroy this value. The path is also threatened if it crosses what is now an open field (perhaps it once followed a hedge which has since been grubbed up). The landowner can plough over the line of the path and, although by the letter of the law it should be flattened and made good afterwards, few bother to make the effort.

The heart of the countryside

Both its own wildlife value and the fact that it leads somewhere make a footpath important. It is usually only on footpaths that the public has the legal right to visit and view many of the types of habitat described in this book.

The Ordnance Survey maps are a good guide to footpaths, and they also show some of the habitat types to be found. Even field boundaries, for example, are marked on the 1:25 000 maps, although whether a hedge or stone wall exists, and if so in what state it is in, can be discovered only on the spot. Similarly with woodland: this is shown on all OS maps, and whether conifer or hardwood is indicated on the 1:25 000, but the condition of the wood can be found only by visiting the place.

Another consideration is that footpaths usually came into being with reference to features already existing in the landscape, such as old woods, unploughed boundary banks and prehistoric burial mounds, and they skirt these or use them as turning points. Footpaths will also often respect the line of scarps, perhaps following a ridge. It is in such places that relic plant and animal communities are likely to be found.

What it's worth for wildlife

Even a short walk can reveal wonderful diversity – paths swing from hill to vale, crossing different pockets of soil, crossing streams and rivers, passing alongside woods. The path surface also varies with its use: even rutted ground can hold permanent trickles of water for the wet-loving members of the buttercup tribe, or perhaps it is the early spring puddles which encourage semi-aquatic plants. Well trodden places may have very successful plants such as annual meadow grass – the grass which is seen everywhere from cracks in pavements to sand dunes – and ratstail or greater plantain which can withstand a certain amount of trampling. In addition, by their very character, paths tend to offer sheltered situations, especially when thickly hedged on both sides. Many insects and birds welcome this.

THE WILDLIFE PATH

The path offers a linear directory of habitats, some like fields and woods of appreciable size, others smaller and occupying no more than a metre or two.

The sunny bank

One of the commonest examples of a mini-habitat, and most often disregarded, is the bare bank. It attracts solitary mining bees or digger wasps. Although these are truly solitary in the sense that the female makes a single burrow and works singly at stocking it as a larder for her grubs before laying her eggs in it, the entrance holes can be clustered on a suitable firm length of bank. Some species will also burrow into hard-worn paths, especially if the soil is rather sandy. Exposed clay might also attract them if it remains dry enough all year. And if a bank is popular with one species, it is likely to be popular with others.

Larger holes will be seen. Like the medieval peasant, nature is a grabby creature and a burrow dug by one species will not go unused by others if the original occupant leaves. Even foxes, which use the path as a track in the way we do, make regular use of rabbit burrows. Positive signs of current ocupancy can include food scraps and footprints and often a noticeable smell from close to. A negative sign will be spiders' webs strung across the entrance.

Memorial flowers

The plants chart the changes in soil and aspect as the path swings from hill to vale. But one frequent fact is that the flowers are often those that have been wiped away from the fields alongside by modern farming. The most usual case is when neighbouring pasture or hayfields have been 'improved'; their indicator flowers (see pages 56–7, 68–9) now remain only on the path. There may also be relic woodland flowers at the foot of the hedge which reflect the history of the area. In Kent and Sussex, for example, primroses can be found along lanes and paths where fields were cleared from woodland, but they are not found where open fields come between woodland and the path – these fields are likely to be 200-year-old enclosure fields.

It is also worth noting any difference between the sides of the path, and the reasons.

Patches of nettles

Nettles are greedy for nitrogen and phosphorus, and can mark ground enriched

GRASSES AND SOILS

DRY

tor grass   wall barley

barren brome

quaking grass

sheep's fescue   sheep's fescue

timothy

LIMY SOIL   crested dogstail   wavy hair grass   ACID SOIL

sweet vernal grass

mat grass

annual meadow grass

most rushes and sedges

tufted hair grass

purple moor grass

Yorkshire fog   cotton grass

WET

THE WILDLIFE CORRIDOR

barn owl

Fence posts are a favourite daytime perch for the little owl.

with rubbish in the past, or mark the site of a stable or hut of some kind. The clumps of nettles on a path create a habitat of their own. Frogs and newts spend the summer in their damp shade (often surprisingly far from water), feeding on the insects which also flourish here.

Nettles also attract familiar butterflies, but their choice sheds light on the complexity of the links between animal and habitat. When mated, female butterflies devote their remaining days to seeking out suitable plants for their eggs, plants that will supply protein-rich fodder for the caterpillars. Usually young, tender plants are chosen, but other factors also play a part.

The peacock butterfly lays only on nettles in full sunshine at midday. The small tortoiseshell prefers those at the edge of large nettlebeds. The red admiral will often lay on shaded plants. The comma, although a woodland butterfly, will lay on sheltered nettles alongside a hedge.

A wildlife corridor

A lane or path offers a corridor along which populations of small animals are maintained. But many larger animals use it as a route across country. Foxes, weasels and stoats are common; they have regular runs. The little owl perches on a vantage point. The barn owl will fly down the lane at dusk.

THE ROADSIDE VERGE

The countryside has uncounted miles of roadside verges, some quite recent but some of ancient origins. They offer rather different wildlife possibilities.

The place of the verge

In earlier days roads were regarded simply as routes belonging to the village, which nobody could plough or block. The actual track taken by the carts twisted and turned to avoid the mud. But animals walking their way to market always made up most of the traffic; until the advent of the railways, even geese were marched scores of miles to their doom. And, of course, the livestock grazed as they went.

Nothing much changed until the days of the stagecoach, when a national system of improved toll or 'turnpike' roads came into being. But this was also the great age of enclosures (see pages 84–5); and, when the new enclosure fields were being laid out, so, too, were roads and lanes. These enclosure roads were as straight as possible (and perhaps changing direction only at the parish boundary), of standard width, maybe 20 metres across, and ditched where it was necessary.

The turnpikes and some of the enclosure roads were macadamised, with a hard-packed gravel surface. Tar was in time added to this mixture to give today's familiar tarmac, and the verge remains as the uncovered strip of green alongside. To this historic store of verges must be added those left alongside today's motorways and by-passes. Flat verge-like grassy areas are also created when curves are straightened on old roads to improve the sightlines.

The lengthman and later

In Victorian times, the village roads were in the charge of a village lengthman, who worked along them season by season, scything back the invading scrub and coarser plants, and controlling the grazing of the passing animals. Today, motor mowers have replaced the scythe (and the County Councils have often taken over the responsibility).

A legacy of history

From a habitat viewpoint, even the most unassuming verge can provide fascinating possibilities. It can have remained un-ploughed for centuries. It can contain

PROFILE OF A VERGE

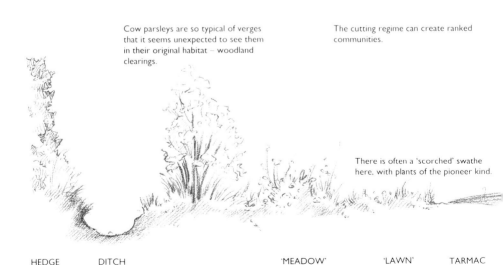

Cow parsleys are so typical of verges that it seems unexpected to see them in their original habitat — woodland clearings.

The cutting regime can create ranked communities.

There is often a 'scorched' swathe here, with plants of the pioneer kind.

HEDGE   DITCH   'MEADOW'   'LAWN'   TARMAC

flowers typical of local grasslands but which modern farming has eradicated from the neighbouring fields. It can carry these old communities of flowers, but modified by centuries of grazing and generous manuring by the passing livestock. Extra boosts of fertiliser can result not in an increase but in a loss of plant variety (see pages 56–7).

Many of the cow-parsley tribe are characteristic of verges. On the other hand, new verges may be ablaze with handsome red poppy, which can wait for years as seed to take advantage of any slight opportunity (see pages 80–1). Oxeye daisy can be common on these, along with yellow rape which has seeded itself in from fields nearby. It is also quite usual today to see patches of cowslip on by-pass and motorway banks; these have been sown, and lines of shrubs planted, for amenity.

A sanctuary

Some verges are famous for their displays of bee, man and other orchids (orchids are known unexpectedly to cover even a steep by-pass bank). Verges are now an important, if not a main habitat for cowslip, rock rose and hay rattle, and also (in chalk areas)

knapweed and its parasitic broomrape companion. Their insects, including butterflies are here, too.

Modern management

Chemical sprays have been tried in the search for a cheap means of keeping verges under control. These would have eliminated all wild flowers regardless, but fortunately they generally prove too expensive. So motor mowers are used.

Sometimes the verge may be mown only once a year, but it often makes economic sense to cut it in swathes, with a short strip next to the tarmac to give clear sightlines, a middle 'meadow' which may be cut early on and then not until late summer, and an inner swathe of even taller growth which has only one cut a year. This creates a welcome variety of different plant communities.

One or two county Wildlife Trusts have lengths of verge which are managed, with the cooperation of the local council, as nature reserves. Orchids are often a feature of these (although it must be said that orchids can also sometimes be found on 'unlikely' newish roadsides).

In places, for example where the road rollercoasters dow to a stream and the soil is damp, a stand of one species (or even just a handful of large plants) may take over the verge, their competitiveness sharpened by the rather different conditions.

Grassy road verges can act as a refuge for plants sprayed away from the fields. However, because the manuring regimes may have been different for centuries, the suites of species may be less varied than those found in the old fields alongside. Verges are now the chief home of cowslip rock rose, hay rattle, hedge garlic and knapweed (and its broomrape parasite). Hemlock is one plant that reflects local disturbance.

DAMP SOIL

THE ROADSIDE CALENDAR

The wild flowers and animals of the verge often mark the passage of the months in obvious ways. But some of the changes can escape the casual glance.

Cow parsleys

The cow-parsley tribe with their umbrella-heads of flowers have laid claim to the tall verge. They are really very attractive plants, busy with humming hoverflies and other insects. Superficially similar, differences in leaf, stem and (for the detail-seeking eye) the 'seeds' (the fruit in fact) are quite noticeable. Furthermore, they flower in a predictable progression through the spring and summer, making an interesting botanical clock. In the south, cow parsley flowers in May, and just as it dies down the heavier, denser heads of hogweed appear, especially strongly in a wet summer (see below). In the northern hills, sweet cicely with aniseed-scented leaves replaces cow parsley as the commonest seen.

If the verge remains uncut, these first umbrellas are followed by rough chervil in June and July, recognised by its purple-spotted hairy stems, and then by upright hedge parsley with unspotted bristly stems.

Slow changes year by year

Slow changes may even escape the notice of those who live along the lanes. Recent research along Akeman Street, originally a Roman road, shows that over half the verge plants are reacting to weather and climate changes. Warmer summers benefit cow parsley, dandelion, creeping buttercup and hedge woundwort, while those which are put at a competitive disadvantage by a good summer include creeping thistle, yellow-flowered crosswort and hogweed, a robust relative of cow parsley.

Takeovers

Some plants notoriously take over the whole verge. Japanese knotweed, a garden escape, is clearly making good in what is for it a 'new' habitat. Its dour ranks are now familiar, and (so far) almost impossible to eradicate once established. Even regular cutting, which looses a vicious fluid, does not seem to weaken the stock. It is now a real threat to many attractive verges.

But perhaps there is hope in what has been discovered about rosebay willowherb. Twenty years after first colonising sites along Akeman Street, it is well entrenched, eventually colonising 25-square-metre patches with thousands of shoots; but then it declines. Although it can seed itself competitively onto 'new' ground unoccupied by it, its seeds are probably at a disadvantage when freshly seeding onto ground it has already occupied, and the colony loses vigour.

Grasshoppers and bush-crickets

These are as typical of roadsides as cow parsley itself. Grasshoppers have short sturdy feelers (antennae) and sing by rubbing hindlegs against wings; they feed on grass and are sun-worshippers, active by day. Bush-crickets are 'long-horned grass-hoppers', with long thread-like antennae; they sing by rubbing wings together and are omnivores, feeding on plants and other insects. The female bush-crickets have a noticeable 'tail' (not a sting but an ovipositor or egg-layer). They are more active after dusk. 'Ordinary' crickets are now rather rare (see pages 114–15).

In the lowlands, the common field grass-hopper is most noticed (in the sense that the house sparrow is the most noticed of birds). It is one of the largest, singing a series of short chirps, usually in chorus. In the uplands, the common green grasshopper is likely to be the common species, with a fast, penetrating ticking song. The meadow grasshopper has a chattery song.

At dusk, the bush-crickets seize the stage. The great green bush-cricket has a penetrating metallic song carrying for over 100 metres on warm summer nights in the south, but it is difficult to track down as it is wary and will stop when approached. The dark bush-cricket is a commoner relative, chirping in chorus.

As the name suggests, the bush-crickets are more likely to be identified with the hedge or bramble clump behind the verge, than with the grass itself.

THE GRASSHOPPER TRIBE TAKE ADVANTAGE OF THE VERGE

Bush crickets seek beds of nettles, brambles and other dense cover, grasshoppers seek long grass.

The song is a form of come-hither, sung by the males to attract the females and to make themselves known to potential rivals. American researchers claim that the song of their US crickets speeds up as the sunshine gets hotter in the course of the day.

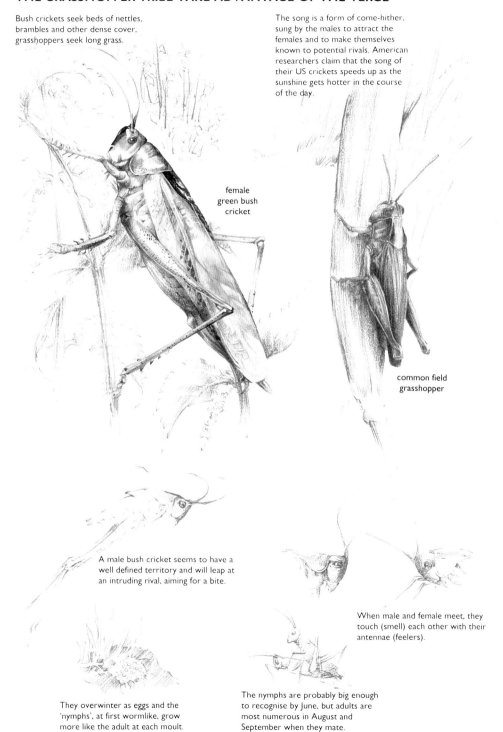

female green bush cricket

common field grasshopper

A male bush cricket seems to have a well defined territory and will leap at an intruding rival, aiming for a bite.

When male and female meet, they touch (smell) each other with their antennae (feelers).

They overwinter as eggs and the 'nymphs', at first wormlike, grow more like the adult at each moult.

The nymphs are probably big enough to recognise by June, but adults are most numerous in August and September when they mate.

THE FARMSTEAD

A MODEL FARM

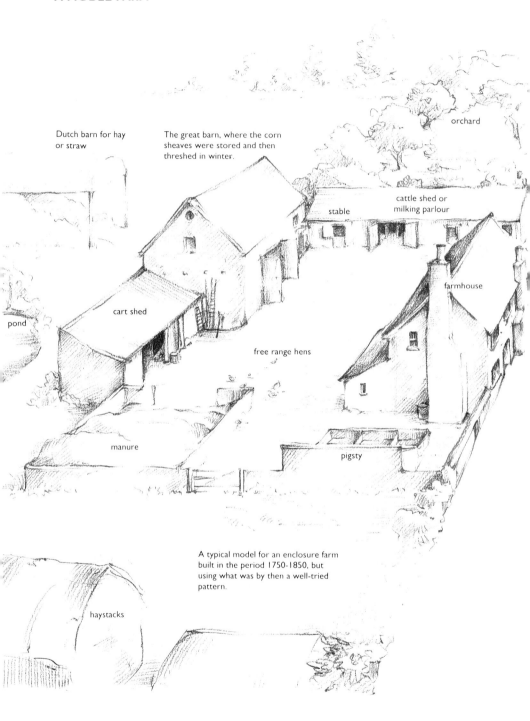

Dutch barn for hay or straw

The great barn, where the corn sheaves were stored and then threshed in winter.

orchard

cattle shed or milking parlour

stable

farmhouse

cart shed

pond

free range hens

manure

pigsty

A typical model for an enclosure farm built in the period 1750-1850, but using what was by then a well-tried pattern.

haystacks

Of the farmstead habitats, ancient orchards are the prize. Yet many have now disappeared, and a host of wildlife and cultural associations have disappeared with them.

The recent farmsteads

At the risk of oversimplification, the site of the farmstead is either very old or comparatively modern.

Prehistoric farmsteads are sometimes seen reconstructed in open-air museums, as a cluster of thatched huts surrounded by a timber fence. Such farms worked their own small 'fields' scattered around them.

By medieval times, these individual farmsteads had in many counties become replaced by villages surrounded by ploughlands, which the villagers worked in common. On the open, hedgeless prairies of this 'manorial' farming were laid out, in Georgian times, the hedged fields we take for granted today (see pages 80–1, 84–5). During these 'enclosures' times, new farms were built away from the village, in the midst of their own fields. These enclosure farmsteads were often built to what had become a standard 'traditional' pattern.

The open-field system was not adopted everywhere. Some countries had small fields carved directly from woodland, and it was here in fact that this traditional farmstead had evolved.

The farmsteads of old countryside

The farmstead pattern was tried and tested in the ornamental small-field countrysides of Devon, West Dorset and other places (see pages 80–1). Many old farm buildings are still found here, and their sites are even older; many Devon farmsteads, for example, occupy sites that were farmsteads in Bronze Age times 4000 years ago.

The shape of the farmstead

Each part had a job, and so old farmsteads had a good deal in common. They were usually mixed farms then, with both arable and pasture. The farmyard, in which the cattle and sheep could be kept at need, is closed in by ranges of open sheds and roofed buildings. One, usually facing out to the south and the sunshine, is the farmhouse itself. Opposite, on the north side, and giving protection against winter winds, is the bulk of the great barn in which the harvest was stored and threshed. To one side lay cattle-sheds and often opposite them stables for horses, with lean-tos for wagons and ploughs. There was a pigsty within the farmyard, and chickens were free-range; outside the farmyard lay orchard and pond.

The old orchard

The orchard would have occupied the same site for hundreds of years, its trees hoary with lichen (and heavy with mistletoe) and replaced only when they came to the end of their natural life. Much of its interest came from the fact that it had a multiple role. It supplied table fruit, but pigs would be let in to feed on the windfalls – the Gloucester Old Spot breed was traditionally fattened on windfalls. Weak lambs would be nurtured here in spring. At a pinch, the grass beneath the trees could even yield a cut of hay.

Established long before the era of herbicides, an old orchard could resemble a small patch of semi-natural grassland. Orchids, ragged robin, cowslips and many other flowers might be found, especially in those warmer southern and midland counties where the farm orchards were quite sizeable. The flowers supported many pollinating insects, including many wild bees. These insects are now in decline, largely as a result of the disappearance of old orchards; almost 90 per cent of Devon's old orchards have gone, for example. Today's regularly sprayed commercial orchards are as forbidding to wildlife as the arable fields.

What's in it for wildlife?

Modern farming has become specialised; mixed farms are now uncommon, and pigs, poultry, fruit – and vegetables – are now intensively produced by separate units. The market garden is more like an arable field. These changes have affected the barn owl and other farmstead birds, and the species seen today are more likely to be those that take advantage of the dilapidation of the unused parts of the old farmstead.

BIRDS OF THE FARM

Links between wildlife and human activities are highlighted in the stories of some of the bird species which have long been traditionally linked with farmsteads.

The barn owl

This bird, with its long wavering shriek, probably became associated with farmsteads because of its instinct to return to established roosts and nesting sites. It was in fact positively encouraged to do so: the round 'owl hole' seen high on the end wall of the barn was an invitation to it to sign up as unpaid rodent operative to deal with the rats attracted by the sheaves of corn stored within.

This bird is equally at home nesting in woodland, and it is the deterioration in the countryside as a whole rather than changes in the use of the barn that have endangered it. Today's countryside offers both the doom of cumulative poisoning from long-lived pesticide traces in the bodies of its prey and the loss of the well-hedged, rough but open ground that it likes to hunt. Modern arable is too well manicured for it.

There are now fewer than 5000 breeding pairs in Britain, and it is ironic that as a species it is a 'successful' bird, in the sense that it has a vast range, being found on every continent except Antarctica.

Yard birds

The pied wagtail is typical, and typical also is its endearing habit of nesting (untidily) on the unused tractor and other odd places. After breeding, it may roost communally in one of the empty outbuildings.

pied wagtail

The house sparrows, not uncommon, look rather neater and cleaner than their town familiars. Its success is in part due to the fact that it is 'tame' enough to suffer disturbance, but maintains its wariness.

The collared dove

This bird is easily recognised by appearance, and even when not seen, by its three-part call 'coo-*coooo*-coo', with the emphasis on the middle phrase.

Over the last half century or so, the collared dove has spread from the Balkans to much of Europe and it has been nesting in Britain since 1955. The reasons for its success are not clear, but it is certain that it is due partly to the fact that it is exploiting a 'niche' associated with man. It remains, however, much more wary than its cousin, the town pigeon. (The town pigeon is in fact the descendant of the wild rock dove.)

Numbers of collared doves can be seen at farm buildings in summer and autumn, where grain is being carted.

Another reason for its success is a long breeding season, with up to five broods a year. As they feed their young on regurgitated crop 'milk', the members of the pigeon family have a fairly flexible breeding season.

Orchard birds

Best known is the bullfinch, one of Britain's most handsome birds. Its heavy bill enables it to feast on ash keys (seeds), but it comes to orchards when this larder is finished, and this will be early in those 'lean' years when the ash crop is sparse. In some years it seems to develop an insatiable hunger for the buds of fruit trees: in such cases commercial fruit-growers are permitted to shoot or trap it.

Far less well known is the wryneck, now maybe extinct in Britain as a breeding bird, but still seen as an occasional visitor. It is one of the woodpecker family, with all their hole-nesting instincts, but it cannot dig holes itself and relies on finding them ready made. Old orchard trees had plenty to offer and were a stronghold of this species. Its name does not imply a weak neck, but comes from the way it twists its neck when startled and also as part of its courtship.

FARMSTEAD BIRDS

collared dove

swift

Every book should contain one real rarity, a bird watcher's bonus, and this is it – the wryneck. It feasted on the ants, beetles and spiders of the old fashioned unsprayed orchard, and also nested in the many holes the ancient trees offered. Its disappearance is certainly partly due to modern pesticides and the felling of trees, yet the diaries of Victorian naturalists show that its decline started 150 years ago. This is a typical ecological puzzle. The bird is at the end of its range here (but still numerous in its Asian strongholds) and even slight habitat changes can affect species in this situation: perhaps the bad summers which set in during Victorian times speeded its demise.

In some lights its dappled plumage resembles the hoary lichens of the old apple tree.

THE VILLAGE

Villages generally offer garden-type habitats. Of more interest are their churchyards, more than 10,000 of them in all, which are potential wildlife havens.

The village as a habitat

Early villages were primitive places. Each peasant had a 'toft' or strip of garden-cum-allotment running back from the huts which stood along the main street. There was often (not always) a green, a kind of common on which animals could be grazed and the village market held. A pond or stream was certain. And of course there was the church and its churchyard of an acre (God's Acre) near the manor house.

In those muddy medieval days, the countryside had its fingers into the village. The green was a wild meadow, the pond was full of frogs and other aquatic life, and it is likely that even kites would visit to scavenge the village refuse, as they did in the streets of London. The trees around the green would have been elms, oaks and other useful natives, and were usually pollarded for their branches. Today, they are just as likely to be flowering cherries or alien horse chestnut, with a fraction of the insect life of native

trees (horse chestnut has four dedicated insect species compared with the 284 of oak, pages 24–5).

Today's village is tidied and tarmacked. Mowing the green changes it from meadow to lawn; and the ducks happily quacking on the pond eat the frogs and scour it for other food (they would themselves have been eaten in the old days). All in all, even deep in the countryside, the modern village may offer only its gardens as a lively habitat.

The garden habitat

In the eyes of wildlife, a garden is a version of scrub, but with usually far less variety of native shrubs and plants. 'Weeds' are cleared out – but they are wild plants with their own dedicated insects. Scrub-nesting birds, those found in the woodland shrub layer, are attracted, but the insect life which thrives with the variety of native shrubs and plants may be conspicuous by its absence.

This is underlined with our most familiar butterflies. Peacock, red admiral and small tortoiseshell are long-distance fliers. They visit gardens to take nectar at the wild flowers, and may hibernate in the garden shed, but, even if the garden does have some

THE VILLAGE FOCUS – THE CHURCHYARD

THE CHURCHYARD

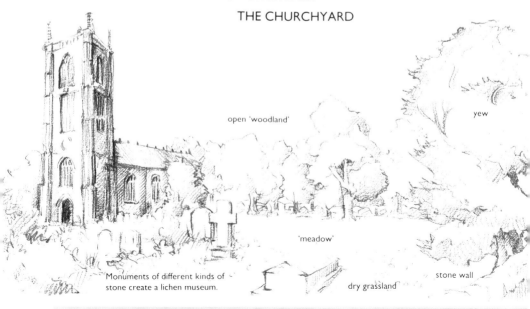

open 'woodland'

yew

'meadow'

stone wall

Monuments of different kinds of stone create a lichen museum.

dry grassland

nettles, they rely on those growing else-where in the fields and woods for their survival (see pages 94–5).

The churchyard

The exception can be the village church-yard. Botanically it can be much more interesting than the rest of the village and offer a haven for insects, birds and (because of its habitual seclusion) for snakes and lizards and small mammals.

Never ploughed, the churchyard may contain meadow flowers which have disap-peared from the fields around. But in this case, perhaps surprisingly, the relatively recent Victorian extension to the church-yard may be the richer. This was enclosed direct from old meadow or pastureland just over a century ago, before the onset of sprays, whereas the original churchyard acre has for centuries been regularly distur-bed by burials.

So, in the old churchyard you are likely to find not lingering meadow communities but competitive individual species. Burials have clearly had a great deal of influence on the plant life. In some churchyards they have raised the soil level above the door sills, and they refertilise the soil (although this effect may be lessened by leaching by rain). It is noticeable that, even in acid-soil regions, the churchyard itself may contain many lime-loving plants.

Where wild flowers are of solemn beauty – wild daffodil, for example – they are likely to have been encouraged by being left uncut or even planted in from the countryside around. To these were added plants intro-duced in medieval times for their medicinal and religious importance. Snowdrop is one of these, now naturalised in many places.

We mustn't forget the churchyard yew of course. Its trunk is worth inspecting – the centre wood may die and rot in old age to give it a bizarre sculptural form.

Modern threats

The modern mania for tidiness threatens many a churchyard. Too many are sprayed to 'keep the place tidy' by those who do not understand ecology. Sadly, the result is often doubly disastrous. The wild flowers are killed, but then nettles and ground elder can take over the empty ground, and the more quickly as the soil is so rich in nutrients and they are hungry plants.

THE GREEN

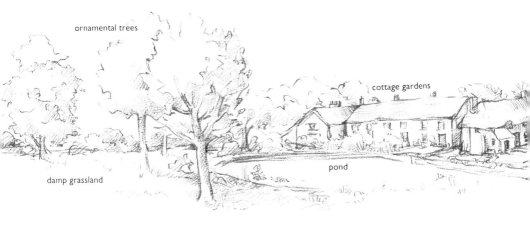

ornamental trees

cottage gardens

damp grassland

pond

AROUND THE CHURCH

The churchyard is likely to be one of the key wildlife habitats in the village, harbouring flowers and wildlife of some significance. There may also be some rarities.

Botany in the churchyard

Although relatively small in area, the churchyard can offer pockets of difference; grassland, scrub, dry banks. The mortared wall creates another opportunity, as do the tombstones themselves. If of local stone, limestone especially, many lichens will now pattern their surface.

The churchyard yew towers over them, 'foreign' in the sense that it has clearly been planted in, but for what reasons nobody now knows. The churchyard tree may have some slight differences from 'wild' yews growing in the countryside.

As in any habitat, the management has the main effect. It is quite customary to keep some areas mown short, so that only 'lawn' plants might be expected, while other areas grow tall to await just one cut a year. These could carry local meadowland flowers.

Churchyard meadow

The most dramatic wild flowers are more likely to be found as individual relic plants than as entire communities (see pages 104–5). Many will originate from meadow grasslands: wild daffodil, for example, which likes damp conditions, or orchids. But certainly in some churchyards there are some unexpected heathland plants, not heather itself but yellow tormentil and (for the more expert botanist) some heathland grasses. The reason is probably that, despite the burials, areas remain undisturbed and leached by the rain of centuries.

Significant plants

Village churchyards can also harbour plants esteemed in bygone days for their religious symbolism or medicinal use. Here they were safe from the grazing of domestic ducks and geese which roamed the village streets at will.

The white purity of the snowdrop led to its introduction into Britain in medieval days to help celebrate Candlemas on 2nd

February. It has now also naturalised itself out into woodlands in some areas.

One or two churchyards are painted pink with flowering bistort in June. This was one of the many plants used by quacks and village wise women; it was thought to combat infertility and aid conception. There are many similar examples. Lords-and-ladies may grow in numbers along the hedgier parts; 'cuckoo pint' is just one of its many phallic names, but the alternative 'parson in the pulpit' may be a Victorian whimsy, or may suggest that it has always been linked with churchyards.

The village rookery

The familiar rook provides a nice example of habitat usage, nesting here but feeding elsewhere. Nesting in a village seems a strong instinct for this bird. The clump of elms near the vicarage was the traditional site of the rookery, but, since the elms died in the 1970s, the birds have often made use of other trees nearby rather than move to the copses of the open countryside which would seem the more obvious choice. It is interesting to see that they will now nest even in tall village conifers.

Bats

Although bats are commonly seen swooping low across the graves in the half light of dusk, bats in the belfry there are not. At least, they will avoid a working belfry: bells would deafen their sensitive hearing, even madden them (hence the origin of the phrase perhaps).

There are many other misconceptions about bats. Far from revelling in Gothicky church cobwebs, they prefer the clean, draught-free attic of a modern semi, where they will spend hours harmlessly preening themselves. They do not attack woodwork, and their droppings (the dry horny cases of their insect prey) are no health hazard.

Bats have reasonable vision, but have a unique sonar. They emit high-pitched squeaks, and catch and interpret the echoes so as to avoid obstacles and to locate flying insects. In fact, as we ourselves 'see' the world about us only because our brains interpret signals passed along nerves from the eyes, it is perhaps possible that bat brains can also create a simple 'picture' of the world from these echoes. At any rate, their sonar system is good enough to prevent them coming too close or trapping themselves in our hair!

Bats are in decline for two main reasons. First, meadows and other rough areas which produced vast numbers of insects have been ploughed up. Second, each year 100,000 roofs are treated against woodworm; the bats are poisoned simply by contact with the treated timbers.

BAT WATCHING

When feeding, bats patrol favourite areas one after the other.

Bat roosts in a modern house.

Half of today's colonies are in modern houses. They need only small crevices.

Estimate numbers by standing outside at dusk to see the emerging bats silhouetted against the sunset or afterglow.

THE ABANDONED RAILWAY

20,000 kilometres (12,000 miles) of railway have been abandoned in the last 30 years. Much has been taken into farming, but cuttings and embankments remain.

Lines across the landscape

Once begun, railways quickly threw a network across Victorian Britain. They totalled more than 32,000 kilometres (20,000 miles), but after the line closures of recent decades, over half have reverted to farmland, been built on or been abandoned.

At their peak, 0·5% of Britain's land surface was railway land. The track could run as a green ribbon flush with the fields alongside, but there were perhaps 30,000 hectares (75,000 acres) of embankments and cuttings and most of these remain, whether in use or not.

Past management

Until the 1960s, railway verges, banks and cuttings were regularly burnt off as a safeguard against fires from sparks from the steam engines. The broken ballast which firmed up the rails was also regularly sprayed with weedkiller. There were proposals in the 1960s to extend spraying to the banks and verges as well, but these were already being recognised as a wildlife refuge despite the regular fires, and spraying was restricted to a narrow strip on each side of the ballast.

Artificial geology

The earliest railway lines hugged the contours but the frequent curves that resulted slowed the trains, and quite soon muscle and money were invested in viaducts, embankments, cuttings and tunnels to straighten the lines. As a result, our railways cross or cut through almost every geological drift and rock layer to be found. Short lengths can produce a whole range of soil types. Even soils from other localities can be found as a result of 'cut and fill', when embankments were created using the material from the cuttings. 'Meadow' mixtures of plants will be expected over much of the flat areas of abandoned railways, although in cuttings the soil is likely to lie only thinly over the bedrock. The ballast itself, which is usually left when the rails are removed, can resemble a well-drained shingle bank, but it can also be quite wet in places, forming a 'mulch' which will suit very different plants.

The plant tally

On the face of it, the harsh management of railway land described above would exile many plants. But the improbable geology of many lengths of line, and the fact that the tracks were set before the widespread use of sprays in the countryside (which meant that there were always seed sources nearby), promoted great variety. If not

ANATOMY OF AN ABANDONED RAILWAY

Waste ground can be overgrown with rank-growing grasses. Look for barren brome, cocksfoot, false oat-grass.

tunnel

bare rock face

soil slides

embankment

ruined signal box

totally scrubbed up, some interesting flowers can be found. In fact, surveys have shown a total of more than 2000 native wild flower species growing on railways, with rarities in some places. To these must be added exotics which have grown and spread from dumped garden rubbish. Railways are also responsible for some intriguing plant movements (see pages 110–11).

What's in it for wildlife?

Overgrown cuttings obviously offer cover and welcome shelter to many animals, as indeed do embankments – a bank always has a sheltered side. In fact, undisturbed banks are rather rare in today's countryside, but even their bare faces attract mining bees and digger wasps and animals such as lizards which need to bask. Survey work has shown that abandoned railways are a stronghold of our commoner butterflies. For nesting birds, it is the structure of the habitat which counts; its bushiness attracts, although some ground nesters can be expected. The bushy cutting could make a popular roosting venue in winter. The abandoned railway will, like lanes and hedges and other linear features, be an obvious route for mammal traffic.

Its linear nature also makes the abandoned railway a good survey strip. Habitats can sometimes be assessed or compared by simple counts along transects (see page 193) – and the abandoned line is a ready-made transect.

It could, for example, make a good site for observations of rabbits. Rabbits appear in many places in this book, as is fitting, for they are quite widely distributed in the country as a whole. What could possibly show up in a railway cutting is some relationship between the warren site and the surrounding plants, that is between rabbits and the particular vegetation structure that their behaviour can cause or create around them.

Rabbits closely crop grass and other low vegetation. However, they find some plants distasteful and these may remain to mark their warren sites. Elder is one such – the rabbits eschew its bark and low copses of elder may disguise their burrow openings. White bryony, a climbing plant with red berries, is another. It's recognised as being poisonous to humans. It's a plant associated with limy soils.

Rabbits can have a considerable effect on the enclosed world of a railway cutting. After decimation in the 1950s from the almost always fatal myxomatosis, numbers have slowly risen again. But while this book is being written, reports are appearing of a rather similar, although not introduced, disease now spreading through domesticated and pet rabbits, although it has not yet reached wild populations.

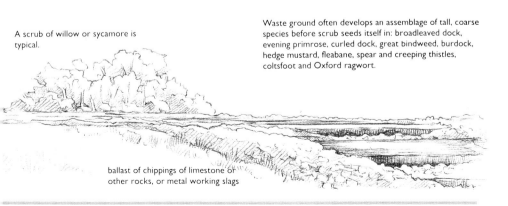

A scrub of willow or sycamore is typical.

Waste ground often develops an assemblage of tall, coarse species before scrub seeds itself in: broadleaved dock, evening primrose, curled dock, great bindweed, burdock, hedge mustard, fleabane, spear and creeping thistles, coltsfoot and Oxford ragwort.

ballast of chippings of limestone or other rocks, or metal working slags

A HALF-HOUR WALK IN A CUTTING

HOW RAILWAYS RATE AS A HAVEN FOR BUTTERFLIES

Results of a survey by members of the WATCH club, the family wing of the RSNC. 'Half hour' walks were made, as described on page 6.

The figures shown are averages: seen on ten walks, each of half an hour. B = Brown, W = Whites, BL = Blues, S = Skippers.

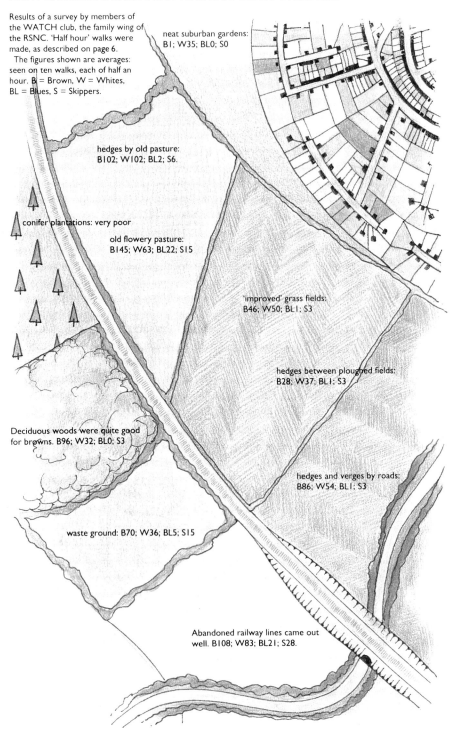

neat suburban gardens:
B1; W35; BL0; S0

hedges by old pasture:
B102; W102; BL2; S6.

conifer plantations: very poor

old flowery pasture:
B145; W63; BL22; S15

'improved' grass fields:
B46; W50; BL1; S3

hedges between ploughed fields:
B28; W37; BL1; S3

Deciduous woods were quite good for browns. B96; W32; BL0; S3

hedges and verges by roads:
B86; W54; BL1; S3

waste ground: B70; W36; BL5; S15

Abandoned railway lines came out well. B108; W83; BL21; S28.

From a wildlife point of view, the abandoned railway line has a potential which belies its modest dimensions; it can be a haven for many species of plants and animals.

Travelling flowers

Until scrubbed up, the commonest community in a cutting is likely to be a meadow of long grass and flowers which reflect the soil of that stretch. This is a background to the oddities that have seeded themselves along this strange linear world, and it is here that the individual stories that are entertaining.

The small, inconspicuous and very rare strapwort was seen only at Slapton Ley on the Devon coast, but now also appears on railway tracks in the area. Oxford ragwort is comparatively common; or it is now. It can be distinguished from common ragwort by the rather narrow pointed lobes of its leaves and its conspicuously black-tipped green 'bracts' beneath the 'petals'. It must be known, unrecognised, to many. Although native to rubbly volcanic slopes in Sicily, it was brought to the Oxford Botanic Garden and by 1794 was on walls in the town; by 1879 it had spread to Reading down the London Line, and now it is seen throughout England and Wales.

Garden and allotment rubbish are another source of exotics, explaining the beds of lupins and red hot pokers seen in cuttings.

Scrub

Although thrusting sycamore making a takeover bid is typical, railway scrub can have a local dialect, with Scots pine in Scotland and whitebeam (a lime-lover) in limestone areas of Lancashire. There may also be a difference between scrub in the cutting and that on the bank. Characteristic of the dry cutting are members of the wild-rose family, hawthorn and also many different microspecies of bramble (see pages 78–9), while the banks usually favour blackthorn together with the brambles.

Butterfly haven

Half-hour walks (see page 203) have shown that abandoned railway cuttings that are suntraps and offer a variety of plants are a good haven for our commoner butterflies. Ploughing and sprays may well have wiped them away from the fields alongside. At their best, total numbers seen can match those of meadowland and other ancient grasslands, although fewer rarities are to be expected. One length of deserted railway in Warwickshire, for example, yielded a count of 586 butterflies seen during the course of nine half-hour walks.

Adders

An adder is probably for many of us our most exotic sighting in Britain. Adders are not really rare; they are our commonest reptile, their population totalling perhaps around half a million. They are to be expected in abandoned cuttings over much of the country, but they are rarely noticed for they are usually shy and retiring and prefer to withdraw at a footstep. A pregnant female, however, may hold her ground. The bite is not a danger to adults in modest health, although medical attention should be sought (it has killed only 14 people in the last 100 years).

They like, and need, to bask, in order to raise their body temperature, and will return to a favourite site for days at a time, and will begin to hunt only when warm enough. Voles are a favourite prey, but they will also climb shrubs to raid birds' nests.

Our other common snake, the grass snake, is, in spite of its name, most often found in damp habitats and is usually seen near or even swimming across water. Soggy-bottomed cuttings could attract it.

The cutting can also be a good place for the slow worm, not a worm, nor a snake although it looks much like one. It is in fact a legless lizard, and the clue is the slight indent where the 'tail' joins its body. It is said that, like its lizard kin, it can shed its tail at this point if seized by a bird, and a new one will grow.

More entertaining is the report, sadly unsubstantiated, of a slow worm living up to its name by failing to catch a slug it was chasing. It can in fact be quite a speedy animal when disturbed.

WASTE LAND

Reliable estimates are difficult, if not impossible, but some sources suggest that as much as one fiftieth of land in Britain is derelict in one way or another.

Kinds of waste land

'Waste' has a particular meaning in early landscape history, signifying the uncultivated and uninhabited land that was used for rough grazing in manorial times. It could carry trees. In fact, unless prevented by grazing or other reasons, most areas in Britain would naturally scrub up and eventually turn into woodland.

Since the Industrial Revolution, however, the words 'waste land' or 'derelict land' have gained ominous overtones. They now imply land that is poisoned and lying derelict after mining or factory use of some kind. Rubbish attracts rubbish, as anyone walking a footpath knows; and such sites have often become refuse dumps.

The soils

Although the soil of such sites may be highly unnatural in origin, it can still have features in common with natural soils. It can be shallow, like heathland soils or those of chalk downland. As happens with heathland soils, the iron in the layers dumped in a tip may have been leached down to form a hard 'pan' some distance below the surface, which, if trees did seed in, would block their roots (see pages 152–3).

The water regime is crucial to any plant trying to colonise. A rubble site can be virtually a desert. But an unshaded site with a soil that cools quickly at dusk can promote a heavy dew, which can make up the deficit for small plants at least.

Waste soils with toxic-chemical residues are the most forbidding, although even here some contaminated mine dumps carry surprising flowers: orchids in some places (see pages 166–7). This apart, the most unfavourable soils are acidic: this releases aluminium and other toxic metals from even ordinary soil minerals, and these affect the nutrient intake by the roots and can also poison processes within the plant, resulting in wilting, discoloured leaves and aborted buds.

Soil creation

If bare rubble is exposed, colonisation starts from first principles as it were, with lichens and mosses and maybe ferns creating a skimpy soil, as they do on a wall (see pages 88–9). The first rooted flowering plants are usually annuals. Plants with leaves lying flat in a rosette or with a low sprawling habitat will be seen. Young thistles, for

WASTE LAND

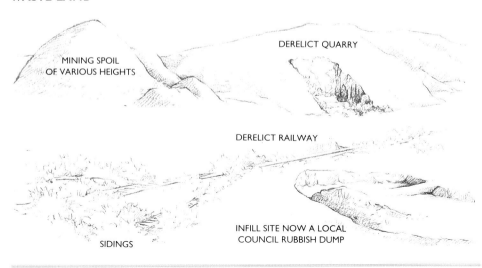

MINING SPOIL OF VARIOUS HEIGHTS

DERELICT QUARRY

DERELICT RAILWAY

SIDINGS

INFILL SITE NOW A LOCAL COUNCIL RUBBISH DUMP

example, have a flat rosette of leaves and a deep tap root to probe for nutrients.

Competition

The competition between different plant species explains what we see – or do not see – in any habitat. For those that can take root early in colonisation, competition is usually slack, and they can sometimes grow in dense and spreading clumps. This can also apply when the habitat they are invading is not bare at all, but simply new to them, and it explains the surprising success of some alien plants. Japanese knotweed is an example; it is now even spreading down crowded verges in Devon and elsewhere. This is also the explanation for the familiar jungles of buddleia on derelict house sites and similar places.

Furthermore, once established, they can take firm possession without needing fresh genetic 'blood' to sharpen up their competitiveness.

Many of these exotics are Mediterranean in origin, or from further afield: pine-appleweed was a native of Asia until the 19th century. Many are escaped garden plants: honesty, with its red flowers and distinctive flat transparent papery seed-cases, can now often be seen on the other side of the garden fence.

What's in it for wildlife?

Once the scars have healed, and with some bushing up, waste land can look attractive; it also houses a far richer wildlife than modern arable fields, for example. Any poisoning affects the worms and other soil invertebrates as well as the plants, and it is they which create a rich loam for plant growth. As is the case with alien plants, some alien animals are now naturalised on waste ground. The house-cricket is now more typical of rubbish dumps than houses, which are generally kept too clean for it; the warmth created by the fermenting rubbish suits it well.

There are and have been reports of other rather more bizarre wasteland denizens. One such is the Sheerness scorpion. Scorpions are not native to Britain although common enough in Mediterranean lands, where their reclusive nature and their nocturnal habits mean that they are rarely noticed by holidaymakers. The Sheerness scorpion, about 1·5 inches (4 cm) long, is found amongst the derelict buildings and old walls of that dockyard and obviously arrived from its warmer habitat by ship – and may well have been here for more than a century.

And tips also attract a good number of scavenging birds.

The birds seen will be scavengers feeding here, such as black-headed gull and starling. Those nesting will reflect the type and amount of cover available.

DERELICT INDUSTRIAL SITE

Indicator plants:
buddleia
sycamore
ground elder
pussy willow

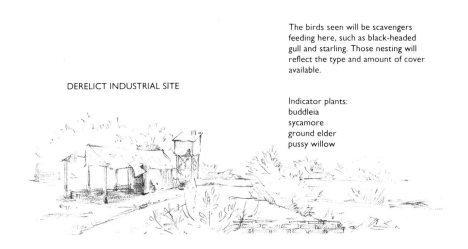

THE NATURE OF DERELICTION

*There are many different kinds of waste
and derelict land, and these harbour many
opportunistic species among the plants
and animals to be found.*

First on the scene

Lichens, mosses and sometimes ferns are
quickly on the scene on bare rubbly ground,
much the same as on a bare rock face (see
pages 88–9). Here, however, quick-seeding
flowering plants can race them in as there is
sure to be some soil exposed. Shepherd's
purse, spurge, groundsel and other 'weeds'
are familiar from the garden flower beds.
Many of them are annuals, and one thing to
notice is that not only are they in flower for
much of the year, but these flowers are often
being carried on successive generations of
plants in the same place – in other words,
they have more than one generation a year.
Another thing to notice is that if conditions
are right these pioneering plants can form
dense carpets.

Of the toadstools, lawyer's wig is the
most likely. It is the fungus most characteristic of piled decaying plant rubbish (it is
often seen along roadsides as well as on
rubbish dumps).

Shoddy plants

A cosmopolitan collection of flowers appears on waste ground, taking advantage of
what is in fact for them a new habitat after
leaping the garden wall (see pages 98–9).
Oxford ragwort is one from Sicily and
pineappleweed one from Asia, both, incidentally, being annuals. Their scattered
distribution interests the botanist, and
many are still colonising: Oxford ragwort,
for example (see pages 110–11), reached
Edinburgh only in the 1950s and Northern
Ireland in the 1960s. New sightings are
therefore of interest. Some of these aliens
are very virulent, thorn apple being one
example. Some are shoddy plants.

One dictionary definition of shoddy is the
yarn or cloth obtained by shredding wool-
len rags. These were (and still are) imported
for treatment here, and the washings can
contain exotic seeds which take root from
the dumped rubbish.

Mysteries of success

Everyone has met earwigs and woodlice
indoors, and they are only two examples of
animals out of place. It is obvious that some
species, both of animals and of plants, are
adaptable, but the reasons why this should
be so are not always clear. Some that would
seem fitted to be ideal colonisers into new
territory are not such. In the case of
mammals, the state of the parent population can be crucial: the dispersal of many
small animals probably occurs when numbers in their home habitat reach saturation,
and the surplus weaker or younger mouths
are crowded out.

But there is always a lot of random luck
connected with animal movements, and if
pioneers are successful they can quickly
breed to create a new and stable colony.

For some insects, the warmth generated
by the fermentation of dumped rubbish is
the key. House-crickets, for example, are
now found only in such places. Modern
standards of cleanliness have ousted them
from houses, where their chirping from the
direction of the fire used to be a familiar
background to bedtime.

Bats are often seen at rural rubbish
dumps, and the insect life also attracts
insectivorous birds. They may drop in only
to feed on the way to elsewhere, but any
handy scrub can attract them to nest. All in
all, the pied wagtail is possibly the most
typical nesting bird of rubbish dumps.

Scavenging birds

There are visits from general scavengers,
too: starlings, rooks, magpies. These re-
enact the historic role once played by the
red kite, which was (so references written at
the time suggest) an important scavenger in
the streets of medieval London.

The habits and geography of birds can
change quite quickly, the collared dove
being one example (see pages 102–3). The
black-headed gull is another: it least deserves the title of 'sea' gull, for only about a
quarter of these birds even nest near the
coast, let alone restrict their scavenging
to it. The black-headed gull is a familiar
denizen of rubbish tips.

THE NATURE OF DERELICTION

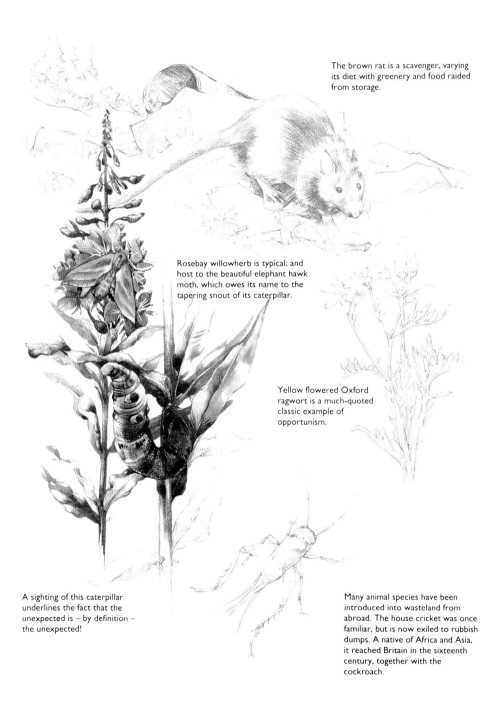

The brown rat is a scavenger, varying its diet with greenery and food raided from storage.

Rosebay willowherb is typical; and host to the beautiful elephant hawk moth, which owes its name to the tapering snout of its caterpillar.

Yellow flowered Oxford ragwort is a much-quoted classic example of opportunism.

A sighting of this caterpillar underlines the fact that the unexpected is – by definition – the unexpected!

Many animal species have been introduced into wasteland from abroad. The house cricket was once familiar, but is now exiled to rubbish dumps. A native of Africa and Asia, it reached Britain in the sixteenth century, together with the cockroach.

LOWLAND LAKES AND MERES

At a generous estimate, lowland lakes, reservoirs and flooded gravel pits have a total area in the region of 50,000 hectares (125,000 acres).

Lakes and meres

Lakes are usually fed by running streams or rivers. In some places shallow basins are filled by seepage through the ground, and these are often locally called meres (from the Old English 'marr'). Otherwise mere is just a poetic name for a lake.

A dying habitat

Reeds and other plants rooted in the mud below the surface can colonise shallow open water. They trap silt, and their decaying stems and leaves add to it, so that a pool or lake tends to fill in from its edges to become first of all a fen and then dry land (see pages 140–1). The flat valley bottoms seen in the hills were the beds of lakes. Drainage has also resulted in the disappearance of many lakes in recent centuries. These losses, both natural and unnatural, may have been made good by the proliferation of flooded gravel pits and flashes (flooded subsidence

of mines). Reservoirs in lowland countryside are now also quite common.

Water quality

One crucial feature of both standing and running water is its nutrient content: whether it is 'rich' or 'poor'. Rich water has dissolved in it chemicals essential for plant growth. In watery habitats a good deal of the plant life which underpins the food chains consists of microscopic one-celled green algae. Individually they are invisible, but if they are there in large amounts they can colour (or even cloud) the water. The decay of these algae also fertilises the mud and allows the plants rooted in it to flourish.

Water colour

The populations of the algae reflect the supply of nutrients brought to the lake by its feeder streams. The chemical content of the rocks and soils that these cross is clearly important, and poor (oligotrophic) lakes are typical of northern hills where the bedrock is hard and usually rather acid. Rich (eutrophic) and middling (mesotrophic) lakes are more typical of the lowlands.

THE LAKE

EXPOSED SHORE

IN SUMMER

Birds equally at home on poor- and rich-water lakes:
  wigeon
  teal
  mallard

Birds preferring rich (lowland) water:
  little grebe
  crested grebe
  mute swan,
  many duck
  moorhen
  coot

sedges

This area is often grazed.

SHINGLE ZONE

OPEN WATER

Being green plants, the microscopic algae need light, and they can be restricted to the surface zone of deep water. They reproduce more quickly when it is warm, and they usually haze the water in summer; indeed, if the water is nutrient-rich and the days are hot, they can rapidly 'bloom' to create a thin soup.

As a result, it is often possible to deduce something about the nature of the water of a lake (and also a river) from its colour alone:

Nutrient level	Colour
poor and peat-stained	brownish but clear
poor but not peaty	clear
middling	slightly greenish
rich	green (or even pink when blooming)
brackish water	often clear
marl lakes	crystal-clear with a blue tinge

The blood-red colour of the mud around some springs and flushes is caused by the oxidation of iron compounds brought to the surface in the water.

Marl lakes

In the chalk and limestone hills, the alkalinity of the water makes it nutrient-poor by locking up phosphate which is vital for plant growth. This phosphate is often precipitated, together with calcium carbonate from the rock, as 'marl' at the bottom of the pool. The water is very clear in these pools, often with the bluish tinge of clean water seen in bulk.

The reason for this is that with the phosphate locked up, the minute algae which normally colour and cloud lake water cannot thrive. On the other hand rooted plants can tap the marl and vast beds of stonewort and pondweeds may flourish, all the more so as the clarity of the water means that plenty of light reaches them. The scarcity of algae means less variety of insects and other small animals, although those that are present, with little competition, may be in large numbers.

SHELTERED BAY

Swamp-nesting birds include:
bittern
mallard
marsh harrier
moorhen
reed bunting
reed warbler

Swamp-fen nesting birds include:
grasshopper warbler
mallard
sedge warbler
moorhen
reed bunting
reed warbler (and hence cuckoo)

reeds and bulrushes

tussock sedge

bushes

water lilies

Birds of the fen zone can include, especially if grazed:
mallard
lapwing
snipe
meadow pipit
yellow wagtail

SWAMP ZONE

WATER LILY ZONE

WATERFOWL WATCH

Summer sees Britain's lowland lakes at their most attractive, but the large flocks of waterfowl in winter more than compensate for the dour weather of that season.

Lake birds

There are no hard and fast lines, but there are two rough groupings of lake birds: those that feed out in open water, and those that are normally restricted to its margins.

The birds that rely on open water for fish or for shellfish and water plants include divers, grebes and sawbills, the last named from the serrations on the bill that enable it to take firm hold of slippery fish.

Most waterfowl, however, are more likely to be seen along the margins of the lake. The ducks divide up into the 'dabblers' and the 'divers'. The dabblers, such as the mallard, patronise the shallows and reach down from the surface to feed, while the divers dive (often with a preliminary jump) below the surface. The pochard is a typical diving duck. But the mallard is often seen feeding on land, and the moorhen spends most of its time on land. Some wild geese graze on fields alongside and only roost out on the open water. The heron nests in trees maybe 800 metres (half a mile) from the nearest water, which it visits to fish from the edge or the shallows.

In winter, waterfowl are freed from the need to remain near a nest, and often fly considerable distances when harsh weather strikes. They then seem to prefer quite open waters and are even put off by such things as a wood too near an otherwise suitable lake. Here, even the highly artificial reservoir can score over the natural lake.

The shore

Nesting songbirds react to the structure of the wood (see pages 24–5), and likewise lake birds reflect the physical structure and cover offered by the shore. This is determined in part by the setting of the lake. The wave action of upland and windswept lakes tends to scour the shore clean.

But the water quality is also crucial, underpinning the food chains as it does (see pages 116–17). Lakes with richer water would be expected to have fringes of dense reedbeds, and the shallower sloping shores which lowland (and usually richer) lakes tend to have also help the reed. Southerly lowland lakes are therefore likely to be better for waterfowl, and this is borne out by surveys. As the list on page 117 shows, however, there are some birds, such as wigeon, teal, and mallard, which are equally typical of rich (usually lowland) and of poor (usually upland) lakes.

Geography and numbers

There is a strong north-to-south bias in numbers of species and a lesser one running from east (high) to west and Wales (low). So (taking lake size into account) East Anglian waters, which include the Norfolk Broads, can provide the best birdwatching, with twice the numbers of species that are to be expected in more westerly areas such as Dorset and Nottinghamshire. This is especially true of duck species.

The territory

Some species make clear choices: dabbling ducks, for example, like plenty of reed or other emergent plants nearby. But the bird's lake territory has a rather different geography from that of a wood or hedge. Dabbling ducks space their nests out along the shoreline, and there will be more nesting possibilities (and hence more ducks) the more sinuous the shore – that is, the longer it is in relation to the areas of open water which acts as larder. For tufted duck, however, different behaviour has often been observed. In spring, the males stake out territories on the open water, but the females nest close together on an island. This is very like the behaviour of many seabirds.

As a general rule, the larger the lake and the more varied its shore, the more (and more species of) waterfowl are likely to be seen.

In winter, as with other birds, the territorial instinct dissolves and they tend to become more mobile. Birds in general can move surprising distances in reaction to adverse winter weather.

WATERFOWL WATCH

The tufted duck is our commonest diving duck, numbers having increased by colonising gravel pits and city ponds (where it is often seen). Do its nesting habits change in these 'new' habitats?

The more varied the shore, the greater the variety of birds able to nest along it.

bushy cover

The numbers in distant flocks can be estimated. See page 202.

reed bed

Tufted duck often associate with pochard.

female

Female tufted duck often nest on an island for safety, and so seem to be nesting communally.

male

Tufted duck are far less common than mallard (7000 as compared to 150,000 nesting pairs), though numbers rise in winter.

tufted duck

PONDS, POOLS AND CANALS

PONDS, POOLS AND CANALS

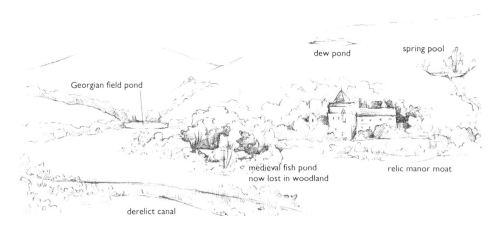

Georgian field pond

dew pond

spring pool

medieval fish pond
now lost in woodland

relic manor moat

derelict canal

In the mind's eye, the countryside is full of ponds, but, unless protected, they tend to be a transient feature, and easily lost. Only a fraction of the ponds of yesteryear remain.

Ponds and pools

A pond is a small body of standing water with no or little flow, and usually fed by seepage or by a gentle spring. The word 'pool' might better be kept for a broadening of a stream which keeps a flow: but the word is used for both.

A short life

Although in the mind's eye a pond is a permanent countryside feature, it has no certain future unless man takes a hand. With little or no current to scour it, dead leaves and plant litter sink to rot at the bottom and build up as mud. The bankside plants root out, more mud collects, and in quite a short span of years only a marshy hollow remains. Hollows marked by a patch of scrub are all that remain of many field ponds.

The history of the pond

Being transient, ponds have a story. They were usually dug or dammed for a reason, and kept open for a reason. There may be no job for the village pond in today's world of piped water, but it is often kept clear as a souvenir. Ancestrally it may have been a fish pond, although village fish ponds were often in the village woodlands (see pages 18–19). Most manor houses, even the most humble, were embraced by a moat: today's village pond may be a fragment of that. Monasteries also had fish or 'stew' ponds.

Field ponds also have a history. Many of those glimpsed in the fields (and many are nowadays hidden in a copse of trees) date from two centuries ago, the great age of enclosures when today's fields were being marked out (see pages 80–1). Dug to provide water for cattle, they are often in corners and shared by four fields. Few farms now have cattle, and, even if they do, many ponds have had their job taken over by an old bathtub. Other field ponds were marl pits: one meaning of this word is a limy clay dug to be spread over the ploughlands to improve their chemistry.

Dew ponds found on the chalk downs are lined with trodden clay or concrete. After rain they collect some run-off from the ground around, but they may also condense a small amount of mist and dew.

Working ponds

Ponds were also created by damming a stream to provide a head of water to drive machinery for milling corn or for iron-forging and other purposes. Mill ponds are common, while in Surrey, for example, there are still many 'hammerponds'.

The canals provide a similar habitat. Some lengths remain full, but muddied by holiday traffic. More useful to wildlife are the derelict lengths, with perhaps less water but less disturbance.

The wildlife eye

Although of many possible origins, a pond evolves a typical structure of open water rimmed by a shallow edge in which emergent plants are rooted. This shallow shore zone merges with a tangled 'meadow' as the ground becomes drier, but not much of this may remain if the field is ploughed. Grazing also trims it, of course. The size of the pond and its depth, whether it lies in full sun or is partly shaded, how much and what kind of nutrients reach it by run-off – these are the things which decide its wildlife. Ponds are easy enough to pollute: run-off from the farm's slurry pit will deoxygenate the water and kill the animal life, while slimes flourish on rich muck and smother the rooted plants. If the tractor's spray tanks are washed out of insecticides near the pond, that, too, can be lethal.

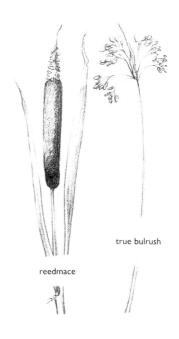

true bulrush

reedmace

The reedmace adopted the name 'bulrush' when the Victorian artist Alma-Tadema showed it in his painting of the biblical story of Moses.

FREE FLOATERS
duckweed
water fern
frogbit

SUBMERGED
water milfoil
several pondweeds
water violet
bladderwort

FLOATING LEAVES
water lilies
(yellow, white
  and fringed)
broad-leaved
  pondweed

Look also for amphibious bistort.

EMERGENT
reed   marestail
reedmace   flowering rush
bulrush   arrowhead
water   bottle sedge
horsetail   water plantain

Reedmace, yellow water lily, arrowhead can tolerate some pollution.

THE LIVING WORLD OF THE POND

*The life of a pond is forever fascinating.
However, it is not quite the separate world
that it seems to be: much of its life has
migrated from land.*

The hierarchies of the pond

We take for granted that in most land
habitats the plants are ranged to the light,
to create recognisable layers. There is a
similar ordering of pond plants, but the
perspective is rather different.

There are, for example, plants which are
completely free-floating; others with floating leaves but rooted in the mud; and those
rooted but with submerged leaves. Another
rank of leaf is found towards the shore,
where reeds, bulrush and others stand with
roots submerged. One or two amphibious
plants, as happy on land as they are in
water, may perhaps be seen where the bank
is firmer.

Invasion from the land

The pond never offers the profusion of
species to be found in even a sparse
meadow. Part of the reason is that aquatic
plants are a rather select group of land
plants that have taken the plunge to adapt
to the watery life. A clue here is that they
flower in air even when they grow totally
submerged. Almost all have familiar land-
based relatives, one exception to this being
the water lilies, whose land-based kin have

presumably become extinct. The amphibious bistort is interesting; it grows short-
stalked leaves when growing on land, but
long-stalked leaves able to sway with any
current when in water. It is a halfway plant,
another, beautiful, example of which is the
arrowhead (see also pages 128–9).

The surface barrier

Unless we angle our gaze, the surface
mirrors the light, concealing the world
enclosed below. But a pond is not quite the
closed world it may seem. Many of its
denizens can in fact break the surface and
fly strongly: both water beetle and water
boatman habitually swap pools at night.
Many insects also have a lengthy water-
bound, immature feeding stage in their
lives, with a final and much shorter flying-
cum-breeding stage; mosquitoes, dragonflies and mayflies are examples. Even
those animals now firmly aquatic may not
always have been. The fact that some water
snails breathe with a lung and must surface
for air, points to a recent terrestrial origin.

The dragonfly

This is truly a birdwatcher's insect, and
moreover one that bestrides two worlds.
The final emergence of the adult from the
nymph which has pulled itself up out of the
water is one of the most spectacular sights
in nature.

The pond in winter

On winter walks, it is easy to forget the
habitat for the scenery: even a wood reduces to cathedral vistas, much of its life
withdrawn. A pond is similar, but some of
the special survival strategies adopted by
the plants are intriguing, especially if we
remember their fairly recent terrestrial
origin.

Surface floaters are at risk from ice, and
water lilies die down to the roots as do many
land plants. But the duckweeds, heavy with
the weight of summer's starch, sink to the
bottom, to rise again by spring when their
food reserves are used up. Frogbit puts out
winter buds which fall off to lie in the mud
and float up again in spring.

dragonfly nymph

Paradoxically, a sheet of ice, although it seals the pond from the air, actually protects the life in it. It seals off the water from further loss of heat, but at the same time lets enough light through for those submerged plants that do remain active. Their photo-synthesis releases oxygen which keeps the pond aerated, to the benefit of all other life. The danger comes when the ice becomes covered with a thick blanket of snow which shades the water below and thus prevents photosynthesis.

THE LIVING WORLD OF THE POND

HAWKERS
Strong fliers, they patrol their territory.

DARTERS
Short and flat in body, they spend much time perched, to fly off to attack passing insects.

DAMSELFLIES
Slender in body, they perch with wings folded back.

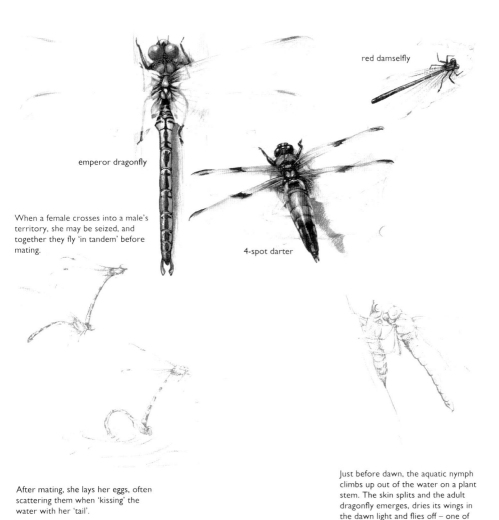

red damselfly

emperor dragonfly

When a female crosses into a male's territory, she may be seized, and together they fly 'in tandem' before mating.

4-spot darter

After mating, she lays her eggs, often scattering them when 'kissing' the water with her 'tail'.

Just before dawn, the aquatic nymph climbs up out of the water on a plant stem. The skin splits and the adult dragonfly emerges, dries its wings in the dawn light and flies off – one of the most dramatic sights of nature.

THE RIVER

The NRA controls over 42,000 kilometres (more than 26,000 miles) of waters in England and Wales. As a habitat they offer aquatic habitats, banks and islands.

The ages of a river

It helps to visualise three ages of a river. These are not ages in years, but stages linked with the varying landscapes through which the water runs. The river in fact helps to fashion this scenery: any view of a river valley is a kind of negative, of land which has been eroded away by water and by the ice of glaciers which once covered most of Britain.

A good many British rivers run through two different landscapes in the course of their journey from source to sea. They begin in the hills as a fast stream or troutbeck running in a steep valley, cascading over a bed of solid rock or tumbling past boulders into pools where the trout lurk. Where the flow eases, fine gravel settles in 'minnow reaches' where these fish are first seen.

Then, often where the first ploughed fields come into sight, their character changes. Cascades are less common and silt begins to settle. The river is starting into middle age, and it is often soon running in quite a wide valley. Later still, when old, the river meanders across what may be a vast lowland plain. Here, rather than scouring the land as it did in its youth, it will fitfully deposit what silt it carries, although the meanders themselves were carved out by the river.

Every river has its own story. Some of those in the far west of Britain rush directly from mountain slopes to the sea, with no real lowland stretch. In the east and south, many rivers are 'born' middle-aged; they rise from springs among slight hills and lack rapid 'upland' stretches.

Fish zones

Trout feed by sight and need oxygen-rich water, but 'coarse' fish, for example, carp, tench and roach, as well as bream feed largely by their well-developed sense of smell and can tolerate murk. Fish can 'zone' a river from source to mouth, in a way which reflects its geographical ages.

THE RIVER

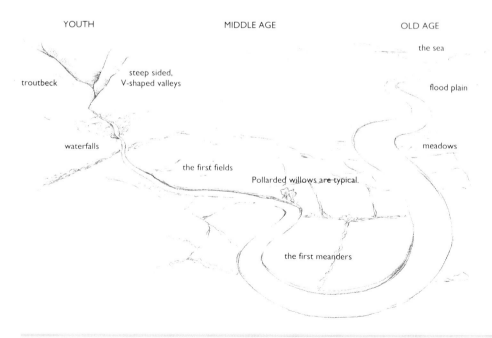

YOUTH — MIDDLE AGE — OLD AGE

the sea

troutbeck

steep sided, V-shaped valleys

flood plain

waterfalls

the first fields

meadows

Pollarded willows are typical.

the first meanders

fast, clear, rocky or coarse gravel bed; well oxygenated current eases.	trout zone; and salmons swim upriver to spawn here
fine gravel	minnow reaches; and grayling bullhead, stone loach
moderate current. silty	barbel and chub zone
sluggish, muddy	bream zone (and other coarse fish,
brackish estuary	flounder zone

Hard and soft water

The river is fed by springs and by run-off from the land around, and the rock and soil give the water a chemical flavour. Over chalk and limestone, the water contains dissolved calcium carbonate, making it 'hard'. Pennine Millstone grit gives soft water.

But a river can change chemically, when tributaries bring in water from another source. Pollution, too, can affect long reaches of river (see pages 130–1).

Steep banks

Although chalk rivers and streams have a fairly even flow, clay rivers regularly spate in winter and scour and deepen their channel, so the slacker summer river runs between the steep banks cut by the winter flood. The banks are an important habitat element.

River engineering

Even 50 years ago, villages were regularly flooded out in winter. Damaging floods are now rarer, but modern river engineering has had a much wider impact on the countryside than we realise. The winter flow is improved by removing obstacles, straightening curves, and deepening the channel and smoothing its banks, grading them to 45 degrees. The cost to wildlife has been immense.

At the same time, old waterside meadows and pastures have been destroyed: with improved drainage they are now ploughed and sown like any other arable field.

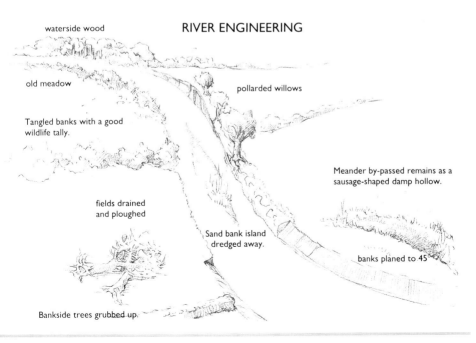

RIVER ENGINEERING

waterside wood

old meadow

Tangled banks with a good wildlife tally.

pollarded willows

Meander by-passed remains as a sausage-shaped damp hollow.

fields drained and ploughed

Sand bank island dredged away.

banks planed to 45°

Bankside trees grubbed up.

THE RIVER BANK

The river bank is one of the many habitats offered by the river. It is worth a half-hour investigation in its own right. There are typical trees and wildlife to be seen.

Mudbanks

In summer when the water is low, shelves of gravelly mud or even short-lived islands are likely to be exposed. They are grand places to explore if you can get to them. Animal and bird tracks remain undisturbed and the flowers you find can be curious; they obviously need to be on the mark for quick growth. Be wary of disturbing nesting birds: common sandpiper and oystercatcher sometimes nest on these temporary refuges.

The river bank

The plants of the bank have their toes in rich river water, and so you would expect a good variety. Willows and alder are characteristic trees, and the pollarded river-bank willow is one of the most recognisable of all trees. The species is crack willow, so named because its weak twigs easily fracture. This trait means that, if the tree is not pollarded, the boughs tend to split themselves off when they are of any size.

The willow tribe are easily muddled, but easy enough to understand. Willows have long narrow leaves, while sallows are broad-leaved willows and often shrubby, with well-known catkins in spring – when they are known as 'pussy willow'. Osiers have long narrow leaves, silvery (with very fine hairs) below, their edges often curled. Poplars are closely related to willows but with broader, rounded leaves. The alder often grows with its feet half in the water. It may be all that is left of a broad strip of wet woodland beside the river. Bankside flowers are those also found in fens (see pages 142–3) and meadows. It is difficult to draw a line between traditional meadow and river bank plants, but habitat boundaries tend to be a human invention anyway.

Bankside animals

The sudden plop means that a grazing water vole (often called, to its misfortune, a water rat) has been alarmed by your steps and jumped in to swim to the safety of its burrow; the entrance is well concealed below the surface. For it, as for much aquatic life, the bank is as important as the water itself. The otter illustrates more clearly than most the fragile dependence of even a bulky animal on the exact quality of many different features of its habitat. Although otters are nocturnal, acutely suspicious and notoriously difficult to catch sight of, their numbers have definitely plummeted in recent decades. Disease and pesticide residues in their food may have contributed to this, but a major cause is the destruction of the long miles of tangled river bank that enabled them to travel widely, meet, mate and perpetuate their species.

Birds of the river bank

Length for length, there is a striking difference between the low bird counts of northern and western rivers and the high ones of the south-east. This is a difference between upland and lowland, with the lowland waterways having comparatively luxuriant vegetation to shelter nesting birds.

This can, however, be changed by river engineering, and so each river makes its own individual offer and it is impossible to generalise. It is clear that the longer the river, the more varied its bird count is likely to be – simply because a greater range of habitats is more likely. This applies both in summer and in winter.

Undisturbed banks are chosen for the holt (den), often hidden away between tree roots.

The cubs play at sliding into the water – look for signs of this.

THE OTTER AND ITS HABITAT

Otters are now rare (and may be absent) outside Wales and Scotland. Pesticide-tainted fish and the destruction of the natural riversides they need are the main causes.

Although often hunting large rivers, it prefers to lie up in streams.

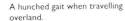

A hunched gait when travelling overland.

Feral mink escaped from fur farms is sometimes mistaken for the otter; but it leaves foul droppings.

Otters need miles of good river – they have the habit of hunting one stretch for a night or two before moving on.

On hard surfaces, spraints are left as territory markers; they are tarry droppings, shiny with fish scales, but not foul smelling.

Male otter (otters have a liking for eels).

THE STREAM

The stream can be a powerful force in the countryside, energetically carving out its own geography. Force and motion also influence the plant and animal life.

The power of moving water

By apt coincidence, 'force' is a northern word for the tumbling waterfall of the hills. The power of water when it starts moving is startling. Its transport ability increases by velocity to the power of five; for the non-mathematician, this means that if its speed doubles it can move stones 30 times larger. At 30 centimetres (1 foot) a second it will carry silt, and at 1·2 metres (4 feet) a second it can move rocks weighing 10 kilos (20 pounds).

Geography of a stream

Changes in flow create their own detailed geography. At a bend the current on the outside is faster, more forceful, and cuts a steep bank or low cliff, while on the inside of the bend the flow is slower and silt is shed to make a gentle slope. Here there may be much more growing: in general, the slower the current, the more bankside vegetation there will be. It is also a general rule that the slower the flow of the water, the more important its quality: whether it is nutrient-rich or nutrient-poor becomes the main factor controlling plantlife and animal life.

Current and shape

The flow does not only shape the streambed. It also affects the actual shape of the aquatic animals. Fish are streamlined not only to improve their swimming, but also to allow them to rest effortlessly, nosing into the current. The dipper, a bird which searches for insects by actually walking on the streambed, takes active advantage of the

THE STREAM

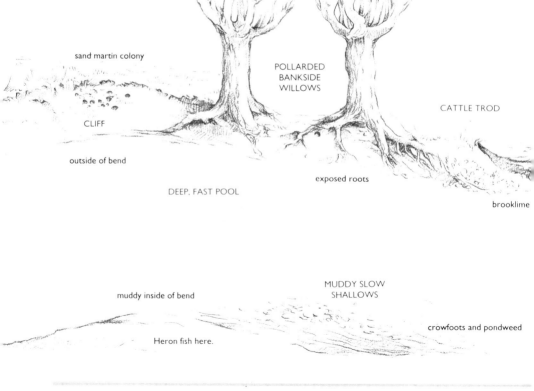

sand martin colony

POLLARDED
BANKSIDE
WILLOWS

CATTLE TROD

CLIFF

outside of bend

exposed roots

DEEP, FAST POOL

brooklime

MUDDY SLOW
SHALLOWS

muddy inside of bend

crowfoots and pondweed

Heron fish here.

current (see pages 138–9). The nymphs of insects found in running water are very often flattened in some way to allow them to hug the stones. There are many examples, but we must not forget that, for small animals, a 'drift' downstream (if not completely out of control) is a useful way of dispersing their numbers. Trout feed at dawn and dusk, the main times of this drift.

The shape of leaves

Plants also adapt to the flow. Underwater leaves tend to be ribbon-like, to enable them to sway, unresisting, with the current. This shape has the additional advantage that it provides a large surface area to volume, to maximise the exchange of gases through the leaf pores and also to maximise photosynthesis, a benefit in the dim light. Floating leaves tend to have a smooth and rather oval shape.

It is only leaves held up above the water that match the exotic diversity of land plants. The most beautiful example of this is surely the arrowhead, a handsome streamside flower. Its arrow-shaped leaves are held above water, floating leaves are oval, and those submerged are long ribbons. In a fast stream only the last are grown.

Fishy geography

'Game' and 'coarse' fish have different needs (see pages 124–5). That said, there are species differences which determine where they locate themselves, as any good angler knows. Some fish prefer deep 'holding' pools, others shallower water. Those that feed on the bottom are often seen in shoals, with more eyes to spot the scattered swarms of insects, worms and other prey and with more eyes to catch early sight of predators when intently feeding head-down in mud.

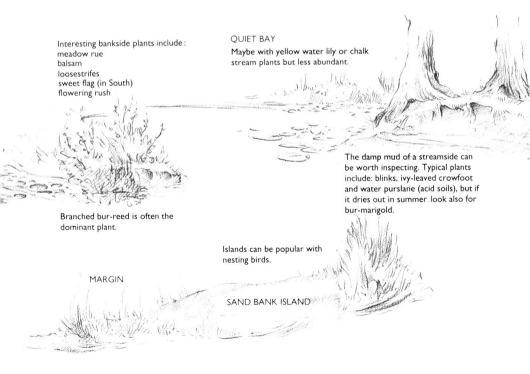

Interesting bankside plants include:
meadow rue
balsam
loosestrifes
sweet flag (in South)
flowering rush

QUIET BAY
Maybe with yellow water lily or chalk stream plants but less abundant.

The damp mud of a streamside can be worth inspecting. Typical plants include: blinks, ivy-leaved crowfoot and water purslane (acid soils), but if it dries out in summer look also for bur-marigold.

Branched bur-reed is often the dominant plant.

Islands can be popular with nesting birds.

MARGIN

SAND BANK ISLAND

STREAM-WATCHING

There is no pollution problem on a stone-dead planet. Its effect on life is what counts. Easily identified animals allow us to estimate the pollution of a stream or river.

Night and day

A casual glance down into a stream will not reveal much of interest. Much aquatic life is small, secretive and hidden away under stones, active only after dark as it is on land. But these small animals (and larger beasts such as crayfish) are often insensitive to red light, and with a red torch you can quite easily watch them after dark.

Pollution

From above the surface, it is often difficult to judge if a stream is clean or polluted. Gross pollution is obvious, of course: dead fish float belly upwards, the water is opaque, and dense growths of slime may mask the bottom. Happily, this degree of pollution is not usual, but lesser levels are. Pollution, by definition, has an effect on life, and so an eye to the life can help gauge the pollution level.

Straight poisoning of the water with pesticides or other chemicals is a matter of accident. Contamination with sewage, which is household, farm and factory effluent, is however, quite common in many, if not most, stream and river systems.

The oxygen equation

All animals need oxygen, and most aquatic species take it from the supply dissolved in the water. The exceptions are those that have a lung of some kind and which come to the surface to breathe. Aquatic plants release oxygen as a result of photosynthesis, some oxygen is dissolved from the air at the surface, and in this way the dissolved oxygen is kept in balance with demand.

Bacteria are key members of this watery world, just as they are on land. They play a part in the breakdown of dead matter, recycling it to release nutrients which will feed new generations of plants and hence the animals that feed upon those plants. These aerobic bacteria need oxygen for this and they, too, take it from the supply dissolved in the water.

The effect of muck

One of the most important, if rarely mentioned 'uses' of Britain's rivers is to act as a dump for sewage, treated and untreated. In principle, there is little harm in this; this muck is only a version of the decaying matter of a healthy stream, and if diluted with enough water no harm is done. But if too much untreated sewage, or even large amounts of treated sewage, get into the water, it is a bonanza for the bacteria. This may occur in summer when the water is low, or when a farm slurry pit overflows into a nearby stream. The bacteria multiply exceedingly rapidly, and use up the available oxygen.

A change in the life

When the dissolved oxygen starts to dwindle, those animals which need an easy supply quickly die. But some are more resistant – perhaps they have red haemoglobin in their blood to store oxygen, as we ourselves have. If the pollution continues, all that may survive are those animals that can breathe from the surface in some way and, because there are no longer any competitors for food, they may now be there in enormous numbers.

As a quick indication, sightings of mayfly and stonefly indicate clean water: much other life such as water louse, freshwater shrimp and caddis fly larvae will also be present. If the mayfly and stonefly are absent, then you should suspect the presence of some pollution. Lack of freshwater shrimp, water louse and others suggests quite heavy polluation. If there is no life except the rat tailed maggot and others which breathe from the surface, the water is very heavily contaminated.

In this way, a handful of easily identified invertebrates can indicate the pollution of a stream. The appraisal can be further sharpened by including the dragonflies and their kin, many of which are linked with running water. Their aquatic nymphs are sensitive to oxygen levels, but the adults also seek out areas of water with good bankside cover. Dragonflies can help identify the best wildlife streams.

STREAM-WATCHING

All should be seen in clean water,
but mayfly, stonefly (and dragonfly)
nymphs die when oxygen is scarce.
In badly polluted water, only the
rat-tailed maggot may survive.

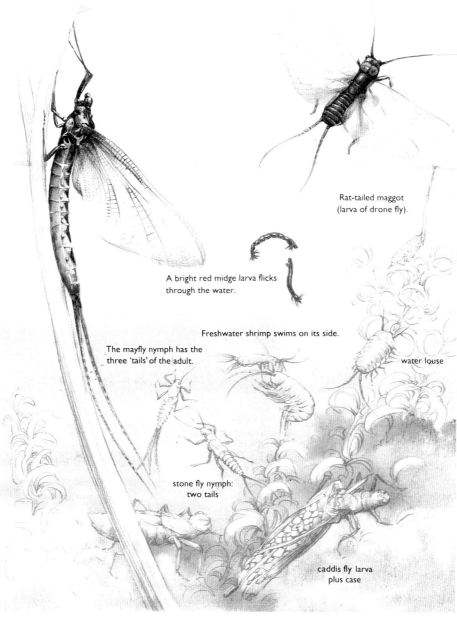

Rat-tailed maggot
(larva of drone fly).

A bright red midge larva flicks
through the water.

Freshwater shrimp swims on its side.

The mayfly nymph has the
three 'tails' of the adult.

water louse

stone fly nymph:
two tails

caddis fly larva
plus case

Dragonfly and damselfly nymphs also
need bankside plants and can indicate
undisturbed streams.

The animal life below the surface can
be seen by scooping a dish through
the bankside mud and weeds and
letting it settle.

THE CHALK STREAM

*Chalk streams and rivers have a character
quite their own. Many famous stretches,
however, are being actively managed
commercially for trout fishing.*

The chalk spring

In clay countryside (which is what most of
lowland Britain is), there is rapid run-off
after rain. Streams and rivers frequently rise
and the winter spates cut deep banks. In
chalk countryside, however, much of the
rainfall sinks down into the porous rock
below the soil. Gravity pulls it down until it
meets a less permeable band, when it perco-
lates sideways and at a hillside emerges as a
spring or a series of scarcely noticed seep-
ages. The same is largely true of limestone,
except that the water tends to find its way
through cracks and fissures in the rock,
which in time become widened into caves.
But springs are as common in limestone
countryside as they are in the chalk.

The water running from the spring is
crystal clear, and where it backs up deeply
as a pool it may be tinged with blue – the tint
of pure water in bulk.

Winter streams

In the chalklands of the south, Winterbourne is sometimes met as part of a village
name. It means winter stream, one which
flows after the autumn rains have topped up
the hidden reservoir in the chalk. From a
wildlife point of view, however, these are
better described as streams that cease to
flow when the rock layers become depleted.

The profile of the stream

Fed by a spring, the flow of the crystal water
is largely regular and without the great
spates of a clay stream. A result is that its
banks are usually shallow, sloping and
marshy, rather different from the steeper
banks of the clay stream. It is not often
noticed, but the arches of bridges in chalk
country are quite low, for the same reason.

Running straight from its underground
cistern, the water is also at a fairly even
temperature, on average about 11 C and
rarely dropping below 5 C in winter. Thus
it feels cool in summer but relatively warm
in winter, when it often 'steams' in cold air.
This even temperature benefits both sub-

THE CHALK STREAM

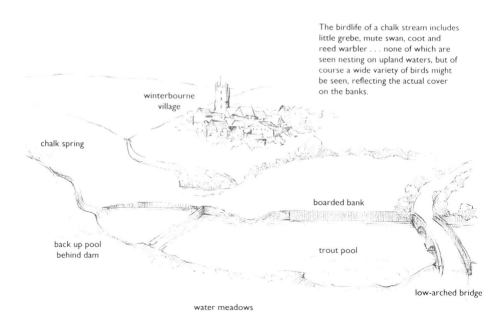

The birdlife of a chalk stream includes
little grebe, mute swan, coot and
reed warbler . . . none of which are
seen nesting on upland waters, but of
course a wide variety of birds might
be seen, reflecting the actual cover
on the banks.

winterbourne
village

chalk spring

boarded bank

back up pool
behind dam

trout pool

low-arched bridge

water meadows

merged and bankside plants. In fact, in winter, the chalk stream often creates a line of vivid green across fields otherwise bleached of colour.

The stream in high summer

As a result of its even flow, long streamers of aquatic plants lie along the streambed – plants that would be torn away in spate. The 'hard' water is also generous with the essential nutrients, most importantly phosphates, nitrates and potassium. These encourage growth; and the summer growth of the aquatic plants can create dense green rafts which fill the stream and raise the water level so that it sometimes even floods over the banks alongside.

Management

The summer rafts of 'waterweed' are often cut back to prevent flooding, but on many lengths of chalk water management is even more rigorous. The streambed itself may be deepened by dredging. This can benefit the trout, and in some trout-fishing streams the 'impact' of the bankside vegetation is also lessened by clearing it and facing the bank with boarding. A rather unnatural water-course is created as a result (and to benefit the trout further, coarse fish in the stream are electrocuted).

Other threats to the classic chalk stream are gravel-digging alongside – when flooded these can contaminate the flow – and the extraction of household water in large quantities direct from the rock reservoir. Many downland streams are now perma-nently dry in their upper reaches as a result. The creation of watercress-beds is less damaging, although there is a danger that the insecticides used to treat the cress may wash down to kill the life downstream.

As crucial as anything else for wildlife is whether the waterway, chalk river or any other, is being used for pleasure cruising. The propellers churn the mud, the water becomes opaque and lifeless. While this book is being written cases are passing through the courts with the county Trusts and other conservation groups opposing proposals that all usable rivers should be open to public navigation.

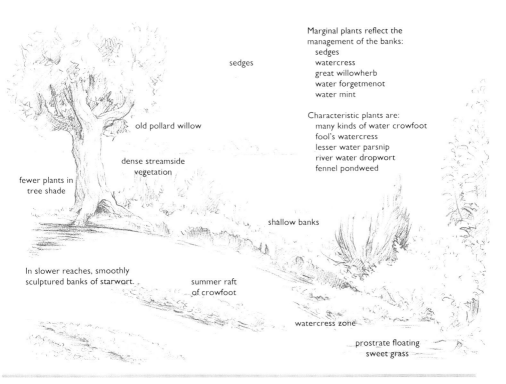

Marginal plants reflect the management of the banks:
  sedges
  watercress
  great willowherb
  water forgetmenot
  water mint

Characteristic plants are:
  many kinds of water crowfoot
  fool's watercress
  lesser water parsnip
  river water dropwort
  fennel pondweed

sedges

old pollard willow

dense streamside vegetation

fewer plants in tree shade

shallow banks

In slower reaches, smoothly sculptured banks of starwort.

summer raft of crowfoot

watercress zone

prostrate floating sweet grass

THE LIFE OF THE CHALK STREAM

Trout often migrate upstream to spawn, lake trout move up the streams.

Trout are very variable: Highland trout are swarming little fish, big headed, and brilliantly spotted.

With their flowing green tresses of waterweed, chalk streams are always an attractive landscape feature. Their wildlife lives up to this fulsome promise.

A mottled green tapestry

The dark green tresses undulating in the swirls of current and sometimes breaking surface are likely to be crowfoots – 'water buttercups'. The leaves can differ; those held submerged are like finely divided bunches of ribbon, but they all have the proud white five-petalled buttercup-like flowers. It is odd but unexplained that they flower earlier upstream – and continue to flower earlier if transplanted downstream. Brighter green starwort often grows with them, although it can create its own sculpted beds.

Look for watercress along the water margins; it also has white flowers, but smaller and four-petalled, and in loose heads. And perhaps there may be, growing up through the matted vegetation of the bank, some water-dropwort, with the umbrella flowers of the cow-parsley family.

A waterside garden

Plants can run riot above the watercress that edges the stream. Patches of colour are added, notably by purple loosestrife and the dusky pink willowherbs.

The mayfly hatch

The stream will hold plenty of mayfly nymphs, one of the classic indicators of clean water (see pages 130–1). The hatch, when the nymphs rise to the surface and the adults shuck their old skins and fly up and away, can be one of the more spectacular events of British wildlife. Although the individuals are far smaller, the effect is on a par with the massed flocks of birds wheeling over the winter saltings.

As with many other insects, these flying adults live only to mate, and they die within a day or two. Alone among insects, however, the flying mayfly which emerges from the nymph skin is still not quite mature. This dull-coloured 'dun' needs to moult again, often after only an hour or two, to become the shimmering breeding adult. Just what biological advantage there is in this two-stage adulthood is not clear. The breeding adults do not feed, but (in good weather) spend their time in endless massed courtship, writhing like wisps of smoke above the stream. Once they are mated, and the eggs laid, they fall exhausted to the water, to be snapped up by any trout that remain ungorged from the earlier hatch.

Trout fishing

At the first sign of the hatch, the fisherman grabs his rod. Made of twists of feather, artificial trout 'flies' do not to our eyes look much like a mayfly. The trout has keen eyesight, so perhaps what is important is the way that the rod dimples the dry flies against the surface of the water, imitating the distressed movements of the spent insect. In the case of 'wet' flies, which are weighted down with lead and trailed underwater, the attraction may be the shimmer of the trapped water bubbles.

The trout

It lurks at the edges of the weed bed, perhaps revealed only by a yawning white gape as it gulps an insect. But beware: as with all fish-watching, make sure you tread softly to prevent your step setting up warning vibrations in the water. Often the trout is noticed only from afar, by the splash as it takes a mayfly. It is territorial, remaining on its own course for long periods, and up to a kilometre from local spawning grounds.

The brown trout which is native to British streams and rivers is very variable. It is practically impossible to find two trout with exactly the same colouring even in the same stream, and indeed there were once wrongly thought to be ten different species. Although both have red and black spots, however, the chalk-stream fish are usually larger and more silvery than their cousins from the waters of the hills. Rainbow trout, a native of north-west America, is bred in fish farms and stocked for fishing in reservoirs and lakes; and it sometimes escapes elsewhere. This fish lives up to its name, as can be seen at the fishmongers.

ABOUT THE TROUT

The fish are linked to aspects of the habitat we are hardly aware of.

Trout need cold water (26°C will kill) and need it richly oxygenated, and also clear, as they feed by sight. Mayfly are a favourite food.

The trout feeds mainly at dawn when insects are active and drift down in the current.

Look for them at the edge of a weed bed.

The eggs are laid in reaches of clean gravel. Spawning (a winter activity) is triggered by a drop to 6°C (43°F). It will not take place above 13°C (55°F).

A typical chalk stream trout is short, thick, small-headed and quite silvery often with yellow about the lower part of its head and with widely spaced spots.

THE WATERS OF THE HILLS

LAKES AND STREAMS OF THE HILLS

Trees grow from rock crevice, out of reach of sheep.

Bogs often accompany headwaters.

A troutbeck cascades over rocks.

Four birds typify this habitat:
  dipper
  grey wagtail
  goosander
  common sandpiper

The minnow reach is where water slackens to allow gravel to settle.

Climate and geology combine to give Britain some of the finest upland lakes and streams in Europe. The setting is harsh, but they have a detailed ecology.

Poor water

The innumerable lakes, tarns and tumbling streams of the northern hills all take advantage of the spadework of the glaciers. Ice sculptured the narrow valleys and the steep rocky slopes, and running water is a comparatively recent influence here. Although sediments carried into the lakes can influence its chemistry, upland water is generally poor in nutrients and also likely to be rather acid as a result of the rock type. A notable exception is the marl lakes (see pages 116–17), which are sometimes to be found among limestone hills.

Poor water is clear, although maybe peat-stained (pages 116–17), and (because of the height) usually chilly and with not much visible in the way of plantlife. A lake need not be the same from one end to the other, of course. Loch Lomond, for example, is largely poor water, but its southern end is fed by richer streams and is muddy, with reedbeds and a good many aquatic plants.

The harsh mountain lake

The nutrient-poor water offers scant welcome to plant life, but the mountain lake is a harsh environment in other ways. Windless days are very rare, and frequent squalls whip up the waves to strip away what peat or soil lies within their reach; exposed shores are often simply bare rock, or, if not, heavy shingle, much the same as found on the seashore. There can also be seasonal variations in the water level, marked by zones of moss or slimes down the lakeshore. These zones do continue below the water, although hard to see in the dappled light.

Plants, if they are there at all, can, however, extend to surprising depths, because the clear water offers far less of a barrier to the light than the greenish water of a lowland lake.

Reservoirs

Living conditions tend to be even more extreme in a mountain reservoir. It is, after all, an artificial addition to the landscape, and may lie fully exposed in a wind gap or be so new that the slowly colonising plants have not yet put in much of an appearance. Its shores are for the most part steep and

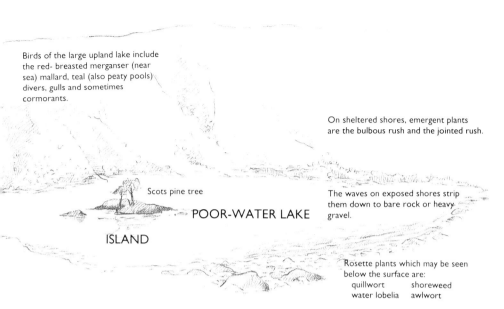

Birds of the large upland lake include the red- breasted merganser (near sea) mallard, teal (also peaty pools) divers, gulls and sometimes cormorants.

On sheltered shores, emergent plants are the bulbous rush and the jointed rush.

Scots pine tree

POOR-WATER LAKE

ISLAND

The waves on exposed shores strip them down to bare rock or heavy gravel.

Rosette plants which may be seen below the surface are:
quillwort   shoreweed
water lobelia   awlwort

continue steeply below the surface, restricting the opportunities for submerged plants. Fluctuations in water level are much greater than for a natural lake; and dry summers with the towns still thirsty can expose the stone walls drowned when the water backed up from the dam.

Troutbecks

On the maps, an upland stream is often a beck in northern England, a nant in Wales, and a burn in Scotland. It has many predictable features: a lot of bare rock in the form of slides and boulders, waterfalls with their deep plunge pools, and potholes in which the currents swirl at times of spate. Sudden rises are common after rainstorms and melting snow. Yet the trout do live and feed here. There are a considerable number of insects and other small animals clinging beneath the stones, and this larder is topped up during rainstorms, when the water cascading down the slopes dislodges soil invertebrates and carries them down.

Acid rain

This has become a familiar doomsday phrase, and it is a real problem. Coal, petrol,

oil and other 'fossil' fuels contain sulphur and nitrogen, which are set free as gaseous oxides when burnt. The rain dissolves these gases and becomes more acid (it is already naturally slightly acid from the carbon dioxide in the atmosphere). This acidity is not so much harmful by itself, but it loosens the chemical bindings of toxic elements and compounds in the soil. It releases aluminium, for example, which clogs the gills of fish. Acid rain causes birds to lay thin-shelled eggs, and kills trees when their roots take up the toxins instead of nutrients.

Conifers seem worse affected than broad-leaved trees. Their needles are shorter, the upper buds abort and the tree crown thins. But acid rain can also cause die-back of the crowns of deciduous trees; the first sign here may be discoloured leaves.

There are claims that the problem of acid water in streams and lakes is made worse by planting conifers in the hills in the first place, for they shed vast quantities of 'acid' needles each year. It is the acidity of the mat of dead needles which helps explain the dearth of other plants in conifer woodlands, although the dense shade may be the harsher feature.

THE WILDLIFE OF UPLAND WATERS

The cold and unproductive waters of the mountain tarn have their own special plant list. Some birds are also characteristic of these harsh regimes.

Cold, clear and empty of life?

Running from hard and often rather acid rocks, the water is poor in nutrients as well as being cold for much of the year. Only in sheltered bays is there likely to be any mud, and here may grow some of the aquatic plants familiar from lowland lakes – such as bulrush or even water lilies. Nevertheless, there are interesting plants to look for in the clear water of the main body of the lake, and they may also be washed up after storms. Quillwort, shoreweed and water lobelia all have bunched, rather narrow leaves. Shoreweed in fact has runners and can form a submerged turf running down to 4 metres or more below the surface. Yet it will flower only when the summer water level falls dramatically enough to expose it – critical behaviour in such circumstances. Water lobelia holds its lovely nodding lilac flowers half above water, but it is clearly at risk where waves are whipped up by the squalls; sheltered bays are a more likely site.

Birds of the upland waters

The streams and lakes of the hills are spared the continual disturbance which threatens any stretch of lowland water, but the benefit is more than outweighed by the harsh conditions. As a result, although in many ways the bird counts complement those of the lowlands, there are far fewer bird species seen here, and that is the case both in winter and in summer. Although several nesting species are found only in lowland habitats, none is restricted to an upland

Divers can be recognised from afar, by their posture, legs far back.

one. Even the divers, as typical of Highland tarns as any, will also nest in coastal inlets.

Four birds, however, are so often seen up here that they can be called characteristic of upland lakes and streams. Look out for dipper, grey wagtail, goosander and common sandpiper. The first two prefer running water when breeding, and, as we can see here, the dipper's relationship with its stream is a close one.

The grey wagtail is cousin to the familiar pied wagtail but (in spite of its name) with yellow underparts. It is often noticeably yellow when seen flycatching, but a keen eye is needed to spot it among the streamside boulders. Like the dipper, it nests in rock cracks and cavities.

The goosander likes wide open water, but it chooses to nest in holes, even tree holes if they are available.

Both dipper and wagtail bob, and so does the last of the four, the common sandpiper, which nests on softer ground alongside the water. Why birds bob is unexplained.

Habitat subtleties

Subtle ties exist between the species and even a bare and seemingly rather simple habitat. Divers are immediately recognisable birds: their legs are set far back, which makes them good swimmers both above and below the surface but ungainly on land. The red-throated diver is the commoner, with maybe 1500 pairs in the Scottish Highlands. Its nests are near the open water of a pool or loch, or sometimes on an island. Where pools are abundant there may be more territories held, but the birds do not feed in their home water and have to travel out. Their breeding success averages 0·45 offspring per pair.

The black-throated diver chooses lochs rather than small pools and is able to feed on its home territory. But there is an obvious disadvantage in this with such a poor habitat, because the breeding success is 0·2 chicks per pair, half that of the red-throated.

On the broad canvas (nature is rarely simple) numbers are maintained, because there is also some coastal nesting. But it is a nice example, nonetheless.

THE DIPPER IN THE HABITAT

It is often seen perched on boulders
in mid stream, spotting prey below
the surface.

The dipper's nest is in a cleft or hole
near the water, sometimes under a
waterfall, and protected by the spray.

The dipper's territory can stretch
along 3 km of stream.

The dipper remains in its territory all
year, a welcome sight in winter,
searching for water kept free of ice
by the fast flow.

To feed on aquatic insects, it walks
into and under the water, angling its
back so that the current holds it
down. Hence its need for fast streams.

WETLANDS

Though in prehistoric times an abundant habitat, nowadays only 2 300 hectares (6000 acres) of swamp, fen and carr remain, mostly in isolated patches.

The names

Wetlands tend naturally to dry out (see pages 116–17) and as a result usually consist of a mosaic of merging communities. Their evolution takes place in recognisable stages, beginning with swamp and ending with wet woodland or carr. Fen is a plashy middle stage between these, but the word fen is often used for all three together, so closely are they linked.

Swamp

The summer water level is the controlling factor. In the lowlands, shallow still water will in time be invaded by dense beds of reeds and other emergent plants to create a 'swamp'. The bottom lies below the summer water level, but in the still and airless conditions the dead vegetation does not decay but beds down to create peat. This gradually builds up to nudge the surface and, when it does, saw sedge or other tussock sedges can root to herald in the fen stage itself.

Fen and carr

Although the peat is largely undecayed and holds its nutrients locked up, the lowland water which bathes it is often quite rich (see pages 116–17) and, when enough peat has accumulated to be covered only in winter, tussock sedges are accompanied by more greedy plants and flowers such as purple loosestrife and yellow iris. Further accumulation sees further drying-out of the ground of this 'rich fen' and then its colonisation by bushes and low trees such as willows and alder, which can do well on damp soil. They grow to create a scrubby woodland or 'carr'. The carr stage is postponed and a kind of meadow created if the fen is grazed or mown

FENLAND

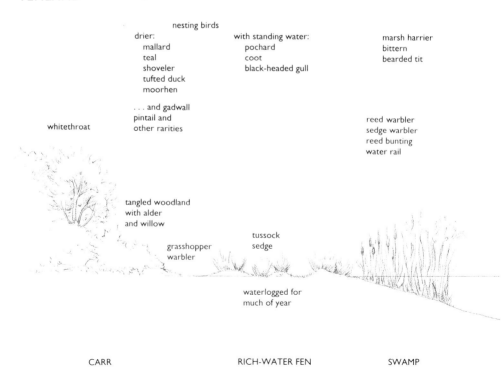

nesting birds

drier:
mallard
teal
shoveler
tufted duck
moorhen

. . . and gadwall
pintail and
other rarities

with standing water:
pochard
coot
black-headed gull

marsh harrier
bittern
bearded tit

whitethroat

reed warbler
sedge warbler
reed bunting
water rail

tangled woodland
with alder
and willow

grasshopper
warbler

tussock
sedge

waterlogged for
much of year

CARR

RICH-WATER FEN

SWAMP

for its very sweet hay. It is a meadow with a rather different suite of flowers from the usual hay meadow (see pages 68–9). If the carr evolves, however, the end point would most likely be tall woodland; and in some woods today alder is common, perhaps as a distant echo of this origin.

If the water is poor in nutrients and slightly acid, when the fen peat nudges the surface it can be colonised by bog moss, which then proliferates to create a raised bog (see pages 148–9). But if sedges flourish, they tend to exclude the bog moss to create a 'poor fen'. Horsetail is now characteristic, and bushes of bog myrtle grow. As the ground dries out, birches will invade, skirted by ferns.

Relic fenlands

Few large areas of fenland remain. Wicken Fen, near Cambridge, is perhaps the best-known example. It gives the impression of wet scrub divided by damp, mown tracks

and cut up by pools and patches and lines of open water. The scrub here is actually a stage beyond the first 'carr' and contains plenty of buckthorn and guelder rose and other woody shrubs which have invaded it.

The Norfolk Broads form another unique area, still containing undamaged areas of swamp, fen and carr. Unlike Wicken, the Broads are not direct relics of prehistoric wetland but were in origin flooded medieval peat diggings; but their interest is none the less for that. It must be stressed, however, that only the private or enclosed Broads forbidden to pleasure craft retain their rich natural diversity.

Marsh

A marsh is waterlogged ground with its summer level at or near the surface, but, unlike the peaty fenland, it has a mineral soil of silt or clay. Marshes often, however, form part of the wetland mosaic alongside swamps and fens.

true bulrush
reed
lesser reedmace
greater reedmace
 (known as
 'bulrush')

sedges
great spearwort
yellow iris
fen bedstraw
skullcap
water parsnip
water dock
water forget-me-not

Grazed fens have a bird count part way between true fen and wet grasslands or meadows with waders snipe; lapwing; redshank and curlew. Skylark, meadow pipit, yellow wagtail and even grey partridge might be seen sometimes.

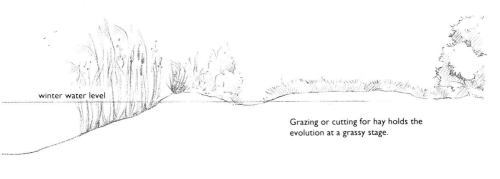

winter water level

Grazing or cutting for hay holds the evolution at a grassy stage.

SWAMP   PEAT BED   FEN MEADOW   CARR

WETLAND WILDLIFE

Even fragments of fenland can contain many typical fenland plants and animals. Migrant birds, for example, are attracted by small stands of reeds.

The fen meadow

The open fen can be an enchanting natural garden. Meadowsweet is one of the fragrant flowers, purple loosestrife another token of its floriferous nature. Yellow flag is striking; you might also look for pea flowers of various kinds, and inspect the paths carefully for they provide an important area of shorter grass where you might expect marsh orchids and scabious. Jostling among these as if drugged on nectar are hordes of hoverflies and lacewings and other insects.

The birds

It says something for human powers of observation that the reed bunting is twice as common as the moorhen (it has twice as many breeding pairs in Britain), but few would care to put a name to it. Fens, with their rather mixed complex structure, are good for amateur birdwatching. Each part, from the reeds with their duck trails to the carr woodland, has its own tally. Keep a lookout for movements of the reeds which run counter to the wind.

The marsh tit and its twin the willow tit illustrate the nice distinctions. The former searches out suitable cracks for its nests, which are as likely in healthy as in decaying trees, while the willow tit digs its own nest hole and so prefers softer, rotting timber. It is the latter which is more restricted to carr woodlands, where rotting trunks and branches are commoner.

Another example is provided by the reed warblers, which sling their mug-shaped nest around the reed stems, and the sedge warblers, which choose to nest low among the tangled plants of drier ground. While the former seeks insects in both reeds and bushes, the latter feeds nearer its nest site and lower down than the reed warbler. There is a hidden geography, a 'zonation' of the birds, a sharing-out of resources, just as there is in a wood (see pages 24–5).

Marsh and willot tit are twins, but can be recognised by their calls: the former a harsh pit-chee, the latter an eez-eez-eez-tchay.

The larder is usually scraped clean. The sedge warbler, a typical migrant, must double its body weight with fat, which will be burnt away by the time it reaches its goal south of the Sahara. Otherwise it will die on the journey.

Butterflies

Many moths are typical (many are linked with the willows growing in these wet places), but few butterflies are restricted to the fenland habitat. The large copper was, but is now extinct in Britain. The handsome swallowtail is really to be expected only in the Broads, although it may breed elsewhere (it was reintroduced to Wicken Fen but seems to have died out again), and occasional strays may reach Britain from the Continent during the summer. The females search out robust milk parsley, a rarish waterside relative of cow parsley.

This is not to say that there are few butterflies: on the contrary, there are at times plenty of brimstones, whose caterpillars feed on the buckthorn bushes, and the nettlebeds here and there support large numbers of peacocks and small tortoiseshells. There are usually many 'browns', identified by the eye-spot or spots on their wings, and most of them linked with grasses of various kinds. The moths, by the way, can attract many bats.

142

The Broads

Naturalists have always had a wonderful time here. It first became a popular area two or three centuries ago, when natural history was first becoming a hobby. There were then many bitterns booming, and the bird list included bearded tits and harriers, and the crystal-clear waters were full of fish. Well, they are still there, but are rarer, and the fish are only present in the few lagoons which remain unsullied by modern farming and boat traffic.

FENLAND FLOWERS

Orchids can be found in wetlands, especially where the water and soil are rather alkaline.

The dusky red marsh helleborine and the pink to rosy-purple southern marsh orchid are typical of fenland.

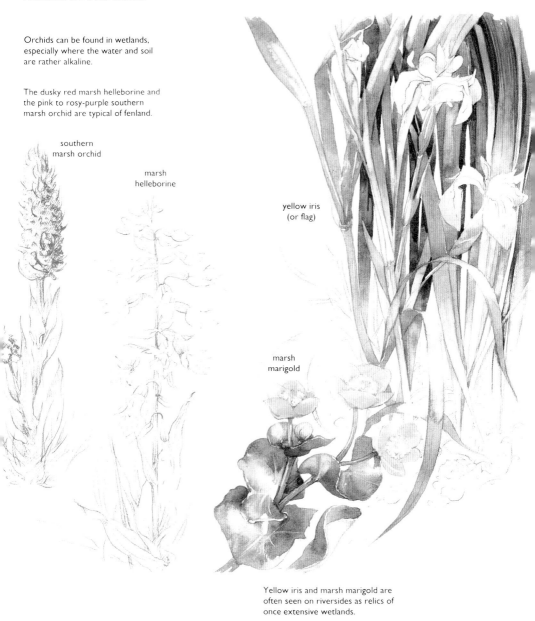

southern
marsh orchid

marsh
helleborine

yellow iris
(or flag)

marsh
marigold

Yellow iris and marsh marigold are often seen on riversides as relics of once extensive wetlands.

143

LEVELS AND WASHES

Wet lowland grasslands are now one of our endangered habitats: only 45,000 hectares (112,000 acres) remain. Those reclaimed from wetland have a distinct character.

The old wetlands

Probably a good eighth of the lowlands were once too waterlogged for dense woodlands to grow. Every river and stream was edged by ground flooded up behind chokes of fallen trunks and loose branches. Even the artificial dams created by beavers contributed: beavers were common creatures here well into historic times (Beverley, in Yorkshire, took its name from them, for example). Vast areas were also brackish, the tides reaching far inland, with the estuaries edged by vast saltmarshes. Added to this, many coastal areas have slowly sunk, to become vulnerable to flooding from both the sea and rivers. As a result, there were once extensive swamps and fens (see pages 140–1).

Five thousand years ago the climate became wetter, and not only did fens take on a new lease of life at that time, but in some wetland areas raised bogs also began to form (see pages 148–9). The consequence of this is that peaty ground is relatively common today.

Drainage

Trackways and artificial timber islands found deep in the peat of the Somerset Levels show that prehistoric tribes did settle the original wetland here. The Romans cut the first canals to carry boats across the Cambridgeshire fens, and these also drained the country around. The drained peat made good soil, and drainage continued. Estuary saltmarshes could also be 'reclaimed', as was Romney Marsh during the Dark Ages. The task required protective banks against the tides as well as drainage ditches, but the effort was well worthwhile as the new ground provided some of the best grazing in Britain (see pages 176–7).

The medieval abbeys were also farming magnates, and they continued the reclamation of vast areas of the peatlands and marshes of East Anglia and the Somerset Levels. In the 17th century, Dutch experts were called in to drain even more of East Anglia; many of today's wide 'drains' are their work.

But winter floods remained a feature of village life well into this century, and became less usual only as a result of modern 'river engineering'. This has also dried out the fields, and by doing so has paved the way for the great ploughing-up of the

LEVELS AND WASHES

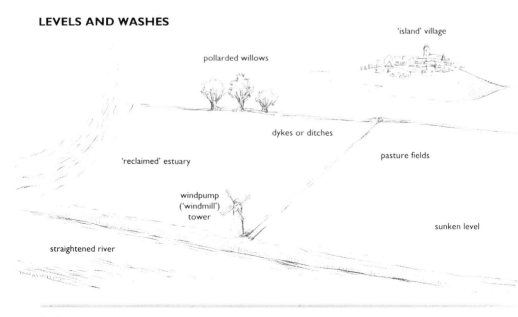

pollarded willows

'island' village

dykes or ditches

pasture fields

'reclaimed' estuary

windpump ('windmill') tower

sunken level

straightened river

traditional grazings alongside the streams and rivers. Old meadows are now very rare (see pages 68–9).

The landscape

Drainage creates an open prairie landscape latticed with ditches, a flat vista broken only by thin rows of pollarded willow and small corners of reedbed. The banks of the larger drainage canals stand high above the surrounding land, which shrank down as it dried out. There may be some peat diggings nearby. These are worth inspecting, for they can reveal the roots and branches of 'Noah's Forest': trees growing before changes in water level waterlogged their roots and killed them.

Wetland words

The word 'dike' (or 'dyke') can, confusingly, mean both a ditch and a bank. There are also local dialect words: in the Somerset Levels, for example, a rhyne is a middling-width drainage ditch. The word 'level' is descriptive of this flat, man-made scenery, as is the word 'wash' as used in the Ouse Washes of Cambridgeshire, which are regularly flooded. The Ouse Washes are a parcel of grassland, about 1 kilometre wide and 22 kilometres long, running between two drainage canals. This acts as an overflow to take winter floodwater and so prevent flooding of the rich fen soils alongside. And this to the delight of vast flocks of birds.

Levels as a wildlife habitat

Though the ditches are highly artificial, if they are not being regularly cleaned out they offer miniature examples of habitat types which have all but disappeared – examples of fenland and the bream zone of rivers (see pages 124–5) with shallow water and plenty of thick but rich mud.

The wildlife interest of an area such as the Somerset Levels is of two kinds. The first is in the aquatic life of these ditches, which can include species now rare elsewhere. The second is in the pasture fields. If they remain unploughed, they can be very floriferous, especially along the ditch sides. Despite the sameness of the landscape, convoluted sandwiches of peat and silt lie beneath it and the local farmers know that, while one field will carry six sheep an acre, the next will be able to take double that number. Plants and other natural life can also be very varied here.

The soft wet ground of these pastures also attracts many waders, both in summer and in winter.

The plant life of the levels can of course contain elements of riverside and fenland.

Damp grasslands provide food for more birds – both species and total numbers – in winter than in summer.

Wildfowl take the seeds, leaves and roots; the other birds take the (sometimes drowning) invertebrates.

peat diggings

Birds present can include: in summer snipe and redshank (which like it wet), curlew and lapwing (which are less choosy), and duck; and in winter wildfowl, inland waders, (e.g. snipe and lapwing) and shore waders.

Bramble and rosebay willowherb can indicate disturbed (drained) ground.

flood meadows

Derelict peat diggings become flooded and colonised by fenland plants.

reed bed

A BRIEF LOOK AT THE LEVELS

Scattered flocks of sheep and cattle belie the wildlife value of the levels, for if unploughed they may be virtually semi-natural in character with many plants and animals.

The peat regimes

Thick peat is often sandwiched with silt below the grass fields. It may be fenland peat, but climate changes in prehistoric times also encouraged raised bogs. 7000 years ago, for example, the Somerset Levels were a swamp of silty lagoons and reedbeds, but, by 5500 years ago, they were peaty fen. The climate became wetter, and around 3500 years ago extensive raised bogs were being created across the fen. It was much the same for the 'mosses' of Lancashire and other northern counties. It is worth having a look at the peat exposed in digging for twigs from the drier stages of this history.

Today's pasture

Out on the grazings themselves, the flowers will reflect how many beasts have grazed, for how long, and when in the year. You can expect to see the damper hollows marked out by rushes, and marsh bedstraw as one typical flower. Traditionally, hay was cut in some fields, the timing of which encouraged taller flowers: look for clumps of meadowsweet, wild angelica and common meadow rue.

Meadowsweet indicates rather damp soil, and grows along the ditches maybe, but there are no hard and fast lines to be drawn. On the wetter ground, yellow marsh marigold and yellow iris flag their presence from across the field. Ragged robin and meadow thistle flower later in the year. It is also worth looking out for marsh orchids, and the marsh fern is one for the enthusiast.

The lapwing's winter roosting repays observation. Small numbers congregate at dusk and feed in the gloom for half an hour. Before it becomes pitch dark they move to join other flocks of lapwings at night 'roosting' sites.

They may feed all night with a full moon: you then see them resting and preening at the roost sites in daytime.

THE TERRITORY HOLDING OF THE LAPWING

In courtship, the lapwing flies slowly up and then dives, ending with an upwards twist with quick wing beats and a peewit call.

The lapwing has the typical plover bill, short and with a swollen sensitive tip which helps it locate its surface food.

rounded wings when flying

The nest is a mere scrape. Not liking cover, the lapwing chooses grassland of a sparse, dull colour, eschewing bright green quick-growing lush grass.

When making its nest scrape, it guards its territory keenly, so spreading its numbers, but feeding at a common feeding ground. But when the eggs are hatched, it often feeds in its own territory.

Signs of disturbance

If the ditches are deepened and the peat does quickly dry out, the result may be rank growths which crowd out the flowers; although 'improving' the drainage in this way is usually followed by ploughing, which wipes them all away anyway. Bramble, hemp agrimony, and rosebay and great willowherbs are clues to disturbance of this kind.

The wildlife of the levels

Three nesting birds are characteristic of the levels, of southern Britain at least: curlew, redshank and snipe. To these can be added the lapwing: surveys coordinated by the British Trust for Ornithology show this to be a common breeder on the levels, although (unlike the snipe) it is also seen in spring on drier grasslands and even bare fields, on the chalk downs, for example. Keep an eye out also for the lively yellow wagtail, a summer visitor, with an endearing habit (which can be noticed from afar) of daintily flycatching around the feet of the grazing cattle.

The numbers of wintering waders can be colossal: the Somerset Levels regularly see 15,000 lapwings and 10,000 dunlins.

Insects can be present in bewildering variety. Most notable are the dragonflies,

together with rare water beetles and water bugs. The ditches harbour many fish, while the Somerset Levels are also a haven for the endangered otter.

The Ouse Washes

In addition to its other waders, this unique block of wet meadowland lying between two drainage canals (see pages 144–5) is famous for two breeding birds now lost from the drained fens alongside: the black-tailed godwit and the ruff (and there are now reports of black terns nesting). The Washes flood in winter, but, as the ground slopes, soggy grassland ranging through shallows to standing water a metre deep is offered. As a result, ducks are attracted as well as waders, and the numbers in the winter flocks are sometimes amazing, with thousands of wigeon and mallard; the migrant Bewick's and whooper swans come here, too.

The Washes also carry many wild flowers, and as a curiosity sea aster grows here 30 kilometres from the sea, a souvenir of the tidal floods that reached far inland in ancient times. The fish are also famous here: large pike indicate the presence of richly varied food chains and plenty of lesser fish – a staple part of their diet.

BOGLAND

Large areas of bog remain in the uplands, but are threatened. In the lowlands, of the original 35,000 hectares of raised bog, only 500 hectares are left.

The character of bogland

Bogs have a bad press. 'Bogged down' describes life at its most dismal. But they are not dirty nor smelly and, although some quake where they overlie small pools, few are really dangerous. Tales of people swallowed up by treacherous bogs owe their origin to the prehistoric habit of burying corpses, or making sacrifices in pools; these can be wonderfully preserved by the tanning acids in peaty boggy water. In the experts' eyes, bogs are a variety of mire – a general word for waterlogged ground which also includes fenlands.

Among the sombre mountain hues, the bright yellowish-green surface of the bog can be seen from afar. This is the colour of the living sphagnum moss (bog moss), but close inspection often shows that this is only part of a detailed mosaic which can include, as well as wet moss mounds, drier hummocks on which heather or even trees grow, although the latter remain checked or stunted by the waterlogging and die younger than they would on dry ground.

Bog moss

There are many types of sphagnum or 'bog' moss, difficult to tell apart, although some are tinted brown or orange or even red. What they have in common is a loose floppy growth which allows them to sponge up water, and even after a dry summer some water can usually be squeezed out. More than any other plant, they testify to our wet climate, thriving in rain which is naturally slightly acid (see pages 136–7).

Types of bog

With reliable daily drizzles more important than weekly downpours, bog mosses flourish. The slightly acid water quenches the activity of decay bacteria, and dead growth does not rot but accumulates as peat below the skin of living moss. This remains sodden with rain and with water soaked up from below, and peat formation can continue and even raise itself up above the level of the surrounding ground. In this way a raised bog is formed, and the bed of peat below its domed surface may become several metres

BOGLAND

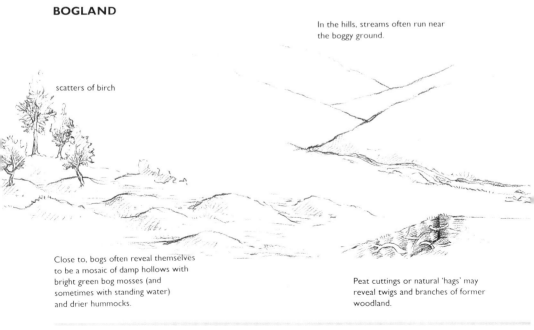

In the hills, streams often run near the boggy ground.

scatters of birch

Close to, bogs often reveal themselves to be a mosaic of damp hollows with bright green bog mosses (and sometimes with standing water) and drier hummocks.

Peat cuttings or natural 'hags' may reveal twigs and branches of former woodland.

thick. As it domes up, its surface becomes a mosaic of drier hummocks and damper hollows, though there are not many pools. In the latter, bog moss actively creates peat until it overtops existing hummocks, which then become the damp areas. Thus the pattern is slowly changing.

Raised bogs are often found in valley bottoms, perhaps built up over fen as they were in parts of the Somerset Levels, the East Anglian fens, and the Lancashire and Scottish lowlands. In wetter regions, flattish ground both in lowland and hills can, in much the same way, be covered by blanket bogs which lap around boulders and even climb slight slopes. These bogs are usually dimpled with open pools of water.

A third type, the valley bog, is found mainly in drier landscapes of East Anglia and the south, in parts of the New Forest (although also in the hills). Here a shallow gravel valley provides the acid conditions for a bog. Some unusual bogs in the south even have a rather alkaline peat.

A living history book

Bogs mark stages in the history of our climate. About 3000 years ago, for example, it was growing wetter and bogs proliferated. Trees dry out the ground and prevent bogs forming, but much of the wildwood had been cleared by then, and it seems that in some areas the bogs overwhelmed the few remaining trees by waterlogging their roots. The trunks and branches of 'bog oaks' and 'Noah's Forest' trees have been uncovered from time to time in peat diggings.

The death of bogs

Most of Britain's lowland bogs are now dead, and peat has ceased forming. Many boglands have been drained and 'reclaimed' for fields, and in some places the peat has been dug for fuel for several centuries. In the uplands, large areas remain, but there has been recent widespread drainage for conifer-planting. In the Pennines, pollution has also had an effect, the smoke from Victorian Manchester and Sheffield killing vast areas of bog moss; these dead bogs are often marked by spreads of opportunists, like cottongrass with its dancing white heads. A rather drier turn of climate over the last centuries may also have contributed to their death.

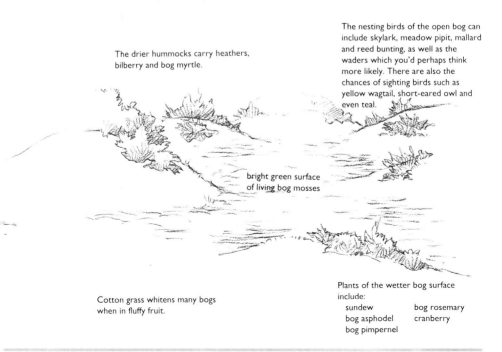

The drier hummocks carry heathers, bilberry and bog myrtle.

The nesting birds of the open bog can include skylark, meadow pipit, mallard and reed bunting, as well as the waders which you'd perhaps think more likely. There are also the chances of sighting birds such as yellow wagtail, short-eared owl and even teal.

bright green surface of living bog mosses

Cotton grass whitens many bogs when in fluffy fruit.

Plants of the wetter bog surface include:
sundew   bog rosemary
bog asphodel   cranberry
bog pimpernel

THE BIZARRE LIFE OF A BOG

Although they come low on the list of favourite beauty spots, bogs do provide examples of ecological survival strategies and some beautiful plants.

The mosaic

Although the water level may be high, the vivid green lawns and mounds of living bog moss usually lie between drier hummocks, a mosaic which changes slowly over time (see pages 148–9).

Poor in nutrients though it be, the peat can be home to 50 different plant species, a surprising number in such inhospitable surroundings. The open pools, moss lawns and drier hummocks each provide different living opportunities, and it is a reflection on the ability of evolution to achieve change that some surprising strategies have become adopted here. One thing to notice in this connection is that there are often plant 'societies' here and there – a patchy dominance of one species which has the competitive edge. The same kind of thing is seen, for example, with bluebells and other flowers in a wood.

Amazing strategies

Faced with a dearth of nitrate and phosphate, both protein-building stuff, some plants have adopted extreme strategies. Furthermore, the nutrient-poor bog in fact provides us with two of our most handsome wild flowers.

Out on the water of the pools grows bogbean, one of the easiest of all our wild plants to identify, with a three-part leaf like a giant clover and lovely pink and white flowers with fringed petals. This plant has bacteria in its roots to help 'fix' nitrogen in the air, though this is not too unusual (clovers and other pea-family plants have the same). Submerged below the surface grows bladderwort, a yellow-flowered plant with drifting stringy stems which have small floppy sacs along them: floppy, that is, until an unfortunate small aquatic insect brushes against trigger hairs, whereupon the sac expands, sucking in water and the insect with it. The insect is then digested for its nitrogen.

Plants of the moss lawn

Far better known as an 'insect-eater' is the sundew, which can splatter the green moss lawn with scarlet. There are, in fact, three species, with rather different-shaped leaves; in all three, however, the leaves are arranged in a flat rosette on the moss, and armed with sticky hairs which gleam like drops of dew and so attract small insects. With the hapless animal stuck fast, the hairs then fold around it and exude digestive juices.

Other notable plants of the moss lawn include cranberry, its stems threading an almost hidden path, the famous red berries autumn-ripe ready for the turkey. Here also grow bog rosemary (its leaves resemble the kitchen herb) and bog asphodel. This last is again a very handsome plant, with green leaves overlapping in iris-like fashion. It has yellow flowers, but later in the year almost the entire plant, fruit capsule included, turns bright orange.

Insect life

Bog pools are clearly haunts of water beetles (look for whirligigs, for example) and water bugs (look for pond skaters energetically rowing across the surface). With scant shell salts, there are few or no water snails or other molluscs; nor many leeches. There seems less life in general: caddis larvae, protected in their cases of fine gravel or twig, but few mayflies or stoneflies which are usually expected in clean water. Midge larvae there may be, and their adults bite strongly to underline the fact. The scant oxygen supply in the still, peaty water may be a limiting factor, for some beetle and hoverfly larvae in fact tap a supply of oxygen from the roots of the plants.

Eight species of dragonfly, however, are linked with boglands (and the counts on southerly bogs can be very high). Being insatiable predators, both when nymph and when adult, their presence suggests that perhaps rainstorms regularly wash insects into the pools from the drier slopes roundabout. What butterflies there are are linked with the drier hummocks: the silver-studded blue or the large heath (a northern species) are typical.

THE SURFACE OF A LIVING BOG

The delicate bog surface is worth inspecting – but carefully, as it is slow to repair the damage of even light footsteps.

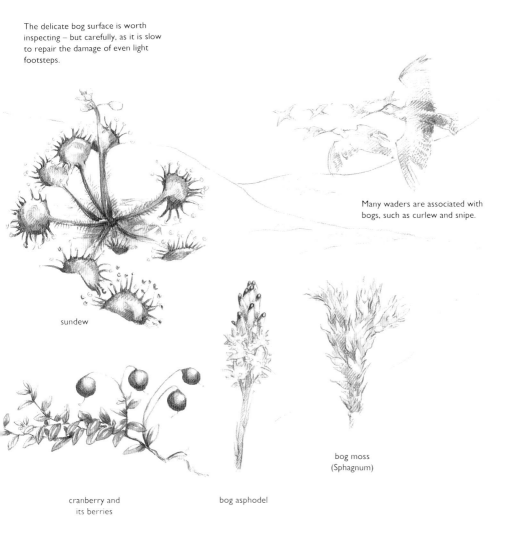

Many waders are associated with bogs, such as curlew and snipe.

sundew

bog moss (Sphagnum)

cranberry and its berries

bog asphodel

Birds

Virgin bogland can attract waders, the soft ground being ideal for their probing bills (especially important for their young, which have to feed themselves as soon as they hatch). Curlew, snipe and lapwing are as typical as any, but the list includes greenshank among others. The drier parts of the mosaic attract meadow pipits and reed bunting (you will hear the cuckoo here). In the northern hills, grouse are firmly part of the picture (see pages 158–9).

The bird count does, however, fall as soon as there is much disturbance, if the area is being drained in preparation for conifer-planting, for example; but skylark, meadow pipit, reed bunting and mallard are all adaptable and may stay on for a few years. Opportunistic birds such as gulls also nest, although perhaps not so frequently as they did in the past.

In winter, the high moorland bogs are all but deserted by birds, except for the red and black grouse.

151

HEATHLAND

Britain has Europe's finest heathland, but it is now a threatened habitat; 60,000 hectares (150,000 acres) remain, only a fraction of what there once was.

Recognising heathland

Heathland is largely restricted to the lowlands south of a line from the Severn to the Wash. It is characterised by sandy or gravel soils and heather, a woody, short-lived undershrub which in late summer unmistakably paints the scenery purple. There is usually quite a bit of golden-flowered gorse, another undershrub, especially at the edges, and in some southerly areas dwarf gorse also mingles with the heather tussocks. But birch and even pine trees readily seed themselves in, followed by oak and hawthorn and others. Left to itself, a heath would in fact gradually become woodland.

Heathland soil

The soil is typically sandy or with a lot of gravel, and is acid and quick-draining; both heather and gorse have leaves and other features suiting them to drought regimes.

The profile of the soil revealed along a sunken lane often shows odd features. Below the surface litter it is bleached an ashy grey, though it may contain quite a bit of dark undecayed peat. Below this bleached band is a hard, concrete-like rusty-coloured layer which often protrudes as a shallow shelf from the exposed face. This consists of iron-containing salts leached from the soil above, and it can be virtually impenetrable to roots. It may also block drainage and allow bogs to form in the hollows where water collects.

The history of heathland

Today's heathland was once tree-covered, but the prehistoric attack by man which elsewhere led to the creation of open downland, for example, here encouraged heathers because of the acid soil. Heathlands are still good places to find prehistoric burial mounds. Its tree cover removed, this soil became leached to make it even more acid. It has remained open ever since, usually because it offered rough grazing as part of the local commons (see pages 76–7). Many warrens were sited on heathlands.

HEATHLAND

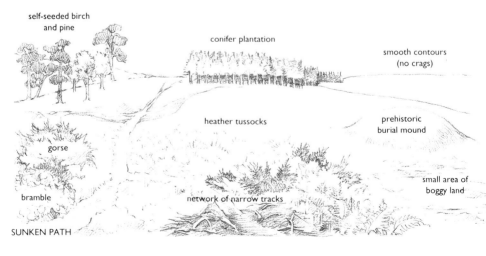

self-seeded birch and pine

conifer plantation

smooth contours (no crags)

heather tussocks

prehistoric burial mound

gorse

small area of boggy land

bramble

network of narrow tracks

SUNKEN PATH

Western heaths also have dwarf gorse growing amongst the heather.

Burned areas are often colonised by bracken.

Grazing itself was not always enough to keep the heath open, and it seems that it was customary to set it alight from time to time. The flash fires cleared the invasive scrub and woody heather tussocks, but left the soil only slightly scorched, so that after a few years sweet young heather and grass would again grow for the livestock.

Heathland destroyed

Large areas of heathland existed in Surrey, Hampshire and Dorset, for example, but over three-quarters of the heathlands on the map in 1800 (when they were at their most widespread) have now been lost. There have been many reasons. Much has been swallowed up by farming; much has been planted with conifers or dug for sand or gravel. Roads and development have eaten away large areas. In recent decades, heathland has been damaged by fires started by accident or by vandals. If deeply scorched, the soil can be completely sterilised for 20 years or more.

From a wildlife point of view, the loss is compounded because the remaining fragments of heathland are often small and many kilometres away from each other, restricting contact between breeding communities, which can weaken them.

Local heaths

Although the heathland stronghold is in the three counties mentioned above, heathlands are found elsewhere in the British Isles. The rocky west coasts often carry something very similar, and the Lizard peninsula in Cornwall has a unique type of heath growing on the soil derived from its serpentine rock.

There were extensive heaths growing on pockets of sandy soil overlying the chalk in the Breckland area of Norfolk. This is, in fact, a botanically bizarre area. The extremely cold winters with their biting winds and hot summers encourage plants not otherwise found in Britain, while the topography of the land creates a mosaic of these acid-soil patches mixed with chalky areas, giving for the botanist some surprising plant neighbours. Newmarket Heath was another famous 'chalk heath' of a similar kind. Both have largely been destroyed by farming and coniferisation.

Heathland flowers to look for include:
ling	heath milkwort
bell heather	harebel
crossleaved heath	lousewort
(in wetter areas)	(in wetter areas)
heath spotted orchid	tormentil
heath bedstraw	wood sage

Some classic heathland breeding birds are now sadly rare:
Dartford warbler
nightjar
tree pipit (if there are trees for song posts)
stonechat
woodlark
hobby

profile of the side of a
SUNKEN PATH

heather

peat

ridge of pan

Look here for the holes of mining bees and wasps.

LISTING HEATHLAND

Rather more clearly than other habitats, heathlands illustrate a basic ecological rule: the larger the area, the greater the diversity of species to be found.

In among the heather

It is sometimes an eye-opener to list how many different plant species there are in a small area, even a square metre, and especially in what at first sight looks a 'poor' habitat. Lay sprigs alongside each other to help the identification of similar plants. The three heathers shown in most field guides pick out slightly different soil: cross-leaved heath prefers damper conditions than common heather (ling) and bell heather (which might mark out the drier areas). But there are also local cousins to be found on south-west heathlands: Dorset heath, for example.

The count should start from the ground up. On heathland, this can be attractively patterned with lichens, which make a miniature garden with clumps of bright green moss. There is often a finely stalked grass to be seen, silvery hair grass, one of our most attractive wild grasses.

Among the flowers, look out for yellow tormentil and trailing bedstraw. The characteristic orchid is heath spotted orchid, and in damper patches some of the bogland species may be found (see pages 150–1).

Bracken is invasive. It can get hold where the ground has been damaged by severe fire or trampling, and it tends to spread ever outwards, which in time creates a ring of young growth around an older, sparser core. This may be clearer on the flat open heath than, say, on hillside or in woodland. Bracken swamps other growth; but which plants arrive back in the core, where its competitive edge is duller?

Spiders

About 250 invertebrate species are linked with heather, and spiders are worth studying in this habitat, especially the way they lessen competition with each other. Various species appear at different stages of heather and gorse growth, from young to full-blown; and as both these plants are evergreen, the spiders can share out much more of the year than is normal with insects, for example, each busy for its own span. This is in addition to obvious distinctions between those of the litter, those of the meshed twigs, the ground-hunting spiders etc. Look here for crab spiders, camouflaged pink or maybe yellow among the heather flowers. Unlike other spiders, they can seem difficult to annoy; perhaps this is when they are comatose after a meal, when other species tend to hide away?

Insects

As well as the heather, the heavily scented gorse flowers are visited by bees and other insects. Even the seed pods are full of minute weevils, while the soil below is a good bed for ants. A clue to the general diversity is the fact that about half our dragonfly species have a link with heathland, breeding in the boggy pools but (in the case of the strong-flying hawkers) flying far out across the heather. One or other are on the wing for most of the summer. Equally colourful, green tiger beetles run actively across the deer and other tracks which crisscross the heather carpet. Few butterflies have a strong tie, but look out for the grayling: its caterpillar feeds on the grasses which may be localised along tracks through the heather. On hot days especially, it demonstrates how these insects control their temperature with distinctive postures. The silver-studded blue is also characteristic of some heathlands, and the small heath and small copper are common here, as they are in other habitats. Look also for the green hairstreak. Typical moths are the fox and emperor, with gaudy caterpillars.

Birdlife and other vertebrates

The hobby and nightjar, both now rare, are characteristic, and buzzards may patrol overhead. The Dartford warbler nests in the gorse. It is our only resident warbler, but still secretive when not breeding. Resident stonechats and migrant whinchats are also typical (whin is an alternative name for gorse), and there is an interesting titbit of ecology here. Whinchats, summer visitors, rear far fewer young. Populations of the

HEATHLAND INSECTS

A camouflaged crab spider waits hidden amongst the heather flowers for a honey bee to land within reach.

hawker dragonfly

burrows of mining bees and wasps

lizard

Part of the eleborate courtship of the grayling: when he bows, she touches him with her antennae.

If its body temperature is too low, the grayling leans sideways to expose its wings to the sun – reducing its shadow also helps hide it.

In hot weather, the grayling stands head to the sun, on tip toe.

resident stonechats fluctuate hugely and can tumble as a result of a harsh winter, but their higher breeding rate allows them to make up the loss.

The palmate newt, which likes pools which are rather acid (and hence is also found on northern mountains), is the most common amphibian of heathland; even so, it is a rare sighting. But lizard, slow worm and adder are common enough and most likely to be noticed in spring, just out of hibernation and still torpid.

MOORLAND

Upland moorland, which includes heather grouse moors, is our largest remaining semi-natural habitat, totalling 1·7 million hectares (4·2 million acres).

The definition of moorland

Moorland is a cousin to heathland (see pages 152–3) but found above 300 metres (1000 feet) in hard-rock landscapes, so (unlike in heathland) bare outcrops are a common feature. Its display of purple heather can be even more spectacular, but gorse is absent because of the harsh exposure, and some moors are dominated by other undershrubs such as cowberry and bilberry (originally a relic of coniferous forest); and grass moors are common. A large area of moorland is often a mosaic of different kinds. There is, or has been, much bogland; unlike heathland, moors are usually bedded in peat, which can be several metres thick. A moor is usually actively grazed by sheep or grouse, and this traditional use can make it a semi-natural community – not quite natural, but so long established that it is the next best thing to true wilderness.

The story of moorland

Today's moorland rather resembles the arctic tundra, and some far-northern moorlands may have been in this state since the Ice Age, but generally, even on the Pennines, it was once tree-covered. The occasional alder or rowan tree growing by a stream – and today's conifer plantations – show trees to be its natural cover. The ground was slowly cleared in prehistoric times, and ancient boundary walls and other features can often be found. It has been kept open by grazing, maltreatment and changes in climate; the wetter regimes which set in in prehistoric times resulted in extensive boglands, which created the beds of peat and waterlogged and killed any remaining trees.

In England, open-commons grazing was usual until around two centuries ago, when quite a bit, even in remote areas, was enclosed into fields. Dartmoor was not fielded, and Scotland had a rather different clan-grazing system, but stone walls are nonetheless a frequent part of the moorland landscape.

MOORLAND

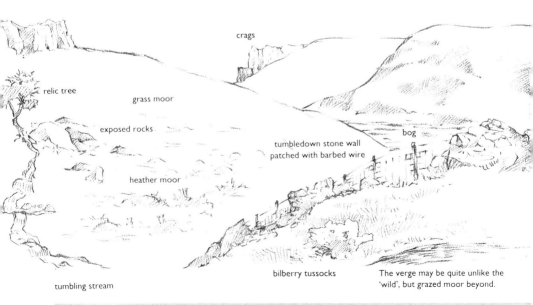

crags

relic tree

grass moor

exposed rocks

bog

tumbledown stone wall
patched with barbed wire

heather moor

bilberry tussocks

The verge may be quite unlike the 'wild', but grazed moor beyond.

tumbling stream

The grouse moors

In the 19th century, large areas of northern moorland were given over to rearing grouse for sport. This has entailed not only ruthless persecution of all birds of prey, but also the regular burning of patches of heather – swaling or muirburn – to create a mosaic of old heather tussocks for shelter and young shoots for grazing. It is odd that, here, birds take the place of four-legged beasts in determining the scenery.

Modern threats

Moorland is threatened in almost as many ways as heathland. Blankets of conifer plantations have clearly changed the landscape, replacing what now seems 'natural' moor. Much bogland has been, and is still being, drained as part of these changes. Changes in the local water regime often dry out other areas, and the peat may be washed away to form 'hags' or deep scars down to the bedrock. These are now a familiar part of the moorland scene, and they often expose the twigs and branches of trees once growing here.

The habitat-reckoning

Uncontrolled or overstocked grazing by sheep, cattle or red deer tends to destroy the heather, grass taking its place; and sometimes there is little else but grasses and sedges. Mat grass can form huge patches, with cottongrass and deer grass (which are in fact sedges) in the wetter areas. Bilberry is typical of more lightly grazed areas. The roadside often provides an insight into how unnatural this seemingly 'natural' wilderness is. It can carry plants, even lowland plants, remarkably different from those over the wall.

Here as elsewhere, grazing destroys the variety of wild flowers. Were it not for sheep (and deer in some areas) many of our high moorlands might be as flowery as the famous high pastures of the Alps. But you will often find that the flowers linger as relics on rock faces out of easy reach (see pages 162–3). One common sight is a tree – often a mountain ash or rowan – rooted into cracks or rock by a stream. Its vulnerable sapling survived here when chance washed its berry into a crack.

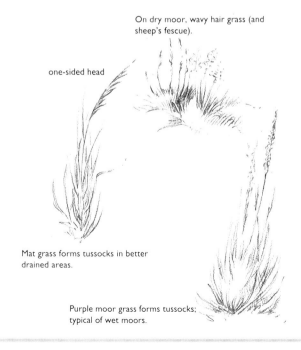

On dry moor, wavy hair grass (and sheep's fescue).

one-sided head

Mat grass forms tussocks in better drained areas.

Purple moor grass forms tussocks; typical of wet moors.

Plants of the northern moors not found on heaths include
bearberry
cloudberry
crowberry
harestail

Three widely met nesting birds are:
golden plover
meadow pipit
wheatear

MOORLAND LIFE

*Dour and bitter though the landscape may be,
moorlands have intricate wildlife communities
and there are also some rather spectacular
individual species.*

Unexpected plant features
It seems odd that the heather's narrow but
thick-skinned leaves are a typical adaptation for drought, yet the plant is typical of
the rainswept moors on the hills. The cold at
these heights, however, inhibits the intake
of water (to say nothing of the days of actual
frozen ground). So thick-skinned leaves, the
reduction of size of the leaf pores to slow
down water loss, and the reduction of the
actual area of leaf surface itself are also
typical of other moorland undershrubs,
such as bilberry and cowberry. Bilberry
grows larger leaves in sheltered places.

Rushes are physically even odder. They
have a stem with drought-resistant character (thin, round), but the spongy tissue
within is typical of aquatic plants which
grow with their roots in water.

A lack of worms
Although there are plenty of slugs (the large
black slug is familiar), lack of salts in the soil
discourages snails. The cold and acid
flavour of the soil inhibits earthworms and
decay, and so there is poor recycling of
nutrients. Nitrate must be gained by other
means, and heather and bilberry are among
those plants that strike up a relationship (a
mycorrhiza) with a soil fungus (see pages
32–3). The sundew and others of the boggy
ground stage direct attacks (see pages
150–1). There are some parasitic plants to
be seen: dodder and the attractive lousewort, which feed from the roots of others.

Butterflies and a splendid moth
One of our most gorgeous moths, the day-
flying emperor moth, is a denizen of moorland. Animals in such harsh habitats are
akin to pioneers: they lay claim to areas that
fewer species care to tackle, but they are at
risk if circumstances change slightly. The
association of a species with a forbidding
habitat can, however, be a tight one. Consider the mountain ringlet butterfly, which

is found only above 550 metres (1800 feet)
in the Lake District, and above 450 metres
(1500 feet) in the Grampians. It flies only in
sunshine, dropping to the ground immediately when a cloud hides the sun. Its nearest
other colonies are in the Alps. Like many
mountain wild flowers, it survives only
where open, early post-glacial conditions
remain, and it forsook lower ground when
this became invaded and shaded by forest.

Other insect life
A noise like a free-wheeling bicycle is the
common green grasshopper, a lowland
species but found further north and higher
up than other grasshoppers. Like many
insects, it reaches the northern edge of its
geographical range in Britain. Ants can still
be quite common, although overlooked:
their nests are usually underground, and
more widely spaced than on heathland.
Look for spiders, too.

Vertebrates
Adders return each day to favourite basking
spots, and lizards and frogs may be found at
surprisingly high altitudes. If a frog is eaten
by a bird, the latter discards the distasteful
eggs, which swell in the rain. The swollen
mass mystified the ancients, who called it
'star slime'. Frog tadpoles may take more
than one summer to mature. Of the newts,
the palmate is most likely.

The dawn call of the cuckoo can come as a surprise. Here it seeks the nests of meadow pipits, our commonest moorland birds – and sometimes successfully: one survey showed that one in five pipit nests held a cuckoo egg. Dawn is a good time for birdwatching up here: the lack of cover means that many are reclusive in daytime. Waders nest on the softer ground of boggy areas. It has long been proved that coniferisation, even when patchy, puts these birds off; they do not like an edge anywhere near them, and so a plantation boundary sterilises a large area of adjacent moorland. It is a general rule that birds of open moorland will not nest if their habitat becomes even slightly covered, although forest birds, which include many songbirds, will continue to nest when only thin scrub is available.

Buzzards can be fairly common and merlins may hunt, not so much in preference to the lowlands but because it is only here that they can live undisturbed. Other birds fly low, close to the scant cover.

The blue hare is perhaps the most typical mammal, in the sense that other species such as voles and foxes are common but are just as likely in other places, while this hare is really restricted to these upland habitats. Stoats are also common up here, and their regular runs can be identified from their droppings and the feral goat has lived wild for hundreds of years in Wales, the Cheviots and the Lake District.

THE RED GROUSE IN ITS HABITAT

A laughing 'go-beck' call is usually heard before the birds themselves are seen.

The youngsters sun themselves in sunny clearings amongst the tussocks.

The grouse uses old heather tussocks for cover, and grazes on the young green shoots.

The nest is a mere scrape.

To a large extent, the grouse (in the absence of birds of prey) controls its numbers itself. The dominant male birds keep others off their territories. They must seek poorer feeding and cover elsewhere, and fewer survive.

In a snowstorm, the birds crouch head into the wind and avoid burial by constantly treading the snow so that they are surrounded by a melt patch. They feed by burrowing into the snow blanket.

MOUNTAINS

THE MOUNTAIN TOP

on the summit patchy greyish 'heath' of woolly-hair' moss

Because of the constant wind, tussock plants may develop as a wave-like mat.

block scree

Juniper bushes hug the ground.

grassy soil showing soil creep

Britain has 600,000 hectares (1·5 million acres) above 600 metres (2000 feet) and 40,000 hectares (100,000 acres) above 900 metres (3000 feet), mainly in Scotland.

The word mountain

By definition a mountain is a mass of high ground, a hill a lower one, although the Scots call their mountains 'hills'. The 'mountain top' often continues upward from moorland, and there may be no very clear division. We have to be wary of trying to impose our own boundaries here, as anywhere else. Geologically, however, mountains are rock stubs not yet eroded away, and so they are likely to have bare rock showing and loose, recently weathered rock pieces. What is also implied in the word is a true wilderness completely free from man's influence, but even in Scotland this is likely only above 900 metres. Elsewhere, sheep and management can be a major influence.

Height

Average temperatures drop as we go higher (and further north, of course). What is crucial is the soil temperature, which controls the rate at which the plant can take up water and hence controls growth. Hill farmers reckon that the length of the grazing season decreases by five or six days for every 30 metres' increase in altitude. Grass stops growing at around 6 C (42 F). Broad-leaved trees do not grow unless the average temperature exceeds 10 C (50 F) for at least two months. But temperature can always fluctuate markedly on these windy exposed heights. Mountain daylight is often obscured by mist and rainstorms (Ben Nevis, like other mountains, creates its own weather, and has only 15 clear days a year).

On the other hand, when the sun does shine from a clear sky, it can be intense up here. Enough for meadows of flowers, but they are largely destroyed by the intensive grazing of sheep and, in Scotland, deer.

The flowers of the mountain have for long been an enthusiast's hobby, and the reason they are so rare is not only due to sheep, but also partly because of the habits of Victorian collectors! Among the loveliest are mountain pansy, moss campion, purple saxifrage, mountain avens, Snowdon lily and spring gentian. The type of rock is as crucial here as anywhere, more so as the soil is usually extremely skimpy.

A salt-rich flush (spring) may be marked by a patch of wild flowers (if they escape grazing).

Physical features

Sometimes the rock faces are as cleanly cut as when first sculptured by ice sheets of glacial times. Freezing and thaws, however, shatter the skin of exposed rock, and the summit is likely to be littered with rock fragments while at the foot of rock faces chutes of broken pieces of every size form a skirt or scree. This may already be invaded by grass and other plants. But mountains differ not only in their rock type (which will influence the plants growing) but also in configuration and bulk. The Cairngorm summits, which seem to be individual mountain tops from the valley below, are in fact the edge of a plateau some 80 square kilometres in area, the largest extent of high ground in Britain and often keeping a patch or two of snow all year long. Ingleborough in Yorkshire has a hard hat of acid grit sandstone protecting the limestone rock which forms the bulk below; two very different rock types here.

Climate influences

High wind accelerates water loss from leaves, and so can kill them and the twigs that carry them. Branches therefore tend to grow facing away from the prevailing wind, and in this way the wind prunes any shrubs and trees that may have rooted. On the mountain slopes, shrubby juniper and birch hug the ground where they grow. Temperature and exposure to wind create a tree line, but the altitude of this can vary from place to place. The western Scottish Highlands, for example, are exposed to the ocean gales and, although this oceanic influence makes it relatively mild, trees do not grow higher than 60 metres up the slopes. But on the western side of the Cairngorms, where the climate is in fact much more severe and where the snow lies late on the ground well into the summer, the tree line is at 550 metres.

Arctic-alpine conditions

These are conditions found at sea level in the Arctic and several thousand metres up in the Alps. But arctic-alpine plants can also be found on British mountains, marooned here when the Ice Age ended and the lowlands became forested and too shaded for them. Some species have an unexpected distribution as a result. Sea pinks and roseroot are found both on Scottish summits and on the coast, but not between the two. The reason is that both these areas have remained open, while trees invaded the swathe between.

Some wildlife is clearly well adapted to the extreme conditions. Ptarmigan and dotterel are two typical mountain birds adapted to keeping themselves alive at the summit, while the moorland waders will nudge up as far as conditions allow. But some other mountain birds are here not so much from first choice, but because this is their last retreat and refuge after centuries of persecution. The golden eagle, red kite and raven are examples. The kite was once so common that it was a familiar scavenger on the streets of medieval London; today it nests only in very remotest areas of the Welsh hills.

MOUNTAIN LIFE

Any high mountain is worth the climb, not only for typical plants and animals that you expect to see, but also for the chance of coming across the unexpected.

The mountain top

Low, stunted and wind-brushed into a drunken slant, any vegetation is surely going to be denser in the shelter of a rocky outcrop. But have a look at the 'bare' ground; here you can expect to see lichens, both ground-hugging and shrubby, perhaps extensive greyish mats of 'woolly hair moss' or *Racomitrium*, making a kind of miniature heathland. It is worth looking at any grass that may be growing up here: it may well be viviparous. Rather than attempting to pollinate by loosing its pollen into the wind (its normal method), it buds off miniature rooted plants which after a while grow independently. Another strategy is that some plants, such as crowberry, which are normally single-sex become bisexual – which also makes good sense in the usual short brisk flowering season up here.

The flowers of the rock faces

It is a real delight to come across a natural rock garden, a cascade of flowers down a sheltered rock face. If they do grow (and they can also be found far below the summit alongside rocky streamsides), it is not simply because they are sheltered from the weather, but mainly because they are safe from the sheep here. Without intensive sheep and (in Scotland) deer grazing, our mountains might be as flowery as the high slopes of the Alps.

What plants you see depends on the rock, of course, and there is likely to be a greater variety on basic (limy) than on acid rock. Mountain avens is an indicator of limestone or other basic rocks; it was probably widespread after the retreat of the ice, but has since become confined to the heights. The mossy cushions of moss campion are easy to recognise.

The plants at one and the same site may include both arctic-alpines from the end of the Ice Age and lowland or even woodland plants. These last colonised the heights when the slopes below were covered with scrub or trees, which have since been destroyed by grazing and climate changes.

Another plant worth looking for is roseroot, quite distinctive in appearance and unusual (but not unique) in being found both high on mountains and on sea cliffs (see pages 160–1). It is well adapted to both these extremes, for its fleshy cactus-like leaves protect it against damaging water loss; both cold and salt reduce the water uptake of a plant.

The plants of the scree slope

Here ferns come in. It is already beginning to be much more welcoming, not only in the nooks of the rocky rubble but also where the snow can lie late. Dry snow provides excellent insulation against cold, which is why the first flowers may be seen pushing their way through late-lying patches (this is quite usual in the high Alps).

Mountain birds

There are those that are adapted to the conditions. The ptarmigan is a bird of rocky ground, hidden by its summer coat of marvellously mottled plumage – it is often noticed as a 'moving boulder'. It eats plant shoots. Though having a white winter coat for snow camouflage, it tends to descend lower when its food (which can include the leaves and shoots of bilberry and heather) is deeply snow-covered. The summering dotterel gets by on skimpy insects, although it can be so indifferent to man that it can arrive unexpectedly to finish the crumbs of a picnic. In summer, moorland waders may be seen quite high. Look also for those birds here as refuges: the golden eagle soaring on updraughts and the raven tumbling in acrobatic play. But there are no examples of incomers colonising the mountains as a new habitat, in the way that the collared dove is colonising the lowlands.

Deer

'Deer forest' of open moorland and mountain is a traditional land use in the Scottish Highlands. There is a regular cull of the animals for sport; a tricky sport, too, for the

MOUNTAIN BIRDS AND PLANTS

crag

raven acrobatics

golden eagle

The late snow patches trap insects wafted up from warmer slopes by rising air: a useful larder for the birds.

The ptarmigan in summer; in winter it is white except for black tail feathers and face patch (on the cock bird).

Patches of mountain avens set with flowers; note the distinctive leaves.

The leaves of moss campion form cushions on which the solitary flowers are scattered.

slightest movement on a distant skyline will alert them. Wild red deer are also found in one or two parts of the Lake District and the Pennines, Exmoor, and also in patches in the south where they are parkland or woodland animals. That they are now so firmly linked with the open moorland and mountain is partly a result of the clearance of the Scottish pine forests; they are by

origin and nature woodland animals, although going high in summer does gain them some relief from the terrible biting blackfly of Scotland.

We can also mention here the herd of semi-wild reindeer, introduced from Lapland some 40 years ago and now to be seen on the slopes of the Cairngorms. They were native to Britain until the Middle Ages.

QUARRIES, MINES AND CAVES

Natural caves are not very common in the British countryside, but there are many abandoned mines and quarries which can offer cave-like habitat features.

Natural caves

Although sea caves are plentiful on rocky western coasts, caves inland are most often found in limestone countryside – in the areas of the Yorkshire Dales, the Pennine White Peak, South Wales, the Mendips and South Devon. Here rain, which is always slightly acid, seeps down through numerous cracks in the fissured rock, dissolving and enlarging them into cavern systems. Much of this work was done by the floods of water created when the ice sheets melted and the soil unfroze at the end of the cold periods of the recent Ice Age.

Caves may open directly to a rocky bluff or cliff, and some gorges such as the Cheddar Gorge are in fact collapsed caverns. But some have been exposed only by quarrying.

Some caves are repositories of the fossil bones of rhinoceros, sabre-toothed tiger and other extinct animals which fell into them through gaps which have since closed. A few even have relics of prehistoric man, who used them for shelter.

Mines

Mining is an industry with very old roots. The first mines in Britain were those dug in chalklands in prehistoric times to gain flint for toolmaking. There must have been many mines dug for metal ores in Roman and medieval days, but the original tunnels are lost among later workings. Tin and copper were sought in the hard-rock countryside of Cornwall and the Lake District, for example, and lead (and silver) could also be gained from the limestone of the Mendips, the Pennines and Wales. In the prime mining areas, many old workings remain as hollows in the ground or as adits (tunnels into the hillside) which, although boarded up for safety, offer a sanctuary for some animal life.

Mine dumps

For plants, mine dumps can offer some useful chemical flavours, and some dumps

THE CAVE

OUTSIDE THE CAVE　　　　CAVE MOUTH

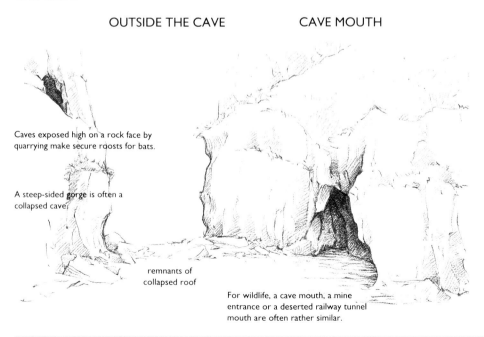

Caves exposed high on a rock face by quarrying make secure roosts for bats.

A steep-sided gorge is often a collapsed cave.

remnants of collapsed roof

For wildlife, a cave mouth, a mine entrance or a deserted railway tunnel mouth are often rather similar.

are famous for their displays of wild orchids. The ore was usually won by digging along a vein and hauling the pieces back to the surface, where they were sorted and the ore-rich fragments kept for further treatment. The rest were dumped, the dump perhaps being used also for the waste from the further treatment.

Perpetual dark

In the rest of Europe, America and elsewhere, breeding populations of animals have become trapped in caves, and in the course of thousands or hundreds of thousands of years have evolved pale and virtually blind forms. Examples include crayfish, fish and salamanders. There have been reports of 'bleached' trout in underground rivers in British caves.

The cave mouth

The cave mouth is the more welcoming, both for animals and for some plantlife. It will have zones of steadily reducing light, and some plants may be found colonising what seems to our eyes a very poor gloom even at midday in summer. In this half light they typically adopt a spindly form, perhaps with larger leaves. Tree branches held in deep shade in a wood also tend to grow larger leaves than normal.

Mosses and ferns can thrive here. Sunlight apart, the humid air can be a positive feature for plants. The air temperature may also remain rather stable, unlikely to become bitingly cold in winter. This even temperature can be an advantage to hibernating bats.

The animals associated with the mouths of caves can range from the minute to the larger mammals – to foxes, for example, which may make a den if a roof fall provides the rather close shelter that their instincts demand.

These conditions may also be supplied by the mouths of tunnels on abandoned railways. Even the fox will be able to squeeze through slight gaps in the safety boarding; after all, it regularly uses empty rabbit burrows as a den, and even very slight crevices between rocks in the Lake District hills and other upland areas.

INSIDE THE CAVE

Ferns can luxuriate in the cave mouth. Some of those which like shade are:
  lady fern (not limestone)
  hard shield fern
  black spleenwort
  maidenhair spleenwort
  parsley fern

filmy ferns
hay scented buckler fern
brittle bladder fern (hart's tongue)
wall rue (especially limestone)
hard fern indicator (an acid rock)
As the names suggest, some have distinctive, delicate fronds.

True cave dwellers:
  cave water louse
  cave freshwater shrimp
  flatworms
  springtails
  one or two spiders

bats roosting

The twilit entrance can offer sanctuary to a fox.

THE LIFE OF CAVES AND MINES

A large number of familiar species can be found in the outer portals of the cave. Those from deeper in often show physical evidence of their seclusion from light.

Mine spoil

The spoil heaps piled outside mine diggings are always worth a quick look, and not only for familiar wasteland specialists. There are reports of sheets of wild orchids, and autumn gentian and mountain pansy, being found on some – not impossible if the chemical flavour of the debris is suitable. Cushions of spring sandwort are a more regular, if less dramatic, example of a coloniser of old lead-mine heaps.

The cave mouth

Ferns luxuriate in the damp and the comparatively steady temperatures of the cave mouth. Look for rustyback, wall rue and (quite rare) maidenhair on limestone faces, and there are similar lists for other rock types, to be found illustrated in the field guides. Mosses will be expected of course, but fungi are worth looking out for. They are decomposers, feeding on decaying plant and animal matter (at the same time contributing to its decay), and the debris on the cave floor may be deficient in this. Deep in the cave, the only fungi may be moulds which will smother bat droppings and the carcasses of what invertebrates there happen to be.

Feeding in the dark

Although the dark recesses tend to be empty, a few animal species are regularly found in the depths of caves, where they ultimately rely on food washed in or down from outside. On the ground there may be numerous springtails. Small (usually well under 5 millimetres in length), they are common in leaf litter and other rotting moulds above ground, and some may find their way into a cave, feeding on the bacteria and the moulds and spores of fungi, detecting them by smell and touch.

Spiders are possibly lying in wait for them in the darkness. One species, *Meta merianae* (few spiders have day-to-day names), spreads a platform of gossamer across a crack used by the springtails and waits patiently until one lands on it and triggers the alarm threads. The more usual home of this spider is in empty rabbit burrows.

The spider population of a cave can be quite varied, if likely to be appreciated only by a specialist. Those that hunt by sight are, of course, at a disadvantage, but the familiar house spider also inhabits dry caves. Others prefer damp surroundings, and a damp portico should attract many. Humid and dark, and free from extremes of temperature, a small cave can offer conditions matching those deep inside a hollow tree, the common habitat of some species.

Hibernating

Some caves are registered nature reserves because of their bats, which use them both as nurseries and as hibernating dormitories, the latter possibly more important. A hibernating animal needs security and ideally an even and dry temperature. Although photographs exist showing hibernating bats covered with beads of condensation, it could be that they are adversely affected if the air is very damp. For hibernating insects this can certainly be a problem. Butterflies such as the small tortoiseshell found hibernating in garages choose dry surroundings. Insect blood tends to absorb water, and they can die of 'water poisoning' if the air is too dank. But the herald moth, a handsome species with wings which resemble a shrivelled leaf and which is seen feeding on sallow catkins when it emerges in spring, hibernates not only in buildings but also in hollow trees and caves. The mosquito family can also make use of caves.

The cave pool

Cave pools and streams may occasionally contain fish washed in by spates. In the depths of the cave, trout, for example, can no longer hunt by sight as they are wont to do, but must smell out water lice or freshwater shrimps from the gravel; their lower jaw is often worn away as a result. Understandably, they are thin and pale, the pigment spots contracted.

WILDLIFE OF THE CAVE MOUTH

roosting bats

herald moth

Choughs sometimes nest inland, in cave entrances: their bill is red, and distinctive.

Some frequent denizens of the deep darkness; the cave-dwelling races are usually much paler and slimmer than those seen on the surface.

freshwater shrimp

water louse

flatworm

Hart's tongue is one of the many ferns which flourish in the damp but mild gloom of the cave mouth.

The cave water louse and cave freshwater shrimp are sometimes rather numerous, at least in southern caves. These animals, also paler, thinner and smaller than their outdoor cousins, feed on specks of detritus washed down from the surface; but they will breed only if enough food is available, and even then they lay far fewer eggs than normal.

If they escape the fish, they may fall prey to flatworms. These leave a sticky, snail-like trail underwater, and retrace their path to feed on any small animals which may have glued themselves to it.

THE OPEN SHORE

Britain is girt with more than 8000 kilometres (5000 miles) of foreshore, and few other coastlines in the world can match the diversity found here.

The interface

The shore is a stark but by no means simple interface between land and sea. Structurally it is very varied, creating a range of habitat types, the living conditions of which fluctuate rapidly with the ebb and flow of the tides. Ecologically it is extremely harsh in a number of ways, posing problems for normal land and sea life both.

The tidal zones

The tides result from the gravitational pull of the sun and moon on the fluid oceans as the Earth spins in its orbit. There are two high tides and two low in each 24 hours, but their heights vary and the spring tides (nothing to do with the season) reach higher and fall lower at around the time of the new and full moons. In between these, the neap tides have the least range. In Britain we have some of the most powerful spring tides in the world, with a range of 12 metres or more in the Severn estuary, for example. The driftline of seaweed and flotsam on the beach usually shows the height of the most recent tides.

This tidal movement means that the shore, whether it be sandy or rocky, is zoned. The upper shore is covered and the lower shore is uncovered only at the heights and lows, respectively, of the spring tides, while the middle shore always receives two dousings and two airings every 24 hours. Above the upper shore, a splash zone regularly doused by spray from the waves is also a feature, and on exposed coasts this can carry the influence of the sea to some height and distance inland.

Currents and geology

Tides and coastal currents help to sculpture the detail of the shore. When waves strongly batter hard rock, bubbles of trapped air are squeezed into cracks and 'implode' under their force. In time the rock fractures and falls away, and the fragments will eventually be worn down to sand and shingle. Further supplies of these come from looser cliffs and other deposits which were maybe themselves beaches at some geological period in the past.

Loose sand and shingle are deposited only where the currents and tidal influence are too weak to carry them further, as in the shelter of the rocky arms of a bay. The prevailing direction of the water movements tends to shift the beach in one direction, to build it up against the rocks at one end of a bay while leaving them bare at the other. Seaside resorts have groynes to prevent this 'longshore drift' nudging their beach on to the next resort. The shingle along Chesil Beach in Dorset is graded thus in size from one end to the other.

Profile of a beach

The powerful 'swash' of the waves crashing up the beach can carry sizeable shingle pebbles with it, but the returning backwash

Waders are typical birds of the open shore. But 'wader' is not a very appropriate name for them, nor is the alternative 'shore bird'. They are seen on the shore, in storm ridge of shingle

Longshore drift piles the sand and shingle on one side of the groyne or rock outcrop.

groyne

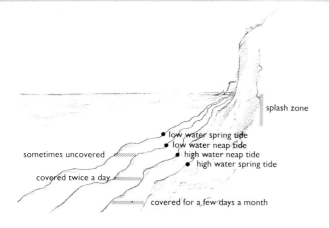

splash zone

low water spring tide
low water neap tide
high water neap tide
high water spring tide

sometimes uncovered

covered twice a day

covered for a few days a month

Some waders to look for are:
  oystercatcher
  dunlin
  golden plover
  godwits
  knot
  sanderling
They have attractive quirks of
behaviour: sanderling for example
dash industriously up and down the
beach following the incoming swash.

The splash zone, the height within
the reach of the salt spray, is a
characteristic feature of the shore. It
can have halophytic plants growing:
those adapted to survive in highly
salty surroundings, rock samphire is
just one example.

is too weak to move them. As a result, sandy beaches are usually backed by raised shingle banks with storm ridges sculptured by stormy seas. In some places, dunes develop behind the beach (see pages 172–3).

The sand itself can consist of grains of quartz originally eroded from hard, granite-like rocks, but it often contains a great deal of shell fragments. Dry sand is loose; when slightly damp it tends to be firm, but with plenty of water it is soft; feet sink into it (quicksands do exist, if rarely) and shellfish live in it, often in vast numbers.

The rocky shore

Although tidal zones are found on sandy and rocky shores equally, they are most noticeable on the latter, where they are marked by seaweeds of different kinds which can tolerate different lengths of exposure to the drying breezes and hot sunshine. Many of the sea snails and other molluscs concealed by the seaweed are also zoned. The various shellfish can be found by picking through the seaweeds, but on exposed coasts, where weeds are absent, barnacles may grow in vast numbers (accompanied by mussels). One of the delights of the rocky shore is the rock pool, but, as we shall see (see pages 170–1), this is certainly not simply a miniature ocean.

Pollution and the shore

As a general rule of ecology, harsh conditions will usually result in fewer species, but those that can successfully combat the problems may be present in enormous numbers owing to the lack of competition for food and space. The exposed headland is one example; it is bare of the normal mixed-seaweed jungle but covered with barnacles.

By disturbing the balance of life, pollution can have the same effect. Shores can be compared in the way outlined on page 205.

Biological survey	abundance	numbers of species	abundance	number of species
green seaweeds	R	3	A	1
brown seaweeds	R	4	R	6
red seaweeds	F	6	R	5
coloured patches (lichens)	F	4	F	4
barnacles	A	2	A	3
limpets	A	1	R	1
sea snails	F	4	R	3
bivalves	F	1	—	—

A = Abundant   F = Frequent   R = Rare

LIFE ON THE SHORE

Both sandy beach and rocky shore make their own separate demands on plantlife and animal life. The limpid rock pool is not the miniature ocean that it seems.

The sandy beach

Unless it is very sheltered indeed, the only seaweeds likely to be seen on the sandy beach are fronds torn from the rocks and washed up along with the flotsam. Some may come from below the low-tide mark. The sand itself, however, can be literally full of animal life. Here we have a major difference from habitats on land, because the primary source of energy is not plantlife which is large and obvious, but a soup of microscopic plants free-floating in the sea itself. The detritus from their death and decay sinks, and as a result the sand is muddied, often very noticeably so even a few centimetres down. This mud can be depleted of oxygen by bacteria, making it black and smelly as a result of waste hydrogen sulphide.

Worms normally inhabit the sand, straining this muck from it. Most of the sand shellfish have siphons to suck in water, and for food they filter the sea water when the tide is in. The mollusc populations can be so numerous that broken shell pieces make up a good deal of the sand itself.

Seaweed zones on the rocky shore

The seaweeds attached to rocks (and other hard surfaces) with a holdfast are of three main kinds: green (which are bright green or yellowish-green), red, and brown (which can be a dullish green). They are all green plants, if lowly ones, on the ladder of evolution, the chlorophyll in the last two being masked by pigments which can allow them to operate more efficiently in dim light. Thus the bright green weeds tend to be found in lighter places, at the tops of the shore or in rock pools, though pools are also colonised by the others.

The brown seaweeds zone themselves down the shore, each species adapted in some way to the length of exposure when the tide is out. Channel wrack at the top of the shore, for example, which is covered for only part of a month at the high spring tides, can stand drying up, its fronds curling inwards when it does so. The largest weeds of all grow below low-tide mark.

Hidden among the weed, the different types of topshell and winkle also zone themselves. Flat winkles with either yellow or dark shells are typical of the bladder wrack of the middle shore.

The effects of pollution

Changes in quality of the sea water can be reflected in changes in seaweed cover. Sewage or other nutrients in the water stimulate the growth of the bright green weeds (have a look at the spot where a stream runs into the sea). The links can, however, be complicated. Where limpets are abundant, they keep much of the rock bare by moving around when the tide is in to graze the young weeds. If they are killed by pollution (perhaps the chemicals used to deal with oil slicks), then seaweed jungles develop. But densely covered rocks are not in themselves a sign of pollution.

The rock pool

The rock pool is not an ocean in miniature. Conditions are harsher by far. Changes in temperature which are normally masked by the mass of open water can be very great in a small pool exposed to the summer sun or freezing winter winds. But what is more threatening to saltwater species is the change in salinity when rainstorms dilute a small pool. Even more toxic could be the acid build-up of carbon dioxide in a small pool by the normal body activity of plants and animals; true, this is removed and oxygen freed when the seaweeds photosynthesise, but they do this only during daylight hours.

Although the rock pool seems to us to be a refuge, its inhabitants are in fact often coping with much more severe conditions than those of the open ocean.

Birds of the rocky bay

Birds are identified with particular shore habitats: the waders with the saltings and marshes where they nest and the open beaches where they flock to feed and roost in winter (see pages 178–9); the gulls with the cliffs where they nest (see pages 182–3), although they are quite mobile in winter. Gulls may from time to time come to pry among the seaweed draping the rocks or pick along the driftline at any season.

All in all, the turnstone is perhaps the bird most closely identified with the rocky shore during the winter months. It energetically searches the weed for sandhoppers and other small animals, turning over seaweeds and marching down to flip the pebbles over in the gullies.

LIFE OF THE ROCKY SHORE

Observe how on soft rock the limpet grinds itself a snugly fitting watertight groove in the rock surface.

mussels

barnacles

bladder wrack, a brown seaweed

retracted beadlet sea anemone

a typical red weed

dog whelk

sea lettuce, a green seaweed

flat winkles

The reason for their different colours is not known: diet may be the reason. However it is known that dog whelks which feed on mussels are dark, those that feed on barnacles are pale.

The shore crab can resist both exposure and changes in salinity and so can be seen everywhere on the shore.

SAND DUNES AND SHINGLE

Shingle beaches border about a quarter of the coasts of Britain, but even when not pounded by the tides they remain a harsh habitat. Sand dunes in time become much more hospitable.

The permanence of the soft coast

It is taken for granted that the coasts guard their line on the map. Hard-rock headlands clearly withstand severe battering by the waves, but mobile shingle and soft-sand features are also near-permanent: sand and shingle accumulate where neither currents nor tides disturb them.

Shingle features

Shingle ranges in size from 6 millimetres to 200 millimetres ($\frac{1}{4}$ to 8 inches) in diameter. In itself, shingle is largely a legacy of the Ice Age, being derived from the scrapings of the glaciers, and beach supplies often come from cliffs of glacial material. Shingle banks lie at the top of beaches (see pages 168–9). But it is quite usual for the profile of a beach to change by the season, and to shift in part of the bay during the winter storms, to expose the previously hidden rock bed.

Shingle is also sometimes found pushed up by the tides and currents into a spit or curved bar at the mouth of a river; one of the best-known examples is Orfordness in Suffolk. The coast also has a handful of larger, and unique, shingle features such as Chesil Beach and Dungeness.

Although shingle that lies within reach of the tides is too mobile for plantlife, even along the driftline there may be some hardy maritime plants, which, unlike the inter-tidal seaweeds, are definitely land plants. Further in, on the stable ridges or in their shelter, other species may even cover the shingle to create patchy carpets of flowers. A brackish lagoon often lies behind shingle features.

The creation of sand dunes

Sand-dune systems form where tide and currents accumulate loose sand and off-shore winds blow it inland. In the way that snow is blown into deep drifts behind a fence, loose sand builds up behind any small feature, perhaps even the hardy driftline plants. If this is out of reach of all but the highest tides, couch and lyme grass can grow, and then the specialised marram grass. These perennial plants can anchor the sand with a network of roots. If their

SAND DUNES AND SHINGLE

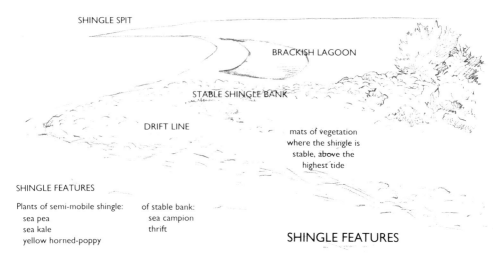

Characteristic nesting birds of shingle are: ringed plover; terns; common gull; black-headed gull and oystercatcher.

SHINGLE SPIT

BRACKISH LAGOON

STABLE SHINGLE BANK

DRIFT LINE

mats of vegetation where the shingle is stable, above the highest tide

SHINGLE FEATURES

Plants of semi-mobile shingle:
 sea pea
 sea kale
 yellow horned-poppy

of stable bank:
 sea campion
 thrift

SHINGLE FEATURES

leaves become covered, a new growing point starts into action, and both leaves and a new root network are created higher up. The dune between the marram tufts is still yellow, with a bare loose surface.

As soon as the sand is in any way firmer, on the face away from the sea, quick-seeding annual plants can successfully germinate. This dune is on the way to being fixed, but a younger one is probably already starting on its seaward edge. Waves of dunes develop in this way. On the older, more stable sand, mosses and lichens create a carpet, giving a greyish appearance, and then other plants invade which are not especially adapted to salty coastal conditions – and with all the more variety if the sand contains broken shell fragments, which provide a ration of lime. These can create something rather similar to a flowery meadow, with orchids here and there. Further habitat is provided by the 'slacks', low-lying damp areas which may even contain open pools in some seasons.

The links

As the dune slowly becomes drier and more vegetated, it becomes favourite country for rabbits, and they can create lawns of short grassy turf. These hinterlands of sand, turf, and scattered bushes and trees are called 'links' in Scotland – and they proved excellent for golf!

Dune systems are under threat from coniferisation and (as are many coastal features) from road-building and house-building. The surface skin of vegetation is always thin, however, and storms (or people) can cause 'blow-outs', exposing areas of fresh pale sand on which colonisation slowly begins again.

Machair

Machair (pronounced mahair) originated in much the same way as links. It is found on the west coasts of northern Scotland and the Hebrides, and consists of areas of shelly sand often lying behind sand dunes and marked out in flat fields today. Machair is noted for its abundant lime-loving plants (and snails). There has, traditionally, been a certain amount of ploughing for cereals and root crops, as well as grazing, but the crop rotation cycle has usually been long enough to allow the flowers to maintain their presence.

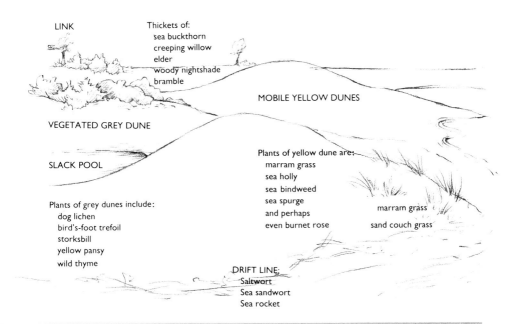

LINK

Thickets of:
sea buckthorn
creeping willow
elder
woody nightshade
bramble

MOBILE YELLOW DUNES

VEGETATED GREY DUNE

SLACK POOL

Plants of yellow dune are:
marram grass
sea holly
sea bindweed
sea spurge
and perhaps
even burnet rose

Plants of grey dunes include:
dog lichen
bird's-foot trefoil
storksbill
yellow pansy
wild thyme

marram grass

sand couch grass

DRIFT LINE:
Saltwort
Sea sandwort
Sea rocket

THE LIFE OF THE BACK SHORE

Once set in train, dunes tend to evolve, and the stages of this evolution can be compared within a short distance. But the sand dunes are always a fragile habitat.

The driftline

The grinding of shingle and sand hit by the waves underlines the fact that constant movement makes a hostile environment. The driftline of seaweed and other flotsam marks the limit of the high tide's reach, but past here some plants may root. Some are annuals; there are advantages in this in a mobile habitat. Look for the yellow horned-poppy, with its unmistakable long seed pods. Sea rocket with sprawling stems which rise to carry succulent leaves is one of these typical annuals. Saltwort is another.

THE WILDLIFE OF THE SAND DUNES

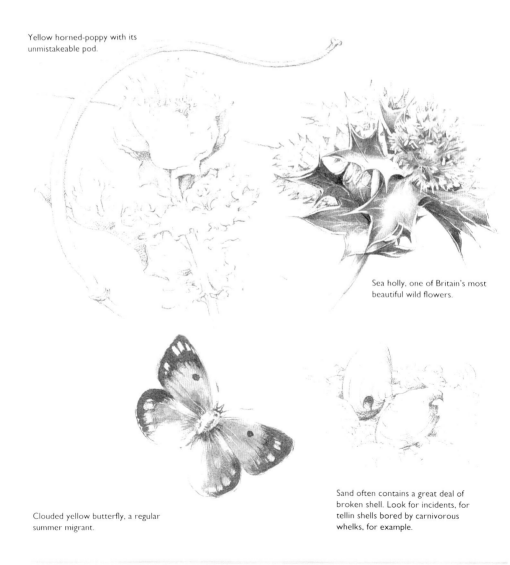

Yellow horned-poppy with its unmistakeable pod.

Sea holly, one of Britain's most beautiful wild flowers.

Clouded yellow butterfly, a regular summer migrant.

Sand often contains a great deal of broken shell. Look for incidents, for tellin shells bored by carnivorous whelks, for example.

The natterjack toad is now on the endangered list. Its tadpoles require warmer conditions than those of the common toad and so it is restricted to sun spots – to sand dunes (and it was previously also found on heathland). It is difficult to observe; It will cease croaking at the slightest disturbance and spends the day dug into the sand to prevent drying out.

The yellow dune

Given the right conditions, the dune evolves slowly but surely. Apart from the dune-builders (see pages 172–3), even the hostile environment of the young yellow dune can produce one of our most beautiful wild plants, the sea holly. Plants lose water through their leaves (therefore sucking up nutrients from their roots), and this plant shows classic adaptations for slowing this water loss, with fewer pores, thick waxy skin to the leaves, and part of the leaf area reduced to spines, as is common in desert cactuses. Deserts and salty habitats both create problems with fresh-water supply. See if any other plants here have similar features. Sea bindweed, its stems creeping over the sand, is also familiar in this habitat.

The grey dunes

A meadow of flowers will slowly develop once the dune surface is stable enough to be painted grey by lichens and mosses. If the sand is shelly (and so able to supply lime) there could be some good orchid counts, but, as with downland, the amount of grazing is an important factor. If rabbit grazing is curtailed, a very dense scrub of sea buckthorn or hawthorn may develop to swamp the shorter flowers. On the other hand, on 'acid' dunes wholly built up from grains of quartz (silica), the tendency may be towards a heathland with heather.

The dune pool or 'slack' in a damp hollow can be a feature. Here may grow many marsh and fen plants, with perhaps creeping willow making a low scrub. There are often interesting orchids in these slacks – slacks – marsh helleborine, coralroot orchid, fen orchid and others.

Unusual invertebrates

Dunes carry a great variety of invertebrates. Moths have a zonation which follows that of their food plants: the gaudy burnet moths, for example, are limited to the older dunes. Quite rare moths are found on the shingle at Dungeness and other places, and the sheltered vegetated side of Chesil Beach has its own species of cricket. The dunes tend to become more populated as they age, and the dark green fritillary, grayling and common blue butterflies are typical of older dunes. Butterflies are not usually seen on the shingle, except maybe for clouded yellow migrants newly arrived from the Continent and perching at this, their first landfall. The shelly dunes can be expected to have a good many snails.

Nesting birds

Remote dunes and shingle stretches are famous for their nesting colonies of terns. The 'nest' of these species is in fact little more than a depression in the ground. The ringed plover is also a famous shingle nester; both eggs and chicks are intricately camouflaged so as to be very difficult to detect among the pattern of pebble shadows, even from close to. Again, its nest is little more than a slight depression.

The Scottish machair is a stronghold for lapwing, dunlin, redshank and other breeding waders. As for other birds, opportunistic gulls (black-headed and common) will nest among the dunes. But for these and for many nesting birds, the crucial factor is the amount of human disturbance.

Winter is a birdwatcher's time. The shore systems of which the dunes and shingle are part attract many waders and others.

SALTINGS AND SALTMARSHES

Intertidal estuary mudflats total some 240,000 hectares (600,000 acres), about a sixth of which is saltmarsh at some stage or other of its development.

The scrapings of the land

An estuary is the shallow muddy area found where a river empties into the sea. It is typically triangular. Here, where the river current is checked by the tide, the silt (mud) it carries is deposited. 'Flats' and 'saltings' are names for areas of sand and mud which are covered by the sea at high tide and exposed at low tide. In Essex and other rather sheltered areas, the saltings stretch out along 'open' coast.

The extent of these areas is seen only at low tide, when a network of channels and smooth banks sculpted by the currents is revealed. At the sides of the estuary, where the current is slackest, saltmarshes develop from the bare mud.

Another important factor for estuary life is that here salt water and fresh water mix; the brackishness of the water depends on the state of the tide, being least salty at low tide when the river is flowing unopposed.

The height of the tide, which obviously influences the area under brackish water, varies not only during the month (see pages 168–9) but also along the coast. The effect of the tides may penetrate surprisingly far inland, recognised by the muddy and often rather steep river banks exposed at the ebb.

Saltmarsh

In slack parts of the estuary, usually in the crook of an arm of land, saltmarshes develop. Here the mud builds up, until it is covered for only a few days each month by the spring tides. A handful of pioneers are first on the scene to fix the loose mud; once these are rooted and some stability achieved, other plants arrive until a meadow-like community as flowery as any other develops. Sheep and cattle are often grazed here, however, and the saltmarsh has a distinct appearance, with a mosaic of small meadowy lawns divided by muddy channels in which the tide still flows. In time these channels become filled with deposited silt, and the whole area becomes invaded by bushes and is to all intents and purposes dry land.

SALTINGS AND SALTMARSHES

The wintering birds tend to feed different levels.	lower flats:	upper flats:	saltmarsh:
	oystercatcher	pintail	snipe
	knot	plovers	golden plover
	dunlin	lapwing	lapwing
	curlew	curlew	redshank
	redshank	redshank	other wild geese
	godwits	brent geese	

FLATS

Fragmentary plant life: green or brown seaweeds on stable mud eel grass.

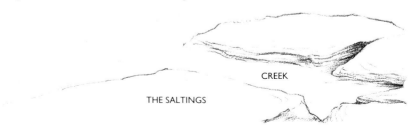

CREEK

THE SALTINGS

Reclamation

The natural evolution of an estuary through saltmarsh to dry land is often obscured by dykes and drains. When drained, the rich estuary mud grows very good grazing grass. Romney Marsh, for example, was already widely drained by Norman times and reared its own breed of sheep (see pages 144–5). In recent times, estuary flats have been reclaimed for other purposes: they are a favourite site for, among other things, power stations which then dominate the landscape.

What's in it for wildlife?

Although seeming a dour place, the saltings are ecologically one of the most productive of all ecosystems, fed as they are by the scourings of a whole river system. The mud supports an incredible wealth of shellfish, worms and other invertebrates. As a result, estuaries can support giant flocks of birds, and their winter numbers are the nearest thing we have to the profusion of grazing animals in the African game parks. These winter flocks are of great international ecological importance.

Some waders and wildfowl also nest here in summer, on the saltmarshes alongside the muddy feeding grounds. The saltmarsh has a simple structure, however, and, as a result of the general rules of ecology, fewer species of nesting birds can be expected compared with a wood (see pages 24–5).

The Scottish sea lochs

These fjord-like arms of the sea have a rather different origin, being valleys deepened by glaciers and since flooded. Sea lochs offer a distinct habitat, with a great difference in exposure between mouth and end which creates a wealth of different shore conditions, and a huge tidal flow which each time brings a tremendous quantity of fresh nutrient in the sea water. Life is much more varied than on the open coast, and there is more of it.

Where the land has been sinking, in Cornwall and Devon especially, valleys have also become flooded to create estuaries with fjord-like features. The Fowey estuary is one of these drowned valleys, with sides notably higher and closer than is normal with estuaries.

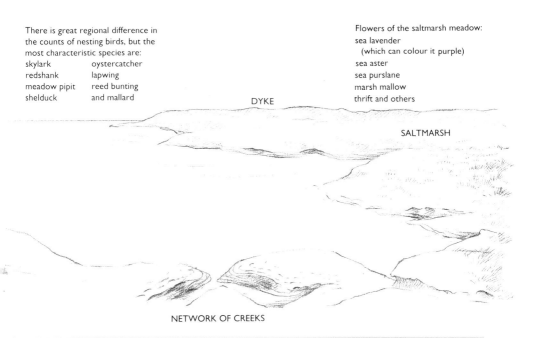

There is great regional difference in the counts of nesting birds, but the most characteristic species are:

skylark	oystercatcher
redshank	lapwing
meadow pipit	reed bunting
shelduck	and mallard

Flowers of the saltmarsh meadow:
sea lavender
  (which can colour it purple)
sea aster
sea purslane
marsh mallow
thrift and others

DYKE

SALTMARSH

NETWORK OF CREEKS

THE LIFE OF THE ESTUARY

Sombre and muddy the estuary may be, yet it is one of the richest of British ecosystems and supports internationally important flocks of birds in winter.

The mud-dwellers

Teeming numbers of molluscs, crustaceans and worms gulp, slither and wriggle in this mud, richly bathed as it is by the scrapings and leachings of a whole river system extending several counties inland. Oysters and cockles are familiar enough, but other shellfish typical of estuaries are less so. One important snail is *Hydrobia*, a snail with a rather pointed spiral shell, but too small and inconspicuous to have a day-to-day name. There can be over 40,000 to the square metre in some estuaries; look for it in pools left by the tide. Of equal relative enormity are the appetites of the birds that feed on these shellfish; an oystercatcher can take 200 small cockles per tide.

Other important members of the fauna are ragworms and the green shore crab (which is, in fact, seen in tidal habitats of every kind).

The saltmarsh

Out on the flat mud only seaweeds will be seen, the green *Enteromorpha* for example, but any brown weeds will need projecting stones as anchor unless the mud is very sheltered from tidal flow. Eelgrass is worth looking for; it is interesting because it is one of the few flowering plants that actually grows in the sea. But where sediments settle out of the main currents, and are exposed for only parts of the tide, glasswort and seablite take root. They are rather cactus-like in some respects, because in this salty environment preventing loss of cell water is as much of a problem as it is in a desert.

They are the pioneers, to be followed when the mud banks are doused only a few times a month by flowers such as sea aster, which grow to create a flowery meadow if left ungrazed. Although growing with one foot in the sea in a manner of speaking (the soil can be salty), these are definitely land plants, although the need to guard cell water can give them succulent features.

Nesting birds

When not intensively grazed, the saltmarsh meadow can attract skylarks and meadow pipits, and perhaps a few scattered waders and mallard, too.

Winter flocks

From a bird's eye view, Britain has a welcoming coast. Both the mudflats and the saltmarshes, whether or not they are grazed, offer seasonal refuge for huge flocks of ducks, wild geese and waders, coming south from their breeding grounds in the arctic tundra, Greenland and northern Europe. They are joined by those waders and ducks which have nested in British hills.

There are two main kinds of wild geese, easy enough to recognise: black-necked (brent and barnacle, for example) or grey (bean and greylag, this latter being the ancestor of farm geese). Migrant swans, the Bewick's and whooper swans, are also seen here in winter.

Sharing out the shore

Waders have rather delicate bills, and many are able to feed comfortably only in soft mud. The state of the tide is crucial, especially in winter when ice may be a threat. The shorter days may mean that the birds will feed at night at low tide if the moon is bright enough.

When you think about it, roosting on the shore with the tides coming and going could be a rather tricky business, especially on long winter nights. The oystercatcher is often the first to hurry to occupy ground out of reach of high tide, a prime spot for roosting. Knots form their own group nearby, while dunlins and sanderlings may share lesser patches of safe ground. But the bar-tailed godwit is more of an opportunist. It follows the tide out and is chased back when it turns, and if caught on the hop has to hope that there will be space left within the roosting stations; a forlorn sight, and not too uncommon according to many birdwatchers, is these birds roosting with water up to their chins.

Species differences also show themselves up in general activity. The dunlin spends

THE OYSTERCATCHER

This wader relies on the tides to
expose its feeding grounds; other
waders often find alternative areas.

Its nest is a scrape in sand or shingle.

Each day it takes its own weight of
mud worms or shellfish.

Unlike other waders, oystercatchers
provide their young with food.

smashed mussel

Cockles and (especially) mussels are
favourite food; not oysters so much,
they are now relatively uncommon.

Cockles or mussels are either stabbed
open or smashed. The youngsters
learn their parents' method.

three-quarters of the low-tide time feeding,
but the curlew less than half. You might
expect the reverse from the shapes of their
bills, as the dunlin's seems the more all-
purpose an instrument compared with that
of the curlew, and so able to exploit a more
varied larder. But it is a deeper larder here
on the mud, and this is where the fine long
curve of the curlew bill is the more effective:
it can reach the succulent lugworms deep in
their burrows (the equal here of juicy
earthworms).

Earthworms they have to search for
when driven inland by storms. The shore-
birds seem to have recognised alternative
night roosts for foul weather.

THE CLIFF

England and Wales have about 4400 kilometres (2700 miles) of cliffs; and Scotland many times that. Inaccessible as they are, ecological threats are minor and local.

Cliff features

Sea cliffs provide some of the most spectacular scenery of the whole of the British landscape. Basically, the power of the storm waves is so great that the slightest differences in rock texture and hardness enable the sea to carve away the more fragile rock and create a bay. Each bay or set of bays, however, has its own particular character.

Cliffs are formed in rather a standard way. Cracks in the rock are exploited by the massive power of the waves, aided by chemical action (if some minerals preferentially dissolve, they weaken the whole face) and by frost and wind. The base of the cliff tends to be hollowed out first, and the rock above collapses. This debris becomes smoothed to boulders, which lie scattered or piled on the flattish platform at the base of the cliff. This platform is more obvious when it is exposed at low tide or seen from a boat; in fact, the best place for viewing both the plants and the birds is from a boat nearby.

Steep chalk cliffs

Chalk is a soft rock, easily eroded, and its cliff faces tend to collapse without much undermining. As a result, chalk cliffs are usually sheer, and more or less free of loose boulders at their foot.

The undercliff

Not all cliffs comprise one single type of rock, a sandwich of different layers being quite usual. Erosion of one layer faster than another can create an undercliff, a no-man's-land which lies below the clifftop but out of reach of the waves. Although we find it difficult to reach, it can be a haven for wildlife, sheltered and nooky and often with its own network of small streams and pools

THE CLIFF

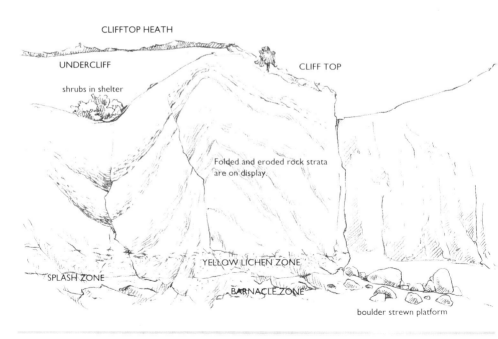

CLIFFTOP HEATH

UNDERCLIFF

CLIFF TOP

shrubs in shelter

Folded and eroded rock strata are on display.

YELLOW LICHEN ZONE

SPLASH ZONE

BARNACLE ZONE

boulder strewn platform

of fresh water, and the sea's influence may be limited to storm spray. Undercliffs are more frequent where the rocks are soft clays or gravels; these can become rather fluid when waterlogged with heavy rains, and the faces often slump down.

Sea caves

Sea caves are formed when the cliff face stays perched in place over the cavities chiselled out by the waves below. The implosive action of the waves can exploit a vein of softer rock, so that the sea cave may extend quite a considerable way inland, even sometimes reaching the surface as a blow hole, which channels up spray on stormy days. In fact, the sea cave may eventually extend straight through the cliff of a headland to create an arch, and when this collapses a free-standing stack is formed which will in time be eroded into a low island. Ecologically, these features provide further opportunities for cliff species.

The cliff and clifftop

Very varied plant and animal communities can be associated with the cliff. The steep slopes and cliff ledges, if they accumulate enough soil, can support plants, but what grows where is decided largely by how much salt spray drifts up to the site (salt is a limiting factor). If the ledges do remain bare, they can still provide secure sites for nesting seabirds.

The clifftop is a separate habitat type, with different conditions. The spray may have only slight influence here (although still evident). The harsh winter cold felt inland may be tempered by the moist ocean air – and the clifftop is always a breezy place. Shrubs and hardy trees are windpruned and lopsided because of the prevailing wind, although they grow fully if there is shelter of some kind behind a fold in the cliff edge. Sometimes an interesting heathland develops up here, with heather and other undershrubs (see pages 152–3).

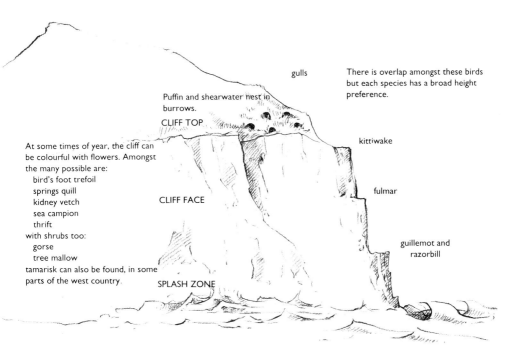

gulls

There is overlap amongst these birds but each species has a broad height preference.

Puffin and shearwater nest in burrows.

CLIFF TOP

kittiwake

At some times of year, the cliff can be colourful with flowers. Amongst the many possible are:
  bird's foot trefoil
  springs quill
  kidney vetch
  sea campion
  thrift
with shrubs too:
  gorse
  tree mallow
tamarisk can also be found, in some parts of the west country.

CLIFF FACE

fulmar

guillemot and razorbill

SPLASH ZONE

CLIFF LIFE

Apart from being visually spectacular, cliffs are important habitats: Britain has international responsibility for a number of cliff-nesting birds.

Lichen bands

The lichens can be quite noticeable from a boat. Much depends on the rock, but on hard granite the lichens can range themselves in three distinct colour bands. The highest zone, above the reach of the regular spray, is greyish owing to bunchy sea ivory and others. Below this is the 'splash zone', with three or four orange lichens. This gives way at about high-tide mark to a black zone; black lichens (often mistaken for tar) can colonise the rocks well down towards low-water mark.

A natural rock garden

Plants tenaciously take root in what seems the merest crack. Much the same is seen on stone walls (see pages 90–1), but the cliff offers a natural habitat on much more grand a scale. Those at the base will be tolerant of salt: rock samphire and wild cabbage and lovage. Higher, thrift and other flowers from the saltmarsh are seen (see pages 176–7). Steep faces here can be a veritable wild rock garden of flowers. The proportion of grass increases with height.

An extra influence can be the bird droppings in nest areas. This rich manure does not lead to increased variety or flowery luxuriance, but the reverse. It encourages ranker and fewer weeds such as sea beet and docks, which then grow to elbow out the rest. Excess fertilisers have the same unexpected effect in other flowery habitats (see pages 68–9).

An undercliff can have a distinct fascination, remote, a private jungle with exotic-seeming horsetails, visible only from parts of the clifftop. Binoculars are useful for glimpsing early flowers in sheltered south-facing corners: a veritable meadow of yellow coltsfoot, for example.

Wild cabbage

It is intriguing that more than one vegetable ancestor is found on the coast. Sea carrot is a close relation of the ancestral vegetable carrot. Wild (sea) cabbage prefers limestone cliffs. Wild cabbage is not seen in Scotland, which makes up for the loss with lovage, growing on sea cliffs and coastal areas, a popular celery-scented relative of the cow-parsley family. As was the case with cabbage, a domesticated lovage was eventually bred for the kitchen.

Cliff birds

Cliff birds are of three basic kinds: those that nest on the ledges and in crevices in the sheer cliffs, those that nest on a gentler slope, and those that burrow into softer soil at the clifftop. There can be astonishing numbers in these colonies: the Pembrokeshire islands of Skomer and Skokholm have 50,000 pairs of Manx shearwaters and 6000 pairs of storm petrels. It is the gannetries, however, that are perhaps the pride of the British coast. There are 13 of them, the largest on St Kilda with over 50,000 pairs of these birds.

Even outside the main colonies, the cliffs can seem to be occupied in every nook and cranny – far more birds crammed close together than in a wood, for example. They all feed out on the open sea, a rather different ecology from that of land birds with their tightly guarded feeding territories. The nests in gannetries, however, are in fact evenly spaced out, and binoculars will show that they are just out of pecking reach, one from the other.

As well as true seabirds, cliffs also attract the raven, peregrine and chough.

The clifftop

Often a kind of heathland exists here, although grazing can affect it. Wind pruning and salt spray sculpture any prominent bushes or trees. It is worth seeing if the vegetation changes just a metre or two in from the edge, and, if so, why.

Some cliff tops have renowned vegetation. One such is the Lizard in Cornwall, which has Cornish heath, a heather rarely found elsewhere in England, although common enough in Spain, and two clovers found nowhere else in Britain.

CLIFF-TOP WILDLIFE

Scots lovage, a stout-stemmed, celery-scented member of the cow parsley family. It has the reverse distribution to the samphire.

Wild cabbage, ancestor of cabbage, kale, broccoli and sprouts, grows on sea cliffs.

Although wild cabbage is typical, rock samphire is the plant par excellence of sea cliffs, its cushion of leaves fitting snugly into rock crevices. It is a southerly plant, trailing out in Scotland.

Guillemots nest in dense colonies on suitable ledges. They are Britain's most numerous sea bird with well over a million breeding pairs compared to the 150,000 of herring gull for example.

183

THE ISLAND

There are about a thousand islands lying off British shores, and ranging in size from mere stubs of rock to sizeable areas little different from the mainland.

Miniature mainland

With the sole exception of Rockall, lying 400 kilometres west of Scotland, Britain's offshore islands all rise from the shallow seas of the Continental Shelf. Mainland Britain itself rises from this shallow shelf, and many islands are clearly tongues of mainland which have become separated from the rest by a relative rise in sea level caused by the sinking of the land. In some cases this was quite recently, measured in centuries rather than thousands of years, and a causeway usable at low tide may remain.

In fact, the Isles of Scilly, a collection of flat-topped granite islets, probably represent an area of land isolated by a relative rise in sea level and cut up by erosion. There are apparently scraps of prehistoric stone wall to be seen below today's low-tide mark:

souvenirs of the mythical lost land of Lyonesse perhaps, or at least proof of the comparative youth of these islands. The Orkneys and Shetlands are a similar example, being an outlying extension of a northern Scottish mainland plain.

The map shows that the narrow Menai Straits between Anglesey and mainland Gwynedd are formed of two rather straight-ish stretches meeting around an irregular bend. There were probably two ice-deepened valleys here which became joined when the sea level rose.

Smaller islands

Smaller islands have usually become isolated by erosion and represent a surviving boss of rock. St Michael's Mount is a Cornish example, but many have been formed at the end of headlands. In a typical case, the pounding of the sea has created caves, which in time bore through the headland to create an arch; this collapses to leave an isolated island, which then weathers down. Clearly the conditions on such a rock knob

THE ISLAND

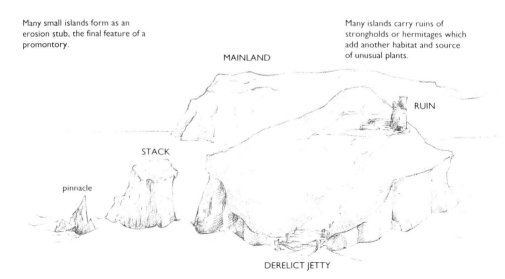

Many small islands form as an erosion stub, the final feature of a promontory.

Many islands carry ruins of strongholds or hermitages which add another habitat and source of unusual plants.

MAINLAND

RUIN

STACK

pinnacle

DERELICT JETTY

Even small islands can be famous for their birds, breeding there or exhausted migrants.

The island coastline is likely to be rather varied, different on each side.

are going to differ from those of a more sizeable area. Far less variety might be expected, but in some cases the bird tally of a small island is remarkable, since it provides a landfall for storm-tossed and exhausted migrating birds: 300 species a year land on Fair Isle, half way between the Orkneys and the Shetlands.

Strongholds

Some islands have been fortified as human strongholds. If large enough, some might hope to be strongholds for plants that have been wiped away from the mainland nearby. Interesting for the chance of unusual plants are those that attracted monastic communities in the Dark Ages or shortly after the Norman conquest. These were not simply secluded hermitages, but often saw a great coming and going of visitors; the monks could also have a lively interest in the affairs of the outer world, including its recipes and medicines. As a result, Steep Holm in the Bristol Channel supports some unexpected species (see pages 186–7).

Islands may have habitats untouched, which are often found damaged on the mainland. At the other end of England, for example, Holy Island off the Northumberland coast has a fine dune system protected as a National Nature Reserve.

What's in it for wildlife?

Even if it is more than a mere knob of rock, the typical island is very unlikely to offer much in the way of habitat variety. Hence there may be fewer species in all than on a comparable area of mainland nearby. Nonetheless, there can be great advantages for those that are present: birds, for instance, may be able to nest free from the threat of fox, rat and snake. Without natural predators, numbers can reach starvation size: rabbits which remain on some islands may be limited only by lack of grass. Where the island is of some size and has healthy stable populations, subspecies may be found. This classic example of evolution in action is described in more detail on pages 186–7.

Typical gannetries are on small rocky islands.

Choughs are found on some islands.

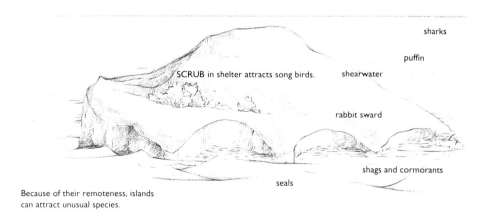

Because of their remoteness, islands can attract unusual species.

SCRUB in shelter attracts song birds.

sharks

puffin

shearwater

rabbit sward

shags and cormorants

seals

LIFE OFFSHORE

A mainland in miniature, a safe retreat, a base for pirate raids, the island can be many things to many species. It also makes an ideal observatory for man.

Safe nesting

Typical gannetries are on relatively small rocky islands, and storm petrels and shearwaters are also attracted to them. Here they may be quite free of rats; shearwaters and puffins, nesting as they both do in burrows which honeycomb the softer soils of cliffs and clifftops, are vulnerable to these. In fact, burrowing seabirds are largely confined to islands when they nest. There are 30,000 puffin pairs nesting on Fair Isle, for example, which is little over 800 hectares (2000 acres) in area. There are also 20,000 pairs of guillemots and 12,000 pairs of kittiwakes nesting on the cliff ledges and flats there.

Bardsey is also notable for its choughs, which nest on inaccessible crags.

The safety is relative, however. Fair Isle may lack rats, but it does have over 100 pairs of skuas regularly nesting. These are the pirates of the bird world, and as well as raiding nests they regularly harass birds on the wing, to steal whatever food they are carrying, even to the extent of forcing their victim to regurgitate the fish it has swallowed as the price of escape.

Seals, too, can find secure refuge and haul out on the rocks skirting the island.

Happy landfalls

Quite apart from offering homes to many nesting birds, many islands have become established as landfalls for migrating birds, and have a tremendous bird count. Fair Isle holds the record (see pages 184–5), but others run it close. The Calf of Man, for example, is better known for its sightings of travelling birds, which include thrushes, wheatears, chiffchaffs, sand martins and goldcrests, than for its nesting seabirds.

Island gardens

In the south-west, Hottentot fig and tree mallow have colonised from gardens to become well established on cliff sides and some islands. The plant lists of some islands are, however, quite extraordinary. The reason can often be traced back to a former monastic settlement, which not only grew its own herbs for medicines and potions but was also perhaps frequently visited by guests from overseas bearing pot plants as gifts. We do the same today, so why not then? At any rate, Steep Holm in the Bristol Channel is an example: its plant tally includes henbane (used in medieval medicine as a hypnotic), caper spurge (a laxative), and coriander (a familiar kitchen spice), as well as the attractive wild peony. All these are by origin from southern Europe or the Mediterranean.

Island populations

The subspecies is typical of island habitats, and mammals provide dramatic examples. The Skomer vole is twice as heavy as the mainland vole, and about 11 centimetres long (head and body) as against 6 centimetres. Other islands have their own subspecies – Jersey, Mull and Ramsay.

In some cases, there are closely similar but separate species which are probably relic populations, an outpost of forms which have or once had a wider distribution. The lesser white-toothed shrew, for example, is found on the Scilly Isles and on Jersey and Sark in the Channel Islands and, apart from that, in southern and eastern Europe. The greater white-toothed shrew, however, is found on Alderney, Guernsey and Herm in the Channel Islands and also in mainland France. Neither of them is found on the British mainland.

St Kilda and Skomer have their own subspecies of wren.

The island effect

The Skomer and St Kilda wrens are an example of the 'island' effect which shows how evolution occurs. A population which becomes separated from the bulk of its kind will in time become inbred, with its own characteristic traits. In time it will refuse to breed with the original parent stock and is then by definition a separate species. An island stock tends to develop physical differences which suit its own environment more exactly, and to develop traits which allow it to exploit its own surroundings more successfully. The most famous example of this is still the variety of beaks that evolved among the finches of the remote Galapagos Islands and which was observed by Charles Darwin.

An actual, sea-girt, island is not essential for evolution to occur: all that is required is that a population is isolated from its parent stock in some way. Apart from the sea, a mountain chain or a desert or other type of inhospitable landscape might create a barrier between the two.

Indeed, the difference may be scarcely noticeable to us, but it may involve a hard and fast difference in diet, with the populations becoming separated by where they feed, and the way they feed. The blue tit and the great tit which feed in different parts of the tree in the wood are an example of the end of this kind of process.

THE GREY SEAL IN THE HABITAT

The annual assembly at the rookery of mothers and pups is seen from September on.

The moulting assembly or 'haul out' usually takes place at a separate site (and separately among bulls and cows) at a separate time of year.

The myth of the singing mermaid originated with the 'singing' of female grey seals.

In fine weather, the seals may also haul up to bask on favoured isolated rocks.

The grey seal prefers a shadowed rocky shore for its pupping 'rookery'.

Its nose and eyes are adapted to hunting in the murk of the ocean.

Dominant bulls stake out territories against others, even fighting off intruders if they refuse to retire. The females also fiercely defend their own pupping ground against other pups and adults.

TOWN FIELDS

British towns have something in excess of 500,000 varied hectares (well over a million acres) of urban garden and garden-like habitat extending an invitation to wildlife.

Attitudes

Although every habitat has its measure of interference, attitudes towards wildlife are most hard and fast in a town, where wild animals are pests and wild plants are weeds.

But even though wild flowers and wildlife are common in towns, and seen every-where, we still continue to regard towns as wildlife deserts. This they certainly are not. Nor is it surprising that this should be so.

Gardens

Gardens are an artificial environment created with native and exotic plants. Some gardens are fussed over almost to the extent of counting every blade of grass. Others veer towards the wild, at least in appearance, with a long meadow of a lawn, dense shrubs, and fences festooned with climbers.

But there are anomalies. Gardeners spend millions of pounds a year on chemical aids of various kinds which by definition create anything but a living ground. And the wild garden, although structurally resembling the edge of a wood or a scrub habitat, will not have the variety of native plantlife of the latter; the insect count will be that much the lower as a result. A clear example is that, although butterflies visit gardens, few breed in them.

In the case of birds, some woodland species have now become typical garden birds – the blackbird and others – although rather more specialised feeders such as blue tits and warblers are not so familiar. The spotted flycatcher makes an interesting example of a bird of woodland glades that has colonised gardens.

To these must be added those birds such as town pigeon and starling which have long since forsaken a 'natural' habitat for the town, although as a species the latter still feeds and roosts in the countryside.

TOWN COUNTRYSIDE

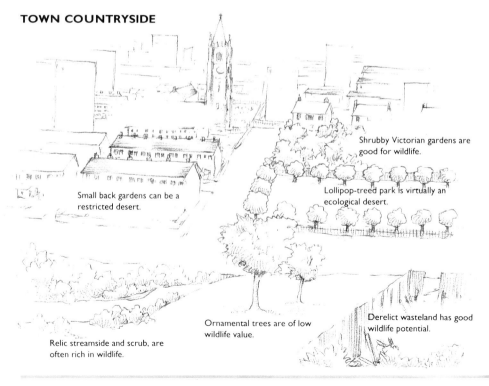

Shrubby Victorian gardens are good for wildlife.

Small back gardens can be a restricted desert.

Lollipop-treed park is virtually an ecological desert.

Derelict wasteland has good wildlife potential.

Ornamental trees are of low wildlife value.

Relic streamside and scrub, are often rich in wildlife.

Parks and commons

Although a refreshing green on the map, and often quite pleasant, these are more likely to reflect the outlook of the local parks department rather than ecology. Bare lawn and lollipop trees do not make a rich habitat. A few blackbirds and magpies may lurk in the shrubbery. The pond may be of more interest, with some surprising water-fowl: pochard, for example, or wild geese. All in all, the secret world behind the keeper's hut where the leaves are piled may be the best place for nature.

Relic countryside

Any town will contain patches of relic countryside, and they can be more interesting than gardens and parks. A surprising number will be found, now surrounded by roads, houses and suchlike. Some will be fragments of recognisable habitat – small areas of wood and meadow, for example. Streamside is fairly common: the habitat structure remains but the water may be foul. Nonetheless, there may be exciting sightings – of rather uncommon or rare wild flowers, including wild orchids.

How much of the original plant variety and animal life remains is another question. As time goes by, species tend to die out from a small area of habitat. Normally the stock is replenished from similar areas nearby, but these town enclaves might be separated from other breeding populations by many kilometres of hostile tarmac and brick.

Derelict land

The other major category of habitat type is waste land of one kind or another. All kinds (see pages 112–13) will be seen. There are usually many examples of the first phases of primary succession (see pages 114–15) on rubble or other solid ground. These are often overlooked, ignored and taken for granted, yet they make an interesting parallel to some of the most dramatic ecology to be found on this planet, such as that of the desert edges and the rock faces.

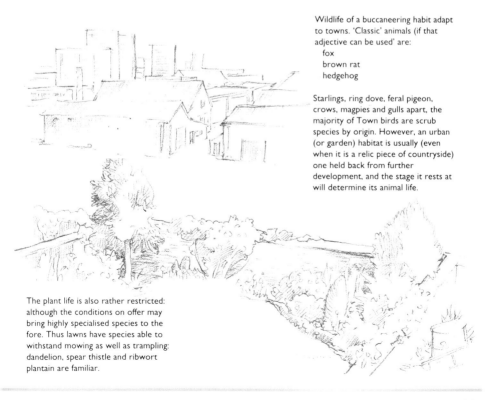

Wildlife of a buccaneering habit adapt to towns. 'Classic' animals (if that adjective can be used' are:
    fox
    brown rat
    hedgehog

Starlings, ring dove, feral pigeon, crows, magpies and gulls apart, the majority of Town birds are scrub species by origin. However, an urban (or garden) habitat is usually (even when it is a relic piece of countryside) one held back from further development, and the stage it rests at will determine its animal life.

The plant life is also rather restricted: although the conditions on offer may bring highly specialised species to the fore. Thus lawns have species able to withstand mowing as well as trampling: dandelion, spear thistle and ribwort plantain are familiar.

THE WILD SIDE OF TOWN

Enclaves of relic countryside apart, a snapshot of animals and plants typical of towns shows that they usually have a buccaneering approach to life.

Butterflies

Butterflies characterise gardens of the older, larger Victorian kind, where a variety of nectar-bearing flowers may be growing. Red admiral, small tortoiseshell and peacock are mobile, are strong on the wing and are familiar visitors to gardens and derelict land; although many gardens do have a nettle patch, they are likely to lay eggs only on the nettle patches of the latter or out in the countryside beyond (see pages 94–5). Sprays have almost wiped out the whites as garden breeders, although they, too, are often seen as visitors.

One exception is the holly blue, a brilliant little butterfly. Though rarely seen in numbers, individuals are frequently spotted in these older gardens. This is a woodland butterfly by origin, and the only woodland butterfly to colonise and lay eggs in gardens in an important way. It lays on holly in spring, but on ivy later in the year.

The feral fox

Now well known from television and other reports, town foxes are very likely to be extremely thin. Their adoption of towns shows up the inherent scavenging character of many animals in the wild: countryside foxes, for example, take carrion as well as live animals, and the young foxes often have to get by on a diet of beetles while they are still honing up their hunting skills. In towns, beetles and worms and birdtable crusts (foxes are good climbers) are regularly part of the diet.

Foxes can make do with what seems to us the slightest cover: the crack beneath the garden shed has been used as a den.

It is not really known if foxes prey on cats; family pets do disappear from time to time, and of course there is a large population of feral cats. In the countryside the unearthly shriek of the vixen calling a mate is a fairly regular feature of January nights, but perhaps these and other calls of the town foxes are lost in the hubbub of traffic and police sirens. Towns are never completely free of traffic or occasional pedestrians, and foxes, being wary animals, may have dropped these calls.

The town pigeon

Today's town pigeons are descended from rock doves, almost certainly brought here from the coasts of the Mediterranean by the Romans. These birds were bred and fattened in dovecots; once accustomed to the home base, they will leave to feed in the surrounding countryside but return afterwards. Working dovecots remained a familiar part of the countryside until quite recent times; they were for a long time a perk for the squire. Pigeons were also bred for racing and as pets. All this led to a melange of plumage patterns. Over the centuries birds escaped from the dovecots and elsewhere, and for these refugees towns, with their windowsills and porticos, may perhaps have awakened echoes of their ancestral homeland.

Many of the feral pigeons seem to have bred back to or retained something like the original rock dove pattern; they are known as bars, with two dark bars across each wing and a glossy green and purple neck. Other patterns are checkers, with speckled plumage of variable colours, and velvets, which are plain birds of many different hues.

Research done some time ago suggested that the 'bars' are more frequent in the north of Britain, and that there are more of them out of the big cities. These plumage differences probably go hand in hand (or feather in feather) with differences in breeding time and success.

It is interesting to observe the relationship between feral pigeons and wood pigeons where they also colonise towns. In Battersea, for example, there is little actual antagonism – simply the fact that the ubiquitous ferals stay away when the wood pigeons are in occupation. Even to the extent of nesting on opposite sides of the same building, but not coming to the same balconies for food put out for them.

THE TOWN FOX

There are foxes in most towns and
cities in the south; fewer in the north.

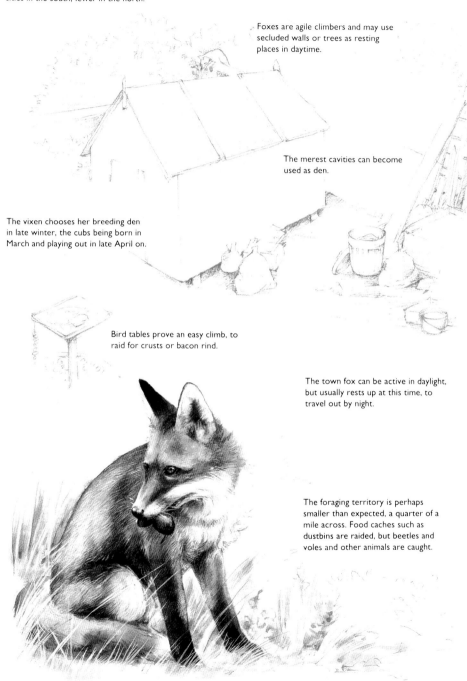

Foxes are agile climbers and may use
secluded walls or trees as resting
places in daytime.

The merest cavities can become
used as den.

The vixen chooses her breeding den
in late winter, the cubs being born in
March and playing out in late April on.

Bird tables prove an easy climb, to
raid for crusts or bacon rind.

The town fox can be active in daylight,
but usually rests up at this time, to
travel out by night.

The foraging territory is perhaps
smaller than expected, a quarter of a
mile across. Food caches such as
dustbins are raided, but beetles and
voles and other animals are caught.

191

HOW TO ASSESS THE HABITAT

If we are interested in a habitat, we want to know more about the plant life and animal life it holds, and perhaps also what it does not.

With plant life, it is often fairly easy to identify and count individual plants and draw sketch maps of various kinds showing what is where. We can analyse this information in different ways and perhaps repeat the work at different times of year.

With animals it is not so easy, simply because they tend to move, or if not, to be reclusive, in daytime at least. Nowadays, of course, collecting butterflies or bird's eggs is in many cases illegal. For scientific research, it may be necessary to trap or snare samples of the animal life, to see what is around. This often requires a licence and is not a layman's job; and, anyway, information of this kind is of little interest without a rigorous context into which to set it. But it is always more interesting to identify things, and to read stories into what we see.

For both plants and animals, there are shortcuts which not only provide information but also provide insights into natural life and sharpen up the interest of what otherwise might become static nature-watching. Some are sketched out here.

Behind plant recognition

Plant recognition is often taken for granted: you see it, you name it, and that's that. Flowering plants, for example, can be grouped into families by the detailed structure of their flowers, seeds and some other features (see 'Classification' in Glossary).

This puts the plant (or animal) into an evolutionary context, for which the habitat is of lesser importance. Thus it is easy to deduce that the waterweeds and other plants of our lakes and rivers are by origin land plants, with close cousins still to be found living in dry land habitats (see pages 122–3). There are some plants which are amphibious, able to grow strongly both in and out of water. One exception is the water lily, which has no land-based relatives, and the assumption is that no fossils of its 'missing links' have yet been found; in any case, plant fossils are not common.

Plant leaves make a rather different study. Although they are not so individual as the flower, nonetheless it is by their leaves that we recognise many plants. There is something of interest here. Aquatic plants tend to have simple leaves which can withstand currents; the handsome arrowhead can in fact produce three different leaf shapes to suit conditions (see pages 128–9). There is clearly a 'best' shape for aquatic plants, but not for land plants, although it is sometimes difficult to understand what advantages there may be in some complex leaf shapes. Leaves can vary on the same plant: shade leaves are larger, while on the holly only the low leaves within reach of grazing animals have spines. Ivy, too, has two shapes of leaf.

Most plants, however, carry no leaves for almost half a year. So winter twigs and leaf buds also help to identify broadleaved trees and shrubs, though they are rather neglected. Young oaks and beeches tend to retain their dead leaves, for reasons unknown.

The age of plants

Annual, biennial, perennial are familiar enough words. It is not generally realised, however, how many annuals are 'ephemerals': that is, plants which can flower and seed more than once within twelve months, some several times if conditions are right for them. They are in flower in any month of the year as a result. Groundsel and other familiar garden 'weeds' are numbered among them.

Perennials with a suckering habit, such as bramble and rosebay, can be some decades old, but only trees, or, to be more precise, woody growths (which include shrubs), reach a good age. Trees and shrubs do not age in the way animals do, and a coppice stool can be centuries old; indeed, some of the oldest living things in Britain are ash coppice stools (see pages 28–9).

It is possible to estimate the age of oak, beech, ash and a few other species of well-timbered trees by their size alone. Measure the girth, the distance around the trunk at head height (1·5 metres from the ground): if the tree is close set with others, 1·25 centimetres ($\frac{1}{2}$ inch) of girth equals 1 year of age; if free-standing, 2·5 centimetres (1 inch) equals 1 year. Rough and ready this method is, but the only alternative is to cut the tree down and count the annual growth rings, which would be rather drastic!

The age of a habitat

There are few shortcuts here. That a hedge is almost certainly older than a tree growing in it is one, but usually the length of time that a habitat community has been in existence has to be deduced from a range of sources. Maps and written records may give an actual age or at least a minimum age in years, although indicator plants and animals can tell you if the wood or grass field is generally an ancient or a recent one (see pages 18–19, 56–7 for examples). A

shrub count can indicate the approximate century age of a hedge (see pages 84–5). In general, after a good many centuries, a habitat tends to develop a varied and balanced 'semi-natural' community, and this itself can be an age indicator. Old meadow land and chalk downland with their abundant flowers are among the examples.

Transects

Details of the plantlife of a habit can easily be gained. The methods are really just ways of focusing our attention on the plant species growing, how much ground they occupy and other things.

One simple method suitable for a hedgerow is a profile transect, an imaginary cut across the breadth of the hedge. A zonation is often clearly evident.

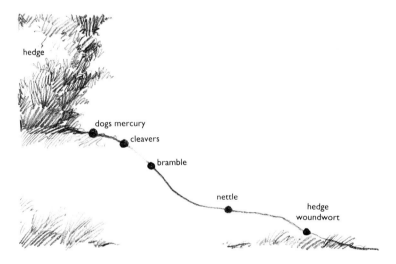

It is quick to do, but only the most conspicuous plants are likely to be recorded. A belt transect (below), which is really just a long thin map, improves on this: belt transects can easily be made across open grassland and other habitats.

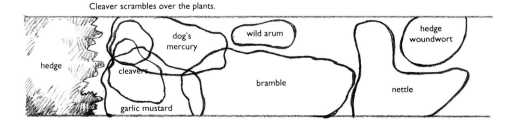

Cleaver scrambles over the plants.

Wild-flower counts

Sample counts of the number of different plant species noticed in a habitat can be revealing. Two separate but similar habitats (pasture fields, for example) can be compared. With habitats which are in the first stage of colonisation, such as sand dunes or waste ground or a burnt area of heathland, the actual total number of plants can be meaningful.

In ecology teaching, a simple light square frame is used, enclosing an area of a square metre (or square yard). It is placed on the ground, and all plant species within it are counted. This is really a method for concentrating observation, for seeing plants which would not be noticed when walking along with a pen and notepad. The positioning of the frame needs to be as random as possible, especially if several counts are being taken in the same field. Some people advise throwing the frame backwards over the shoulder to a site unseen, but there is no need to go to such theatrical extremes.

It is unlikely that the names of all the plants will be known without hesitation, especially when they are not in flower. At any one time, only some of them are likely to be in flower, so that it can be worth simply counting up how many different kinds of leaf there are (the leaves of different species are often distinct enough). Ancient chalk turf and meadowland can have over 30 different species of flowering plant to the square metre, including up to a dozen wild grasses in the latter case.

It is interesting to decide whether a high count increases the chance of rarities.

Maps

Plant societies can be mapped, although this is a time-consuming business. Their presence is often the direct result of unseen changes in the soil below; an obvious example is the plant tally of the top of an ancient ant hill which becomes leached and perhaps rather acid as a result, compared with that of the flatter ground around. Some of the most dramatic examples are found in surviving areas of Norfolk's Breckland (see pages 152–3), where patches of acid gravels carry a very different suite of flowers from that of the chalk turf which surrounds them.

TRACKING MAMMALS

Britain's wild mammals are rather difficult to observe. A faint scream from the grass may be all that is revealed of an angry incident between two shrews; a flash of tan coat the only glimpse of a roe buck. Even grey squirrels, although familiar enough, are comparatively secretive. In addition a large number of mammals are active only or mainly by night. Nevertheless, they cannot but help give some indication of their presence.

Night calls

These can be extraordinary, and eerie when first heard. The screams of the vixen on January nights are startling, and the weird rasping coughs of the buck roe deer and the far-carrying high-pitched rhythmical cry of the doe are truly alarming on still July and August nights, if they are not recognised for what they are.

Pathways and runs

Mammals which graze or feed on plants usually tend to have fixed periods of activity; and they also tend to keep to regular pathways between the 'safe house', whether it be a burrow or simply a regularly used daytime lying-up place, and the feeding ground. Their larder does not move, and so this path usually takes a short route between the two. It is also for some species an emergency escape route back to the safety of the burrow. Shrews, moles and badgers which raid a larder of insects and worms – more or less a sitting larder – also tend to have regular runs. Mammal predators such as stoats also make use of regular tracks along the foot of a hedge when they are on reconnaissance in their territory.

The vegetation of the pathway becomes flattened with use or even worn to bare soil; this is often seen on a track across a heath.

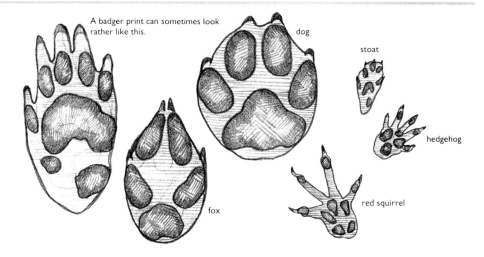

A badger print can sometimes look rather like this.

dog

stoat

hedgehog

red squirrel

fox

The width of the path can be misleading. A deer track can be quite narrow, but the height of the fences and fallen boughs and other obstacles under which it runs can be more of a clue to its usual traffic. Hairs caught in snags can be a clue, those of the badger, which are dark but paler blue at each end, being easily recognisable, though their paths will also be used by others.

Have a look along hedge bottoms or the bases of stone walls. The bottom of an overgrown ditch is a less obvious route, but one that is often chosen. Mice, voles and shrews create pathways (which can become tunnels) through longish and tussocky grass, as do rabbits if the grass is tall enough.

For most of its length such a pathway may be too firm or too littered with leaves and twigs to take any footprints, but from time to time it may cross a muddy patch. This is the place to look for tracks.

Tracks

These are unlikely to be as clear as they are shown in illustrations in field guides. It is best to look for them in early morning or late evening, when the light is at a slant and casts shadows. The ground which gives the clearest track is fine dampish mud, damp sand or dry snow, but the tracks will quickly slump or merge in around the edges in all three, and in some weathers quickly become silted up with wind-blown dust.

There is always a chance of finding prints 'fossilised' in mud which has since dried and hardened; even dinosaur prints originally formed in this way have been found.

There is often a difference between fore and hind prints, and confusion can arise because the gait of the animal affects their planting. When moving fast, for example, rabbit tracks seem (at least to our eyes) to point logically in the backwards direction because the hind prints are in fact being placed ahead of the fore. The distance between hoof prints in deer tracks relates to the speed, which can change, as will be seen if the tracks are followed. The further apart they are, the greater the speed.

Territories

Many mammals keep rather clearly defined territories. That of the badger is explained overleaf.

Red deer hinds have summer and winter territories, and the successful stags join them in the latter, which extend over about 10 hectares (25 acres). The weasel's territory can occupy 2 hectares of woodland, a stoat's ten times as much of open countryside. The roe deer buck takes about 5 hectares (12 acres). These territories are instinctively fixed, and are of an area which will comfortably feed the animal, its mate or mates and youngsters.

The tracks may respect the territory bounds, of course.

Deer-tracking

There are several species of deer living wild in Britain, and some also roam semi-wild in parklands of one kind or another. Deer-tracking is worth a book in itself.

The favoured browsing areas of red deer in wooded areas can become grassy 'lawns' as a result, such as can be found in the New Forest. The way that deer graze grass can be distinctive.

On the way, the animals may snatch a mouthful at a favourite bush alongside the track, virtually coppicing it (even holly will be raided in this way). Shrubs browsed by roe deer look rather as if they have been clipped. Roe deer will also browse back the leaders and side branches of young conifers, which is why they are often fenced out of young plantations. In winter, roe deer especially may make do with blackberry, and thickets may be stripped bare of leaves as far as they can reach.

Changes created by deer browsing in woodland can be more extensive than realised, and perhaps really noticed only when two areas are compared: one might have much denser undergrowth than the other for no apparent reason, for example. The wild flowers can also suffer: it is notable that fallow deer are very fond of wild orchids, and can wipe out colonies of tway-blade in woods that they graze.

Or the tracks may lead to a wallow. This is typical of red deer, being an often deepish wet hollow into which the stags forcibly throw themselves, to roll and smear themselves in mud. It may be a reaction against the irritation of ticks and other skin parasites; but it is curious that the females also do rather the same, but choose no more than a dry and dusty patch of earth.

The courtship of deer is elaborate. Unlike the red deer, the roe bucks seem to occupy their territory for the whole year. The courtship chase is often circular, and a 'roe ring' – a racing ring – can result, worn into the grass often round a bush or tree. (Rabbits also run rings around each other in courtship, but these are likely to remain only in sand, rabbits often being present on sand dunes, of course.)

Another common clue to a deer's territory is the fraying of saplings – rubbing the bark off them with the forehead, and scenting them as a territorial marker. This is sometimes connected with clearing the antlers of the skin, or 'velvet'. The young tree may be pushed sideways by this activity. Rather different is the hunger gnawing of strips of bark in a hard winter: fallow deer (but not roe) will strip roots and lower trunk in this way. Roe deer will, however, use the foot of a trunk or exposed roots to scrape their short antlers free of velvet.

Beginnings and endings

If found, tracks can be followed. On an open clear canvas such as sand dunes, there is always the chance of finding evidence of an incident: of one animal coming across another and finishing it off, maybe.

The origin of the track is often a clue, but one that should be closely quizzed. The burrow may identify the owner of the tracks leaving it, but burrows made by one species are often hijacked by another. Tracks from a tree will suggest a squirrel, especially if they lead to a series of frenzied diggings when it makes random attempts at finding its buried cache of nuts (see pages 72–3). Tracks are often purposeful in this way: little in nature is accidental. But other animals are also good climbers, including the mink (is the tree near water?).

Badger-watching

Badger-watching is a rewarding pastime. Because of the habitual nature of most animal behaviour, a regular programme of activity can be expected. Foraging areas reached by the track can usually be easily identified: the badger digs up roots and bulbs, and also worms, leaving shallow scrapes in the ground (often lawns in the wood are chosen, or pasture outside it). But badgers, like most animals that are not strictly herbivorous, are scavengers, and on the watch for anything they can get. So a badger will also raid a rabbit's stop if it finds one (see page 199) and kill the helpless youngsters, leaving their nipped-off heads scattered over the ground; foxes will also do

THE BADGER IN THE HABITAT

Grooming and toning up muscles by scratching bark.

Pushing a ball of grass or bracken for bedding.

An early visit to a shallow dung pit.

The set is often in sloping ground, its many entrances fronted by piles of soil. Here footprints are found, and wisps of old bedding.

The holes are about 30cm across (rabbit holes narrow to 15cm or less).

Unused entrances may be spanned by spiderwebs.

First to emerge to the sow. She raises her snout to scent danger. (When badger watching, stand hidden and down wind, an hour before dusk.)

Hours are spent out in the territory, up to 50 hectares (120 acres) in area. It becomes networked with their well marked tracks.

this. Another thing to look for is the exercise trees where it cleans its claws – these are likely to be near the sett – and latrine pits, which are found both near the sett and out in the territory, where they act as territory-markers.

Droppings

These are often relatively easy to recognise, and a favourite in field guides. The otter spraint is described on page 126. Rabbits doubly digest their droppings; the first green droppings are re-eaten in the burrow, the hard, dry pellets left as territory-markers on ant hills or other bumps in the ground.

Somewhat similar are the pellets coughed up by some predatory birds after the first stage of digestion. They contain the bones, feathers and fur of their prey (see page 200).

Food remains

The actual method of feeding can be a distinctive feature. Even the way that the grass is grazed can be a clue. Deer often nibble the tips of the grasses, easy enough to pick out when you are looking for it. The grazing of livestock is described on pages 58–9.

Food remains can be persistent. Badger setts and fox dens are usually easy enough to distinguish: apart from the massive earthworking of the former, its entrances are usually relatively clean, perhaps scattered only with some old grass or bracken bedding, whereas the fox has the habit of leaving an entrance scattered with debris of meals – with bones, feathers and other food rubbish.

Trout or salmon taken by an otter can be recognised, for this animal has the habit of peeling the skin back over the tail and picking clean the bones, including the cartilages of the head.

Wood mouse and bank vole also leave identifiable clues. They both take hazel nuts; the empty shells left by the wood mouse have radiating toothmarks on the inner surface matched by faint scratches on the outside, whereas those left by the vole lack these outside toothmarks. Squirrels tend to split the nuts into two parts with their powerful incisors, while birds tend to leave jagged holes where they have drilled and broken their way through the shell.

Mice and voles also share out berries, including hawthorn berries (haws). Here we have another example of the 'fit' of species, for the wood mouse tends to take the pips and leave the pulp and skin, the bank vole to be more interested in the latter (though sheer hunger may distort this rule). Both may store the berries, and nuts, too, in an empty bird's nest, often quite a way from the ground since both are agile climbers.

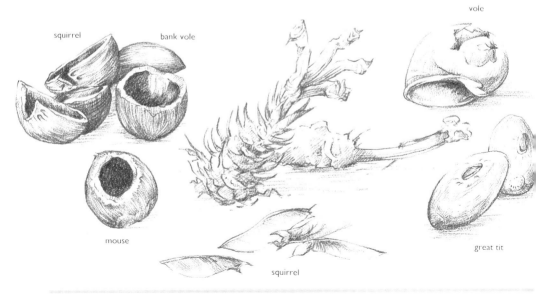

squirrel   bank vole   vole   mouse   great tit   squirrel

Burrows

The size of the entrance is sometimes a clue. Smallest of the mammal burrows are those of the shrews, about 2·5 centimetres in diameter. Mouse holes are larger, and those of rats maybe 10 centimetres in diameter. As with rabbits, the width should be gauged a short distance into the hole, since the actual opening tends to slump wider.

Rabbit warrens have many entrances, and the whole interconnecting complex may extend across an area of almost 200 square metres. Apart from the communal system, the doe will often dig a solitary blind burrow or stop, where her young are born. Here, they are left alone for much of the day (the entrance is usually closed up when the doe leaves it). Foxes, however, may make use of the rabbit's burrows, as may stoats and others.

There are several ways of discovering if a burrow is in active use. Watching it may sometimes be possible; although most mammals are active only by night and are shy of any light, many seem to be relatively tolerant of red light. Footprints in the excavated soil are a clue, as are fresh food remains. A rank pungent smell is sometimes proof of rabbits; the smell of foxes is also recognisable. Undamaged spider webs strung across the entrance are a sign that the hole, if not the burrow, is not in use. You can also leave a pattern of grass stalks at the entrance to see if these become disturbed.

Mole hills are pushed up when new tunnels are being cleared in the soil below. A network of tunnels lies below the grass, through which, on a regular four-hours-on and four-hours-off shift pattern, the mole patrols, snapping up any worms or insects that have fallen into the tunnel.

Nests

A few mammals manufacture identifiable nests. The dormouse creates a domed summer nest which may be several feet above ground, while the winter one for hibernation is on or near the ground. The former is often a woven mass of the bark of honeysuckle: hence stripped honeysuckle may be a clue of its presence in the wood.

The harvest mouse makes a tight ball of a summer nest, about 6 cm across and about 40 cm off the ground, woven around and between vertical plant stems. These nests are very unlikely to be found in the modern cornfield, but perhaps in its undisturbed edges. They are also found in the reeds of undisturbed watersides. The winter nest is a snugly padded cell on the ground or in a short burrow.

Most likely to be seen is the drey of the grey squirrel – an untidy, football of twigs high in a tree, seemingly loosely jammed together, but surviving strong winds and gales. Otherwise it will take over a woodpecker hole, or make itself at home in a hollow trunk or bough.

Counting mammals

The numbers of herding mammals such as seals and deer (and rabbits) can usually be estimated without too much trouble. As with a flock of birds (see page 202), count out a manageable fragment of the whole visual area, with perhaps ten or twenty individuals, say, and multiply up to get an approximate estimate of the total.

There are professional techniques for estimating populations. Many involve humanely trapping a sample number, and marking and releasing them. After a while, long enough to allow complete dispersal, the trap is again set to see whether the population is static or fluctuating. The estimated population equals:

$$\frac{(\text{number in first sample}) \times (\text{number in second})}{\text{number of marked individuals in second sample}}$$

One complication is that mammals, whether they be predators, scavengers or herbivores, are often strongly territorial, and this will clearly bias the results in any given area. Shrews may have a range of not more than 30 metres, for example, and voles about the same. All in all, mammal populations are best related exactly to the given habitat area, by marking on a sketch map actual sightings and such clues as food signs and tracks, recorded over a period of time and, if possible, relating these to particular plants or features.

FOLLOWING BIRDS

Birds leave far less persistent tracking clues than mammals, and observing birdlife is much more of a three-dimensional business. Unlike mammals, however, birds do tend to press themselves on our attention, and on the whole birdwatchers want to see the real thing and are not satisfied to see the tree where the bird sat the day before. Nonetheless, some tracking clues are useful.

Footprints

These are likely to be of any value only on streamside mud or on the estuary flats or sand of the coast. Many species have distinctive prints and these, when clear enough, may reveal confrontations and other incidents.

Waders and other shore feeders can make distinctive patterns where they probe the mud for shellfish and worms.

Feathers

These are lost in various ways: accidentally when fleeing through the branches; or moulted; or dusted off in a dust bath. Many birds seem to enjoy this last activity, which may relieve the itchings of lice.

Pellets

These are coughed up by predators – owls and raptors (the daytime birds of prey such as hawks, falcons, eagles and buzzards) – and also by gulls and others. They contain the compacted feathers, bones and other indigestible parts of whatever the prey happened to be. These pellets have a characteristic shape, as these examples show:

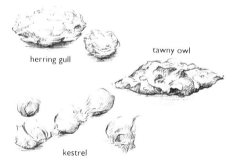

herring gull

tawny owl

kestrel

Many raptors choose a favourite perch or plucking post, below which both pellets and dismembered refuse including bones and feathers may be scattered. Birds taken by hawks are carefully plucked before being eaten. The sparrowhawk, for example, likes to use a 'block', a tree stump perhaps, although an old nest or (it is claimed) a specially constructed platform may be used; often close to the ground.

Other food remains

Thrushes hammer snail shells, taking them to a favoured area of hard ground or an 'anvil stone', which becomes surrounded by a litter of broken pieces.

The nuthatch crams a hazel nut into a bark crevice and hammers through the shell, a sound that can be heard from some distance. The empty nut shell may remain in place.

Tree or other holes

These are of two kinds. Feeding holes are typically bored by woodpeckers in the trunk or branches or in the rotting stump of a tree. The birds probably detect a clutch of beetles or other grubs by the resonance of the timber or even by scent and hammer through the bark to reach them. These colonies can be smelly: the goat moth gains its name from the odour of the caterpillar.

Nesting holes are sometimes freshly made, by woodpeckers generally, but many birds adopt holes that they find. Owls make use of what is available. The coal tit and others adopt, which is why nest boxes are so successful, although what seems to us the merest crevice might be called into use.

Some tits will excavate a hole. The willow tit burrows in soft wood, although its twin the marsh tit will adopt a hole, and this leads to a separation of these two similar-looking species (see pages 142–3).

It is quite common for the nest of one species to be adopted later by another. Woodpecker holes frequently play host to redstart, starling, tits, pied flycatcher and others. When the nuthatch adopts the hole of a woodpecker, it narrows the entrance with mud to reduce the risk of raiders.

The burrows of the sand martin and kingfisher are worth looking out for along the riverside (see pages 126–7).

Birdsong

Outside the breeding season, for much of the year in fact, many birds are mobile. They can turn up in all kinds of places, and even blackbirds and others which seem fairly residential make long journeys to seek food.

Nesting time is different. Instinct now comes to the fore, and territories are held against all rivals. What the holding of territory does, in fact, is to spread the species out over the available larder, dispersing them down the hedge, or across the wood. In this context, the colonial nesting of seabirds is interesting (see pages 182–3).

Birdsong can be part of territory awareness. Birds make many calls – of alarm, of recognition, and of warning – but songbirds and some others also have elaborate song, often with complicated phrases. In the simplest case, the male chooses a songpost near the nest and sings from it at regular intervals. This song warns off intruders of its own kind; if they fail to heed the message and approach closer, threat postures are adopted (equal to our clenched fist). If these fail, feathers may fly in actual physical attack, although it is unusual for this stage to be reached.

The robin provides a good and familiar example of how well defined in the bird's instincts this territory is. It is relatively unafraid of man, and will often accompany or precede a walker down a path or across the garden, until its territory boundary is reached, whereupon it turns back. If a rival robin encroaches onto its territory, it will adopt its threat posture, raising its head upright to show its throat, giving its body a sagging sack-like profile. As with many wildlife sightings, this can be done so quickly that there is scarcely time for us to notice, but it usually has its desired result.

The dawn chorus

Birdsong is clearest in the morning, although stormy weather tends to diminish it. The birds start singing in what can be a regular order:

blackbird – half an hour before sunrise
songthrush
wood pigeon
robin
mistle thrush (maybe the only one
    to continue in wild weather)
(pheasant)
willow warbler
wren

After some time many of these will fall silent. Song usually recommences in late afternoon or evening when feeding slows down. Some may continue after dusk – the nightingale is by no means the only one to sing at dusk's end (see pages 26–7).

Estimating numbers

The fact that birds do hold territory allows us to estimate the number of songbirds (or, more precisely, the number of nesting pairs). On an early-morning walk down a hedgerow, for example, the different species will reveal themselves by sight and sound.

Transects

Walks of this kind can also be used to determine the total population of an area. The basis of the method is to walk slowly along a fixed path, taking note of all birds heard or seen within, say, 25 metres of the path on each side.

A set of such transects, parallel to each other and 50 metres apart, will enable an estimate to be made of bird numbers in a wood. If it is a fairly uniform wood, only part of it need be surveyed, the total for the survey area being multiplied up for the wood as a whole.

Relative abundance

One problem in hoping for absolute totals by transect counts is that some bird species are easier to see and hear than others; some may have a day off when you are surveying. Transects are thus perhaps more useful for gaining an idea of relative abundance. The path is walked as before, but now it can dogleg or zigzag through the habitat providing the separate lengths remain more than 50 metres apart. The relative abundance equals:

$$\frac{\text{number (average) of that species seen}}{\text{total of all birds seen}} \times 100\ (\%)$$

One 'top-ten' list, with relative abundance (%), may be:

wood pigeon	16%	jackdaw	7%
wren	10%	blue tit	7%
blackbird	9%	willow warbler	5%
robin	8%	chaffinch	3%
song thrush	7%	starling	3%

with a further 20 or more species also present but less abundant.

Spot census

This is a rather similar method, but, instead of walking, choose, say, ten points in the wood about the same distance apart and spend ten minutes in each, noting all birds seen or heard within a 25-metre radius.

Such methods provide a handy way of monitoring changes in birdlife through the seasons. They also allow two different woods to be compared, and perhaps draw attention to the differences resulting from deer browsing, which changes the structure of the lower layers of the woodland.

Absolute counts

It is possible to try to make counts of absolute totals in a habitat. This means drawing a sketch map and marking actual nest sites and other observations on it, using standardised symbols. Census work of this kind is coordinated by the British Trust for Ornithology, and examples of the symbols used are enough to illustrate the calibre of the information gained. Here for a bird species coded B:

B♂	male
B♀	female
(B)	singing male
B	alarm call
B food	seen with food in beak
B*	nest
—B B—	two birds fighting; the arrow shows direction of retreat of one
(B)–(B)	singing bird changes its position

Bird flocks

Estimating birds on the wing or far out on saltings or a lake is not so difficult as it may seem. The knack is to count a group of ten or 20 (or 50 or 100 if they remain still long enough) and to estimate the number of similar groups in the whole flock.

× 8

Bird nests

Sitting birds and nests in use should never be disturbed. Nests can often be seen, however, on a winter walk. Their structure is fascinatingly diverse, as one common example shows: although the blackbird and its cousin the song thrush both use grass, the former lines it with grass but the latter with mud. Field guides give examples.

REPTILES

As snakes and lizards are relatively light of body and utilise existing holes for cover, traces of their activities or passage are likely to be very faint. The only exception may be on fine, slightly damp sand or windless dry dusty heathland soil, where adder, smooth snake and slow worm may leave characteristic but puzzling tracks, and lizards leave their prints.

The grass snake, however, is most frequently seen swimming on a pond or ditch.

Snakes shed their skins from time to time, and the loosed skins can occasionally be found.

INSECTS

Indicators of the health of a habitat
Insects can provide signposts to the health of a habitat. Unlike birds, which may nest in a hedge (or in a disused tractor, come to that) and feed well away, an insect is more closely linked to the actual plant species. Many are typical of classic habitats as well as other countryside features – the gatekeeper butterfly, for example, is typical of hedges, being more often seen along them than in other places (its alternative name is the hedge brown).

Although insects have a broken life cycle, at least one span of it is often highly visible. The presence of the flying adult mayfly or dragonfly, for example, speaks for the cleanliness of the water in the stream or river (see pages 130–1).

Estimating numbers
Numbers in a flying swarm of, for example, hoverflies or mayflies can sometimes be estimated using the same method as for bird flocks: by counting a small area and multiplying up. Flying insects are quick on the eye, and this cannot be very precise. Swarms of greenfly or similar species motionless on a plant can be estimated in the same way.

Butterflies
The above method can be used to estimate numbers in a butterfly colony. Many blues are colonial, their presence reflecting the plants present as well as conditions (see pages 62–3).

Carefully planned butterfly counting, however, can reveal some interesting information. There are five main family groupings of British butterflies:

browns
blues, copper and hairstreaks
skippers – with moth-like flight
whites and yellows
nymphalids – large and colourful, and often familiar because they are wanderers (fritillaries, peacock, red admiral are examples)

Comparative numbers in habitats can be gained quite simply by means of half-hour walks. The walk should be made at a fairly slow speed and take 20–30 minutes. That represents just over a kilometre (about $\frac{3}{4}$ mile), and the walk can be circular, ending at the start point. It should be taken between 10.30 a.m. and 4 p.m., on at least five fine days, and only during warmish, stillish weather which encourages the butterflies to fly; if the wind is sweeping up a lot of dust, or big branches are swaying, they are unlikely to be out and about.

Imagine a path 2 metres wide, and keep a record of how many butterflies are seen on that path and 5 metres ahead. The average (or total) for five days can be compared with those in other habitats. In this way, abandoned railway cuttings have shown their value as a refuge for the commoner species, although some also had rarities (see pages 110–11).

Coming to the light
Lighted windows attract insects at night, and some of these visitors appear as regularly as clockwork by the season or by the time of night. The maybug, for example, must be familiar to anyone near an oak wood during the month of May, while the dainty green lacewings are familiar on country window panes after dusk has ended.

Attracting moths
The professional ecologist might try exposing a captured female moth; the males of

some species can scent a potential mate from many hundreds of metres. This keen sense of smell (the feathery antennae house the receptors) means that moths are attracted to sweet molasses, with perhaps a spoonful or two of wine or beer mixed in, smeared on a trunk or post; they will visit and perch alongside to sip it, when they can be observed with a red torch.

PONDS AND STREAMS

Mammals
The otter leaves recognisable clues (see pages 126–7), but the feral mink is now quite common. The mink, originally an escapee from fur farms, now roams widely, exacting a toll on waterfowl in some places; it leaves droppings which are foul compared with the spraints of the otter.

The familiar plop from a short way ahead as you walk down a stream bank is a water vole leaping to safety. Commonly called a water rat, it is a true vole with the vole's vegetarian habits. It has a complex tunnel system running along the bank, with entrances both above and below the waterline and perhaps others some metres inland away from the bank itself. It has a regular territory which it patrols, swimming or on foot, and some of the paths may be visible. When above ground it is usually actively grazing, creating a shortish 'lawn' among the bankside vegetation.

Water shrews are probably commoner than realised. Their home range can extend along 140 metres of stream, with bankside burrows with exits just above and below the waterline.

Birds
Waterfowl can be investigated in some of the ways used for woodland and field birds (see pages 200–202). Large numbers of waterfowl flock in winter. Two bird species make burrows, usually in a cliff-like stretch of bank, to provide safety from marauding rats. The sand martin's burrows are to be seen grouped together. The kingfisher's is solitary, and very often its entrance is

streaked white with droppings: in comparison with the martin, it keeps a foul nest.

Reptiles
The grass snake, despite its name, is most usually seen swimming on or moving near water rather than on land.

Amphibia
Frog spawn is such a familiar image and folk memory of spring that it comes as a shock to discover that frogs are now rather an uncommon sighting. Indeed, in many parts of Britain, their stronghold is now the suburban garden. The reasons are that almost all the once common field ponds have disappeared in today's manicured countryside, and pollution has also taken its toll.

Frog and toad spawn are easy enough to distinguish (the latter is laid in strings rather than clumps). Toads seem to 'remember' ancestral breeding ponds, to which they move each spring, often on traditional routes across country and across a variety of obstacles ranging from old tumbled stone walls to modern by-passes. Some conservation organisations mount toad-watch patrols to protect them on the latter. How toads manage both to 'remember' the pond and to navigate to it is unknown.

Fish
Different stretches of river are characterised by different assemblages of fish (see pages 124–5), while pools and mature lengths have their own holding areas. Some fish are notable migrants: salmon return to their ancestral headwaters to breed, while trout also migrate (see pages 134–5). Eels were often found making cross-country journeys from one stream to another. They, too, are migrants, and young eels swarm up some westerly rivers.

Water pollution
The damaging effects of pollution on life are well known, and the health of a stream can often be deduced from its animal life (see pages 130–1).

THE SHORE

The seashore offers good opportunities for watching wildlife, and it is particularly strong in some respects.

Tracks

Damp sand and wet mud are ideal media for tracking. Even the delicate footprints of birds can remain clearly on view for hours until the next tide. Signs of feeding activity usually accompany these. Waders probe the mud for worms and shellfish, and the surface around the prints can be dimpled as a result. The plovers are among the birds that 'paddle' the mud, agitating it with one foot. This may have the effect of drawing the invertebrates to the surface, either out of curiosity or perhaps because these vibrations resemble the slaps made by the wavelets of the incoming tide. On the other hand, the webbed feet of the gulls when they patter act rather like a suction valve, of the kind used to clear bath plug holes.

Feeding traces

Gulls cough up pellets containing the fish bones and skin of their prey, but these do not linger long in this environment. Broken shells may remain: oystercatchers have two methods of opening shellfish (see pages 178–9). It is in the small shallow pools out on the saltings at low tide that you are likely to see the small *Hydrobia* shells, which play such a vital part in bird diets here.

Relative abundance

Shores can be compared quite simply, by walking down them and estimating the relative abundance of plants and animals in a transect about 10 metres wide. The main groupings are noted: green seaweeds, brown seaweeds, red seaweeds, sea anemones, worms, barnacles, shrimps and so on. The actual species need not be identified, but note how many different species there are of each group:

> rare – only one or two
> frequent– several
> abundant – a lot

If a plant or animal is abundant only at one level on the shore, it still counts as abundant since its distribution is probably controlled by the tidal levels and zones, such as red seaweeds which may be abundant at the bottom of the shore and lichens at the top.

Imagine that one area has few green seaweeds but three species of them, while another which has similar exposure to the waves has abundant green weed but only one species. These green weeds are favourite grazing of limpets, and these two results suggest that limpets are still active and numerous on the first sample but less so on the second. If it was pollution that harmed them, then one green seaweed in particular – *Enteromorpha* – is quite resistant to many kinds of pollution.

And indeed this example is based on a real incident some years ago, when a tanker came to grief on the rocks off south-west Wales. Oil flooded into the sea, and polluted the nearby shores.

It was found that the limpets and sea snails in the second sample area were at first being drugged rather than killed by the oil, but in that drugged and helpless state they dropped off the rocks to be eaten by seagulls. The resistant seaweed flourished and in some places smothered out other animal life.

Certainly this simple survey will show up the effects of exposure on different sides of a bay, one sheltered from and the other facing the main waves. It can also pinpoint areas affected by pollution, perhaps a long time ago.

Rock pools by night

As with some other habitats, it is worth inspecting a rock pool with a red torch at night. Many of its denizens are virtually blind to, or at least untroubled by, red light, and continue their lives undisturbed. Exposed limpets, for example, roam the rocks, grazing barely noticeable seaweed slimes. They return to the same spot exactly, the edge of their shell tailored to fit perfectly that part of the rock surface if the rock is hard; on soft rocks the edge of the shell sits in a groove worn in the rock.

USEFUL ADDRESSES

The following short list is of the main organisations which are open for membership to the general public and which own or manage land of wildlife value, which is either open to the public at large or restricted to their members. Others may also have holdings. The Forestry Commission for example, although mainly concerned with timber production does some conservation work. Many societies produce magazines or enable their members to take part in monitoring or other activities.

The Royal Society for Nature Conservation (RSNC),
The Green,
Witham Park,
Waterside South,
Lincoln LN5 7JR
(0522) 544400

This is the linking body of the county-based Wildlife Trust Partnership who together own more land which is managed as a nature reserve than any other organisation.

ADDRESSES OF COUNTY TRUSTS

Avon Wildlife Trust
The Old Police Station
32 Jacob's Wells Road
Bristol BS8 1DR
(0272) 268018

Bedfordshire & Cambridgeshire Wildlife
    Trust
5 Fulbourn Manor
Manor Walk
Fulbourn
Cambridge CB1 5BN
(0223) 880788

Berkshire, Buckinghamshire & Oxfordshire
    Naturalists' Trust (BBONT)
3 Church Cowley Road
Rose Hill
Oxford OX4 3JR
(0865) 775476

Birmingham & Black Country Wildlife Trust
Unit 213
Jubilee Trade Centre
130 Pershore Street
Birmingham B5 6ND
(021) 666 7474

Brecknock Wildlife Trust
Lion House
7 Lion Street
Brecon
Powys LD3 7AY
(0874) 5708

Cheshire Conservation Trust
Marbury Country Park
Northwich
Cheshire CW9 6AT
(0606) 781868

Cleveland Wildlife Trust
The Old Town Hall
Mandale Road
Thornaby
Cleveland TS17 6AW
(0642) 608405

Cornwall Trust for Nature Conservation
Five Acres
Allet
Truro
Cornwall TR4 9DJ
(0872) 73939

Cumbria Wildlife Trust
Church Street
Ambleside
Cumbria LA22 0BU
(05394) 32476

Derbyshire Wildlife Trust
Elvaston Castle Country Park
Derbyshire DE7 3EP
(0332) 756610

Devon Wildlife Trust
188 Sidwell Street
Exeter
Devon EX4 6RD
(0392) 79244

Dorset Trust for Nature Conservation
39 Christchurch Road
Bournemouth
Dorset BH1 3NS
(0202) 554241

Durham Wildlife Trust
52 Old Elvet
Durham
County Durham DH1 3HN
(091) 386 9797

Dyfed Wildlife Trust
7 Market Street
Haverfordwest
Dyfed SA61 1NF
(0437) 765462

Essex Naturalists' Trust
Fingringhoe Wick Nature Reserve
Fingringhoe
Colchester
Essex CO5 7DN
(020628) 678

Glamorgan Wildlife Trust
Nature Centre
Fountain Road
Tondu
Mid Glamorgan CF32 0EH
(0656) 724100

Gloucestershire Trust for Nature
 Conservation
Church House
Standish
Stonehouse
Gloucestershire GL10 3EU
(045) 382 2761

Guernsey
La Société Guernesiaise
Candie Gardens
St Peter Port
Guernsey, C.I.
(0481) 25093

Gwent Wildlife Trust
16 White Swan Court
Church Street
Monmouth
Gwent NP5 3BR
(0600) 5501

Hampshire & Isle of Wight Naturalists' Trust
71 The Hundred
Romsey
Hampshire SO5 8BZ
(0794) 513786

Herefordshire Nature Trust
Community House
25 Castle Street
Hereford HR1 2NW
(0432) 356872

Hertfordshire & Middlesex Wildlife Trust
Grebe House
St Michael's Street
St Albans
Hertfordshire AL3 4SN
(0727) 58901

Kent Trust for Nature Conservation
The Annexe
1a Bower Mount Road
Maidstone
Kent ME16 8AX
(0622) 753017

Lancashire Trust for Nature Conservation
Cuerden Park Wildlife Centre
Shady Lane
Bamber Bridge
Preston
Lancashire PR5 6AU
(0772) 324129

Leicester & Rutland Trust for Nature
 Conservation
1 West Street
Leicester
Leicestershire LE1 6UU
(0533) 553904

Lincolnshire & South Humberside Trust for
 Nature Conservation
The Manor House
Alford
Lincolnshire LN13 9DL
(0507) 463468

London Wildlife Trust
80 York Way
London N1 9AG
(071) 278 6612

Manx Nature Conservation Trust
Ballamoar House
Ballaugh
Isle of Man
(062489) 7611

Montgomeryshire Wildlife Trust
8 Severn Square
Newtown
Powys SY16 2AG
(0686) 624751

Norfolk Naturalists' Trust
72 Cathedral Close
Norwich
Norfolk NR1 4DF
(0603) 625540

Northamptonshire Wildlife Trust
Lings House
Billing Lings
Northampton
Northamptonshire NN3 4BE
(0604) 405285

Northumberland Wildlife Trust
Hancock Museum
Barras Bridge
Newcastle upon Tyne
Tyne and Wear NE2 4PT
(091) 232 0038

North Wales Wildlife Trust
376 High Street
Bangor
Gwynedd LL57 1YE
(0248) 351541

Nottinghamshire Wildlife Trust
310 Sneinton Dale
Nottingham
Nottinghamshire NG3 7DN
(0602) 588242

Radnorshire Wildlife Trust
1 Gwalia Annexe
Ithon Road
Llandrindod Wells
Powys LD1 6AS
(0597) 3298

Scottish Wildlife Trust
25 Johnston Terrace
Edinburgh EH1 2NH
(031) 226 4602

Shropshire Wildlife Trust
167 Frankwell
Shrewsbury
Shropshire SY3 8LG
(0743) 241691

Somerset Trust for Nature Conservation
Fyne Court
Broomfield
Bridgwater
Somerset TA5 2EQ
(08234) 51587

Staffordshire Wildlife Trust
Coutts House
Sandon
Staffordshire ST18 0DN
(088) 97534

Suffolk Wildlife Trust
Park Cottage
Saxmundham
Suffolk IP17 1DQ
(0728) 603765

Surrey Wildlife Trust
Powell Corderoy Annexe
Longfield Road
Dorking
Surrey RH4 3DF
(0306) 743404

Sussex Wildlife Trust
Woods Mill
Shoreham Road
Henfield
West Sussex BN5 9SD
(0273) 492630

Ulster Wildlife Trust
Barnett's Cottage
Barnett
Demesne
Malone Road
Belfast
Northern Ireland BT9 5PB
(0232) 612235

Warwickshire Nature Conservation Trust
Montague Road
Warwick
Warwickshire CV34 5LW
(0926) 496848

Wiltshire Trust for Nature Conservation
19 High Street
Devizes
Wiltshire SN10 1AT
(0380) 725670

Worcestershire Nature Conservation Trust
Lower Smite Farm
Smite Hill
Hindlip
Hereford and Worcester WR3 8SZ
(0905) 754919

Yorkshire Wildlife Trust
10 Toft Green
York
Yorkshire YO1 1JT
(0904) 659570

In addition, there are also numerous Urban Wildlife Groups and the WATCH Club for young people. Details of these can be obtained from RSNC.

The National Trust owns considerable habitat. In England and Wales for example, amongst its 573,000 acres it has ten National Nature Reserves managed by English Nature and seven similar in Wales; 514 SSSIs, 21,000 acres of ancient woodland, 7000 acres of heathland, 16,500 acres of peatland and 3700 acres of old grassland and meadowland. Scotland has its own organisation.

The headquarters are (there are many local offices):

The National Trust
36 Queen Anne's Gate
London SW1H 9AS
(071) 222 9251

The National Trust for Scotland
5 Charlotte Square
Edinburgh EH2 4DU
(031) 226 5922

The Royal Society for the Protection
   of Birds
The Lodge
Sandy
Bedfordshire SG19 2DL
(0767) 80551

The Wildfowl Trust
Slimbridge
Gloucester
Gloucestershire GL2 7BT
(045 389) 333

The Woodland Trust
Westgate
Grantham
Lincolnshire NG31 6IL
(0476) 74297

GLOSSARY

This gives a brief definition or explanation of certain words used in the text. One or two common words, such as 'classic' and 'dedicated', are used in a special way in this book which is explained here. In addition, there are a few brief explanations of differences which sometimes cause confusion (e.g. that between a vole and a mouse, a gull and a wader, a butterfly and a moth).

Numbers in brackets are page numbers for more detailed explanations:

Abundance relative abundance allows us to compare habitats

Abundant numerous, and maybe not confined to one type of habitat

Acid 1) see Soil; 2) acid rain is one result of air pollution

Acre 4 840 square yards (about 70 × 70 yards); 0.4 hectares

Adaptation evolved characteristic fitting a living thing to its niche

Alga (plural algae) simple green plants, many of which are one-celled but including seaweeds

Alien species of plant or animal whose natural range does not include Britain

Alkaline opposite to acid, see Soil

Alluvial of river sediment

Amphibian soft-skinned, cold-blooded vertebrate, e.g. frog, newt

Ancient long-established habitat such as woodland or pasture with semi-natural character

Animal mobile for part of its life and feeding on plant or animal matter; often taken to mean Mammal (which see)

Annual plant which germinates, flowers and seeds within a 12-month period

Aquatic of (fresh) water

Arable ploughland, sown with cereal and other crops

Arctic-alpine a plant typical of those two areas

Arthropod a member of a large animal Phylum; animals with external skeleton (a hard 'shell' of some kind)

Assart field(s) cleared from woodland

Association stable, broad plant community

Atlantic of climate, wet and mild

Bacterium (plural bacteria) microscopic organism often involved in decomposition

Barren 1) with poor soil; 2) old-fashioned name for heathland

Basic (of soil) alkaline

Berry fruit with flesh around the seeds

Biennial 'two-year' plant, flowering and seeding in its second year, then dying

Biomass measure of an ecosystem

Biotic factor the influence of living things on a habitat or an ecosystem

Bivalve mollusc ('shellfish') with a shell in two hinged parts

Bloom 1) a flower; 2) rapid algal growth

Blue (butterfly) a butterfly family

Bog(land) wet, peaty habitat

Bolling stump of pollarded tree

Boreal a prehistoric climate period

Brackish (water) tainted with salt

Brashing clearing the lower branches of trees in a plantation

Broadleaved trees other than conifers and usually (not always) deciduous

Brown (butterfly) a butterfly family

Bryophytes mosses and liverworts

Bug 1) an insect with sucking mouthparts; 2) in daily speech an imprecise word for an insect

Bush general name for low woody growth

Bush-cricket distinctive grasshopper

Butterfly day-flying insects with large patterned wings and club-tipped antennae

Calcareous containing lime (see Soil)

Calcicole a plant liking (or confined to) limy soils

Calcifuge a plant that will not usually thrive on limy soil

Canopy upper branching of trees

Carr wet woodland which develops from fen

Carnivore usually an animal which preys on another, although sundew is called a carnivorous plant

Casual an alien plant growing wild but not (yet) widely established

Catkin tassel of small flowers

Cell microscopic living unit of animal or plant body

Cereal grain crop, e.g. barley

Characteristic typical of a habitat, often so as to help define it

Chaser type of dragonfly

Chlorophyll green plant pigment, seat of photosynthesis

Classification the naming of plants and animals and groups of them in a way that reflects their evolution and relationships. One example is
Phylum – Arthropoda
Class – Insecta
Order – Lepidoptera (butterflies & moths)
Family – Lycaenidae (the blues)
Genus – *Lysandra* ⎫
Species – *bellargus* ⎭ the Adonis blue
(The species name *Lysandra bellargus* is unique to that species, Latinised, international and in italics)

Classic in this book, a long-established semi-natural community

Climate the long-term character of weather, which influences distribution

Climax the stable final stage of plant succession at any place, influenced by climate, exposure, etc.

Climber a plant that uses another for support

Coarse (fish) not a game fish; adapted to muddy conditions

Colonist early invader of a 'new' site

Colonisation the invasion of a 'new' site, usually in waves of specialised species

Colony 1) a number of animals (or plants) of one species breeding in close proximity; 2) a well-organised community, e.g. ants

Common 1) not rare, and often widely distributed; 2) an area of land to which local people have (or had) grazing and other rights

Community assembly of plants and animals linked together in some way and relatively independent

Compartment area of managed woodland

Conifer cone-bearing tree with needle leaves, usually evergreen

Conservation protection of species or a habitat; in practice this usually means care and management in a traditional way

Continental of climate, dry, with hot summers and cold winters

Coppers a group of butterflies closely related to the blues

Coppice woodland cropped by regularly cutting shrubs or trees to a stump

Copse a small wood

Covert small wood, often sporting

Crown the head of a tree

Cultivar cultivated variety

Darter type of dragonfly

Deciduous of trees, shrubs, shedding leaves in autumn

Decomposer category of plant or animal active in the decay cycle of an ecosystem

Dedicated in this book, a species of animal (especially an insect) closely linked to a plant (tree) species

Den (breeding) lair of fox and other mammals or rodents

Derelict abandoned habitat or area

Distribution the range of a species

Dominant dominating, and usually the tallest, plant species in a community

Down(land) chalk hills; their pasture

Drift 1) movement of pebbles on a beach; 2) soil or other surface deposits, especially those of the Ice Age

Duck small waterfowl with webbed feet, broad bills – divers or dabblers

Dun immature mayfly adult

Dune sandy coastal habitat

Ecology study of the relationships between plants, animals and their surroundings

Ecosystem a (self-contained) balanced unit of plant and animal life, influenced also by climate, etc.

Edaphic of the landform and other physical features of an ecosystem

Enclosure a field; The Enclosures – historic period when many of today's fields were created

Endangered rare and in danger of extinction (usually globally)

Environment surroundings; setting; a collective term for temperature, light, humidity, etc. which affect living things

Ephemeral quick-growing plant ('weed') with more than one life cycle a year

Epiphyte plant which habitually grows on another

ESA Environmentally Sensitive Area – area of recognised habitat value in which special grants are available to encourage farmers to maintain traditional methods

Estuary the V-shaped mouth of a river

Eutrophic of fresh water, nutrient-rich

Evergreen retaining leaves in winter

Evolution snowballing process of change whereby new species arise 'fitted' to their 'niche'

Exotic foreign plant or animal species

Extinct no longer found in that habitat or country; or globally

Falcon long-winged bird of prey

Family group of related animals or plants (see Classification)

Fauna the animal life of an area

Fen 1) distinct wetland habitat with peaty soil; The Fens are a part of East Anglia once a wetland of this kind

Feral domesticated but now living wild

Fertiliser (artificial) manure

Field 1) farming enclosure; 2) as an adjective, of trees, etc. of open countryside

Field layer layer of a wood, with grass and herbs

Fir (tree) name commonly used for conifers in general, but in fact one kind

Firebreak corridor in woodland to curtail fire outbreaks

Fittest in evolution and ecology this does not mean the healthiest, but the best suited to a habitat or niche

Flood meadow pasture lying beside a river and frequently flooded as a result

Flora 1) the plants of an area or region; 2) a field guide describing them

Floriferous with many flowering species

Flower 1) definitive part of flowering plants; 2) often used of a herbaceous flowering plant as a whole

Food chain, web linked ladders and networks of food and feeder

Forest 1) general name for (usually a large area of) woodland; 2) land set aside for the Royal hunt and perhaps wooded in part; 3) High Forest is timber-producing woodland

Forestry the commercial growing of timber

Form shallow lair of hare

Fry newly hatched young fish

Fungus (plural fungi) 'plant' of simple structure which usually plays a role in decay and decomposition. Fungi are so unlike green plants that they really form a third living kingdom

Gall cancerous plant growth

Game of fish and some birds, caught or shot for sport

Gastropod mollusc with spiral shell

Gene inheritable unit of matter which controls cell growth and development

Genus (plural genera) a group of closely similar species; genera are grouped into families

Grass a flowering plant with narrow leaves and small petal-less flowers

Glade woodland clearing

Grazing (land) pasture

Greenwood Romantic name for woodland

Ground layer in a wood, below the field layer, with mosses, etc.

Gull family of grey or black and white seabirds

Hanger hillside wood (in Hampshire)

Hard (of water) with dissolved salts; chalky water

Hardwood (timber of) broadleaved tree

Hatch one meaning is the massed emergence of adult mayflies

Harrier birds of prey characterised by a low hunting glide

Hawk general name for small day bird of prey

Hawker type of dragonfly

Hay dried grass, winter fodder

Heath(land) particular lowland habitat characterised by heather

Hectare 2.47 acres (see Acre)

Hedge(row) field division

Herb in contrast to its kitchen meaning, here a non-woody green plant generally perennial but dying down in winter to a rootstock or low rosette of leaves

Herbaceous of a plant (herb), with no tall persistent parts

Herbicide a chemical toxic to plants

Herbivore general name for an animal that consumes plants or parts of them

Hibernation winter 'sleep', but different from normal 'sleep'

High forest 1) close-growing timber woodland; 2) occasionally used for tall woodland in general

Higher plant green plant with well-developed sap system, e.g. flowering plants

Honeydew sugary exudation of some sap-sucking bugs

Humus decaying matter in soil (see Soil)

Hybrid progeny of two different but closely related species

Ice Age(s) geologically recent series of advances of polar ice; we are now in an interglacial (a retreat)

Improvement the ploughing, draining, fertilising of farmland to increase yields, resulting in the destruction of ancient habitat and wildlife

Indicator in this book, a species of plant or animal which relates to some stage in the history/health of a habitat

Introduction non-native species now established in the countryside – that is, naturalised; see also Casual

Insect arthropod with body in three distinct parts and (usually) a separate life stage between egg and adult

Intensive of farming, using modern high-yield methods (see Improvement)

Intertidal the zone of the seashore exposed between high- and low-tide marks

Invertebrate general name for 'lower' animals without an internal skeleton

Irruption long-distance mass movement of birds to find food e.g. when seed crop fails (not the same as migration)

Key ash-tree fruit

Lane general term for (green) trackway

Larva immature ('grub') life stage of insect (e.g. the butterfly caterpillar)

Lawn (laund) grassed area in a wood created by deer or cattle grazing

Laying (layering) cutting and binding hedges

Leaching the action of rain washing nutrients, minerals out of the soil

Leaf that part of a higher plant which is the seat of photosynthesis and (as important) transpiration

Levels drained wetlands of e.g. Somerset

Ley ploughed and sown grassland

Lichen lower plant type with fungal and algal elements

Lime calcium carbonate, constituent of chalk and limestone rock

Limestone pavement unusual limestone formation

Limiting factor an aspect of an ecosystem which restricts life – e.g. the amount of oxygen dissolved in the water of a stream

Ling alternative name for a common heather

Link sandy-grassy-treed area backing sand dunes

Linnaean relating to Carl Linnaeus, who perfected the Latinised two-part system of naming species (see Classification)

Litter layer of partly decayed leaf and twig matter on the soil surface

Loam a good rich soil, see Soil

Loch Scottish term for lake and also inlet of sea

Longshore drift movement of a beach

Lowlands general name for countryside below 1000 ft (300m).

Machair flowery, flat sandy area typical of some Scottish coasts

Maiden standard timber tree

Mammal Class of animals with fur etc.; often called 'animals' in general speech

Management care and use of a habitat or site for conservation or farming

Marl 1) lime; 2) descriptive of some ponds in limestone or chalk areas

Marsh waterlogged wetland with mineral soil (by contrast a fen has peat)

Mast crop of (e.g. beech tree) seeds

Master woodland tree adopted by butterflies

Meadow general name for (long) grassland, but really the name of a special hay-producing field

Mediterranean (climate, plant) of that area

Mere 1) local name for pool; 2) general name for wetlands in East Anglia

Mesotrophic fresh water of middling nutrient content

Metamorphosis change of e.g. insect from larva to adult

Microclimate localised humidity and other conditions of a small-scale habitat, e.g. the foot of a hedge

Microspecies species differing from close kin in small ways only, e.g. brambles

Migration instinctive regular yearly and often long-range journey between breeding and wintering grounds

Mining of bees, wasps, those that excavate individual nests

Mire general name for soggy wetland; but in particular referring to peat wetlands

Mixed of a wood, with more than one main species of tree

Molluscs Phylum of shelled animals

Moor(land) (usually) high open ground with acid soil with heather or (if grazing is heavy) grass

Mor raw humus, and referring to (acid) soils with slow decay and few worms

Moss 1) northern word for a bog; 2) a Class of lower green plants liking damp areas

Moth (usually night-flying) insects with whirring flight, feathery antennae

Muirburn regular burning of areas of moorland to benefit grouse

Mull mild humus, and referring to rich (e.g. woodland) soils with plenty of decay and worms

Mycorrhiza association of fungus with roots of higher plants

Name see Classification

National Park area in which planning is aimed at the protection of landscape but not necessarily habitat and wildlife

Native plant or animal whose natural range includes Britain

Natural of nature; see Semi-natural

Naturalised alien species established in the countryside

Natural selection mechanism of evolution, by the survival of those living things best adapted (best fitted) to their 'niche'

Nature reserve area in which management is planned to protect habitat and species

Nest breeding structure of birds and some mammals (and in general speech also used of colonial home of ants, wasps, etc.)

Neutral of soil, neither acid nor alkaline

Niche 1) a crevice, platform on wall or rock face; 2) in ecology, the role of a plant or (especially) an animal in the life networks of an ecosystem: a niche is occupied by a species

Nutrient a chemically simple 'food' required by plants and obtained from the soil; also used of animal food

Nursery area or site where young are reared; herons, bats have distinctive nurseries

Nymph young of (a primitive) insect species which rather resembles the adult

Nymphalid Family of large and usually colourful butterflies

Neap the slightest tides of the month

Oligotrophic of fresh water, poor in nutrients

Omnivore eater of both plant and animal food, often a scavenger

Orchid wild orchids are often a signpost to an old-established habitat

Order grouping in Classification (which see)

Oygen demand the oxygen requirement of (aquatic) plants and animals, the supply being dissolved in the water around them

Organic derived from or in some way connected with living things

Pan dense mineral layer of heathland soils (podsols)

Panicle loosely branching flowerhead, e.g. of many grasses

Parasite a plant or animal gaining nourishment from another living plant or animal

Park(land) grassland dotted with trees, with a historic origin

Passage (migrant) a bird passing across Britain on its migration route

Passerine Order of birds: the song (perching) birds

Pasture grassland, grazing land

Peat 'soil' of largely undecayed plant matter usually accumulated in waterlogged conditions, but also on heathland

Pellet capsule of indigestible matter coughed up by birds

Perennial a plant which continues living from year to year

Pest emotive word used of insects and other small animals which reduce the yield of a crop plant in some way; also sometimes used of scavenging mammals

Pesticide chemical (spray) used in farming, to eliminate pests (see above)

Photosynthesis process whereby plants synthesise sugars from water, carbon dioxide, 'locking up' the energy in sunlight and releasing oxygen; green chlorophyll acts as the catalyst for this

Phylum major division of animal kingdom

Pioneer animal or plant in the forefront of the colonisation of open ground or new habitat opportunities, e.g. birch trees in a woodland clearing

Pine (tree) an Order of conifers

Plant one of the great Divisions of the living world. A plant is a primary producer and storer of energy by means of photosynthesis. Fungi are still usually called plants though they are nothing like. Plants are divided into lower (algae, mosses, liverworts, lichens) and higher (flowering plants), the latter having a well-developed sap system

Plantation planted timber woodland, either conifer or broadleaved

Pleacher stem bent in hedge-laying

Podsol leached heathland-type soil

Pollard tree with branches lopped at head height

Pollen flower spores, thick-skinned and in some soils long-lasting, so preserving the story of the vegetation cover

Pollution a result of human activity which degrades a habitat and damages plant or animal life

Population the number of individuals of a species in one place, or generally

Predator animal (especially a vertebrate) preying on another

Prevernal early spring, a season

Primary 1) of colonisation, on to virgin ground; 2) of woodland, never anything but woodland since the end of the Ice Age

Protected species which receive legal protection because they are rare or endangered

Pure (of woods) with only one species of dominant tree

Quickset ability (able) to grow from a cut shoot which roots when bedded in soil

Race local breeding population, not yet a species

Range geographical distribution of a species

Raptor day-active bird of prey – e.g. hawks, falcons, eagles, buzzards

Rare in ecology, the word implies very exact habitat needs and with the habitat itself hard to find, the species is rare; it may be quite abundant where found

Reclamation the draining, ploughing, fertilising of semi-natural habitats such as fen, saltmarsh, heathland

Regeneration regrowth of a habitat after damage or destruction

Relic fragment of former widespread habitat or community, e.g. woodland, meadow

Reptile cold-blooded, rough-skinned vertebrate

Ride access path in woodland

Ridge and furrow broad corrugations resulting from medieval ploughing, still sometimes visible

River engineering flood control and drainage works

Rodent Order of mammals with gnawing teeth, e.g. rats, mice

Roost 1) night station of birds (usually in numbers together and hence out of the breeding season); 2) also used as verb

Rosette leaves held flat on the ground, e.g. dandelion

Rotation in farming, alternating the crops each year so as to vary the demands on the soil

Runner (or stolon) creeping stem

Rush Genus of plants of damp soil with pithy round stems and grassy flowerheads

Sallow broad-leaved willow

Salting or saltmarsh coastal sand, mud, with areas covered only by some tides and becoming colonised by plants

Sapling a (very) young tree

Saprophyte a plant feeding on decaying matter (e.g. fungi, some orchids)

Scavenger animal feeding on decaying matter or debris

Scree fallen debris below a rock face

Scrub patch of bushes rather than trees, a stage in succession towards woodland

Seaweeds marine algae (green, red, brown) which often zone themselves down the shore

Secondary 1) of colonisation, on to open land but which has previously been wooded; 2) woodland resulting from this

Sedge grass-like plant with solid stems and often of damp places

Seed reproductive unit of flowering plants; a seedling germinates from it

Semi-natural vegetation or habitat which although modified by man has a rather natural character, e.g. ancient woodland, unploughed meadowland

Set (sett) badger burrow system

Shellfish marine molluscs

Shrub a woody plant branching near ground level

Signpost in this book, a species which illustrates some aspect of a habitat; a storyteller (see also Indicator)

Smallwood poles etc. gained from coppice

Silage grass cut green and sappy and stored as cattle fodder (cf. hay)

Silviculture forestry

Skipper Family of moth-like butterflies

Slime general name for loose algal or fungal growth

Slug mollusc with shell inside body

Slurry liquid farm dung

Society minor plant (plus animal) community within a habitat

Soft of water, with few dissolved minerals, easily lathering

Softwood conifer timber, tree

Soil the surface covering of the land in which plants root and many animals live. A mull soil is rich in decaying humus, a mor soil is leached and poor and rather acid. Soils can be acid, neutral or basic depending on their constituents

Songbird a bird with highly developed song, a Passerine

Species a population of similar plants or animals which habitually interbreed; the only natural grouping in Classification and usually with both a day-to-day name and a scientific Latinised name, e.g. great tit (*Parus major*), dandelion (*Taraxacum officinale*). Each animal species has a niche (which see) or role in its habitat, and animal species do not generally compete with each other directly

Sphagnum bog moss

Spinner final, mature adult mayfly

Spinney one name for a small wood

Spore reproductive unit of e.g. fungi, mosses

Spring 1) the season; 2) of the largest tides of the moon-monthly cycle

Spruce Family of coniferous trees

SSSI Site of Special Scientific Interest, a top-grade habitat

Standard timber tree in coppice woods

Stool newly cut coppice stump

Stop rabbit breeding burrow

Storyteller see Signpost, Indicator

Strategy in this book the (instinctive) way of life adopted by a species

Structure (of wood, etc.) the arrangement of different layers of vegetation

Succession the colonisation and development of a plant community culminating in the climax community (usually woodland)

Sucker shoot arising from roots

Suite in this book, a few key plants or animals which typify a habitat type

Sulphur dioxide gas released by burning coal and oil, responsible for acid rain

Swaling burning areas of heather moorland for the benefit of grouse

Swamp wetland habitat marked by reedbeds and with open water for most, if not all, of the year

Symbiosis union of two different species to mutual advantage, e.g. a lichen

Terrestrial of the land as opposed to the water

Territory area which animals defend against members of their own species, especially when breeding

Thicket general name for patch of dense (often spiny) scrub or a low dense wood

Thinning part of woodland management

Thorn general name for spiny shrub species, e.g. hawthorn, blackthorn

Timber (tree) tree grown or valued for the timber of its trunk

Traditional in this book, an old-established way of managing habitats such as woodland, pasture, but which has died or is largely dying out

Transpiration evaporation of water through the leaves of a plant, enabling nutrients to be sucked up from the roots

Tree woody plant branching from the top of a vertical trunk

Tree line the altitude above which trees do not naturally grow on a mountainside

Troutbeck fast upper reaches of a stream

Tundra treeless, cold lands of the Arctic Circle

Tussock bunched growth typical of sedges, rushes and some grasses

Typical of a species, more often seen in a certain kind of habitat than elsewhere

Umbellifer Family of wildflowers with umbrella-shaped flower heads

Undercliff pocket habitat below the clifftop

Undershrub low, woody but relatively short-lived plant, e.g. heather, gorse

Understorey layer of woodland beneath the canopy, alternatively called underwood or undergrowth

Unimproved farmland or habitat which has not been recently drained, fertilised etc. to raise its crop yields

Uplands areas of Britain which are generally over 1000 ft (300m)

Variety a form of an animal or plant species with distinct colour or other character

Verge grass strip alongside roadway

Vermin an emotive word used for buccaneering or predatory vertebrates which scavenge in domestic or farm or sporting holdings.

Vernal of the spring season

Vole blunt-nosed plant-eating rodent

Vulnerable a species with small breeding population: possibly en route to extinction

Wader (usually) long-legged and long-billed birds of coasts, wetlands and moors

Wallow mud bath of deer

Warbler Family of small songbirds. Of those seen in Britain, all but one (Dartford warbler) are summer visitors

Warren rabbit colony; in medieval days an area set aside for them

Washes the Ouse Washes are a regularly flooded area in East Anglia

Waste 1) Neither arable nor good pasture; traditionally unenclosed rough grazing; 2) derelict land

Waterfowl general name for aquatic birds – duck (and geese and swans)

Water meadow riverside grassland with sluice systems

Weed a plant which competes with a crop

Wildfowl birds shot by wildfowlers – duck, geese, swans, waders

Wildlife native and introduced animals in general, but in day-to-day speech often implying only vertebrates, especially mammals and birds

Wilderness virgin land, untouched by man. There is very little if any in Britain

Wildwood name for virgin woodland which spread across Britain after the Ice Age

Willow catkin trees of damp places (sallows are broad-leaved willows)

Wood(land) tree-covered ground

Wood pasture 'waste' used for rough grazing; it could be quite thickly covered with trees, although it was not an important source of timber

Wort old-fashioned term for a herb

INDEX

Page numbers in *italics* refer to illustrations